foreword by **JOHN RALSTON SAUL**

edited by **ANDRÉ PRATTE**

translated by **PATRICK WATSON**

CANADA

QUEBEC FEDERALISTS
SPEAK UP FOR CHANGE

D1004395

Douglas & McIntyre

Vancouver/Toronto

Douglas & McIntyre Ltd.
2323 Quebec Street, Suite 201
Vancouver, British Columbia
Canada V5T 4S7
www.douglas-mcintyre.com

Library and Archives Canada Cataloguing in Publication
Reconquering Canada : Quebec federalists speak
up for change / edited by André Pratte ; foreword by
John Ralston Saul ; translated by Patrick Watson

Translation of: Reconquérir le Canada.
Includes bibliographical references.
ISBN 978-1-55365-413-1

1. Federal-provincial relations—Québec (Province).
2. Nationalism—Québec (Province). 3. Federal government—Canada.
I. Watson, Patrick, 1929– II. Pratte, André, 1957–
JL246.S8R4213 2008   320.471'049   C2008-904989-6

Editing by Lucy Kenward
Cover and text design by Peter Cocking
Printed and bound in Canada by Friesens
Printed on acid-free paper that is forest friendly (100% post-consumer
recycled paper) and has been processed chlorine free.

We gratefully acknowledge the financial support of the Canada
Council for the Arts, the British Columbia Arts Council, the Province
of British Columbia through the Book Publishing Tax Credit, and
the Government of Canada through the Book Publishing Industry
Development Program (BPIDP) for our publishing activities.

CONTENTS

JOHN RALSTON SAUL

FOREWORD

FEDERALISM IS the political solution for societies that accept their complexity. This simple fact explains how Canada has become the oldest continuous democratic federation in the world. *Reconquering Canada* brings us a broad group of Quebecers who believe in federalism.

These writers would be the last to suggest that our country has had a blemish-free run. But then every country, including every democracy, has its own list of warts, failures, shameful acts and unachieved dreams. Only in the most extreme cases—what we now call *failed states*—are these seen by some as sufficient reason to explode the state.

Although our list of failures is shorter than those of most other countries, Canada's dark moments have been all too real. There is, however, an advantage to having a shorter list: you are less likely to believe your country can only go on existing if you learn to forget about your failures. This concept of *forgetfulness as the key to progress* was a central idea in nineteenth-century European nationalism; of Charles Péguy, for example. The Canadian view has been that it is better not to forget—better to build the future through a state of consciousness of our past failures. As for our friends and allies, most of whom have devoted their history to removing the differences within their countries, they have built up particularly long lists over the same 160 years since 1848 when Canada became a democracy.

What has kept Canadian federalism more or less on track has been the combination of political balance and social conditions, which together have created a very particular atmosphere. We have come to accept that a problem solved does not mean there will be less complexity. By accepting the complex nature of our society, we accept the necessity of equally complicated solutions.

That is why André Pratte's book, with its fourteen writers and thinkers, is both important and interesting. And that is why it has attracted so much attention in its original French version. For almost forty years, even the most rudimentary ideas of federalism and complexity have been difficult to put forward in Quebec as a mainstream approach to organized life. Even in the 1970s and 1980s, when federalism was being expressed in a muscular manner, it was as if it were an old, marginal, out-of-date theory. At best, whether in mythological or utilitarian or political arguments, federalism was treated as a consolation prize. Indeed, the federal government and many of the governments of other provinces often talked and acted as if federalism were not really a system, let alone a philosophy of social organization. It was just a fancy name for a crude power struggle between rival governments, a matter of money and administration. As for complexity, well, in an era of utilitarian obsessions with efficiency, federalism was seen as suffering from overlap and was therefore full of wasteful inefficiencies.

There were, of course, real problems to be dealt with by Quebec society, to say nothing of Canada as a whole. There was historical baggage to be unpacked on all sides. And there are still unresolved issues to do with constitutions and ever-evolving balances of power. But then federations always involve ongoing debates over how to balance the country's interwoven elements. That is the nature of the beast. As a number of the writers point out in these pages, many of the problems of the 1970s and 1980s were internal to Quebec, not the result of federalism. Provincial institutions had to be created—some in order to catch up with the rest of Canada, others to lead the way for the rest of the country. French had to be anchored into this new modernity. Most of this has been done very successfully, sometimes by Liberal governments, sometimes by the Union Nationale and sometimes by the Parti Québécois, and it has all been done within the federal system.

What *Reconquering Canada* deals with is the underlying assumption of Quebec public life. This has never been about nationalism. After all, the writers of this book are federalists and nationalists. Nationalism exists everywhere. There is lots of it throughout Canada. British Columbians and Newfoundlanders are just as nationalistic as Quebecers, each in their own way.

It is far more accurate to understand the underlying assumption of Quebec public life over the last few decades in religious terms, as if a new religion had appeared in the 1970s; new, yet still an expression of the old Judeo-Christian idea of faith as necessarily monolithic. There is still only one god, who just happens to be a secular expression of myth and the state. Thus, there is only one possible faith, which is secular and tied to an inevitable destiny, itself stripped of the complexities of federalism and the interwoven relationships with *the other*, which federalism assumes exist. It is those relationships that make life in a federation, its myths and politics, so complicated. The accompanying argument was that Quebec's minority situation created a need for a more monolithic nationalism: that is, a nationalism closer to the nineteenth-century European sort, one in which clearly defined tenets were to be subscribed to by all loyal citizens.

In truth, Quebec has never functioned in the monolithic manner of the sovereignist/*indépendantiste*/separatist faith. Quebecers are far too sophisticated for that. If anything, they have lived as comfortably with federalism as most other Canadians—and perhaps more effectively. Being an integral part of the Canadian experience, Quebec has always been filled with complexity, whether social, linguistic, religious, secular or regional.

But mainstream public discourse has not really reflected this reality, because of the domination of what might as well be called the Parti Québécois faith—a faith built upon the impossibility of a messy, complicated place like Canada.

This book is all about creating a new mainstream discourse, a new language that reflects Quebec's reality. Creating a language—a vocabulary, phrases, paragraphs, arguments—in which federalism and complexity are neither marginalized nor on the defensive, but are seen as normal expressions of a modern state—is an important project. The language that André Pratte and his friends are seeking to create is not one that attempts to exclude, for example, long-time sovereignists. Rather, it is an attempt to reach out to any Quebecer who will listen to a complex and inclusive message.

There can be little doubt that, as the decades have gone by, many Canadians outside of Quebec have gradually tired of the Quebec Question. Some feel they have been worn down, others that it is always the same questions no matter what issues are dealt with, others that there are many non–Quebec-centred but nevertheless key national issues from which they are being distracted. But we have no right to tire of a question so central to our existence as a country and as individuals. And here, with *Reconquering Canada*, is a mass of words and phrases and arguments from a group of successful, intelligent and interesting Quebecers who believe in federalism, in the ongoing Canadian experiment and, of course, in Quebec.

RECONQUERING CANADA

ANDRÉ PRATTE

INTRODUCTION

FOR MORE than four decades, federalists and sovereignists have been debating the future of Quebec and Canada. After a string of endless and fruitless constitutional negotiations, three referenda, and innumerable gaffes and disruptions, the debate has now bogged down. The two sides continue to exchange the same dull old arguments, each holding rigidly to its own convictions.

Since the failure of the Meech Lake Accord some twenty years ago, the sovereignists have generally led the debate. They successfully made fun of the Charlottetown Accord and caused the whole country to hold its breath during the 1995 referendum. They have considerably strengthened their voice by setting up a federal wing and they have pushed their opponents to the wall over the sponsorship scandal.

During this time, the federalists have never actually been able to advance their agenda. At first they thought that silence—the "let's just get on with it" approach—would allow them to gain the upper hand over the sovereignists, but this strategy only brought things to a head. Then they thought they should make Canada more "visible" in Quebec, a plan that quickly went sour. The sponsorship scandal not only tainted the credibility of every proponent of Canadian unity living in Quebec, it also had a terribly demoralizing effect on them.

To make matters worse, a lot of Quebec federalists and Mario Dumont–style autonomists see the association between Quebec and the rest of Canada in much the same light as the sovereignists do. In their view, this relationship boils down to a list of endless demands, a systematic resistance to any federal initiative and a kind of isolationism, an indifference to what is going on in Ottawa and in English Canada.

During the past few years the political order seems to have been changing. The combined efforts of Jean Charest's provincial government and the federal government have allowed Quebec to make some meaningful advances. The provincial election of March 2007 and the federal by-elections in September of the same year showed the sovereignist parties to be weakened. What seems to be emerging is a willingness for renewed political dialogue. This is especially true on the federalist side, which for much too long has been content only to counter the arguments of the *indépendantistes*. The time is right for Quebec federalists to rethink their views, question their beliefs and get over their fear of speaking out.

The contributors to this book come from diverse political and professional backgrounds. However, they share four convictions. 1) They appreciate that today's Quebec is better off developing within Canada rather than trying to become a separate country. 2) They believe that Quebecers need to change their approach to dealing with the rest of the country and their view of federalism, realizing that constitutional demands, while important, are not an immediate priority. 3) They think that Quebecers would be smart to become more involved in the evolution of the country, to take full advantage of belonging to Canada rather than staying on the sidelines. 4) They are convinced that Quebec now has in hand the tools it needs to meet the challenges it faces.

These are the convictions that these writers have tried to convey, each in their own style and according to their own personal and professional experience. The book is not really a manifesto: that is, the authors have not tried to come up with one common text. Each chapter is independent of the others: its writer is the sole author and the only person responsible for the ideas contained within it.

There will be those who call this a useless exercise, who claim that the sovereignist movement is already in retreat, but that would be to misunderstand the reason for our undertaking. This collection is not a denunciation of the sovereignists. It is a call to the Quebec Nation to reconceptualize Canadian federalism and to review the province's relationship with the rest of the country.

ANDRÉ PRATTE *is the Editorial Pages Editor at* La Presse.

DANIEL FOURNIER .

SAYING YES TO CANADA

IN THE LATE SUMMER of 1971 I was seventeen and had just received a scholarship to the Phillips Exeter Academy in New Hampshire. Upon arriving in the "Live Free or Die" State, I found myself studying the history of the American Revolution. This led, somewhat ironically, to my discovering from an American perspective why my native province, Quebec, had refused to become the fourteenth colony of the United States despite a generous invitation from the Continental Congress and the great Benjamin Franklin himself.

At the time, I read with fascination the passionate debates among the Founders about the appropriate roles for the federal and state governments, exchanges that brought forth the eloquence and intellectual persuasiveness of distinguished men such as Thomas Jefferson, James Madison and Samuel Adams. I was learning with pleasure, not to mention relief, that great polemical arguments between the centre and the regions were hardly exclusive to Canada.

I can honestly say that this was one of the most stimulating periods of my life. To be transported from the football field of

Loyola High School in downtown Montreal to the auditorium of
Exeter, where we heard the various presidential candidates make
their case to the voters of New Hampshire, was a big change. And
although I continued to play football in New Hampshire, I had to
get used to moving around a smaller field, catching a smaller ball
and playing against bigger and faster opponents than any I had
known until then.

Every morning while at school I was first in line for breakfast, and I was served by a woman whose family, like so many
others from Quebec, had moved to New England during the
depression of the late nineteenth century to seek a better life.
This all seemed very new and inspiring to a young man intent on
finding his way in the world. During that fall of '71, I began to
speculate about what might have happened had Quebec accepted
Benjamin Franklin's invitation. Would the citizens of this puta-
tive fourteenth state have continued to speak French within the
framework of the American form of government? Seeing so
many New Englanders with francophone names who spoke not a
word of French—like the woman who served me breakfast every
morning—I did not have far to look for the answer.

Also that fall, I followed the heated discussion over a nuclear
power station that had received approval to be built in Seabrook,
New Hampshire. As I followed the controversy, I realized how
fortunate we were in Quebec to have such an enormous capacity to produce hydroelectric power. I became acquainted with
classmates both from the great old families of America and from
some of the country's most depressed communities, and I came
away with the impression that the gap between rich and poor
was smaller in Canada. In short, I became aware that while my
country was different from the United States, it stood up well in
comparison. And the more I thought about this, the prouder I
was to be a Canadian and a Quebecer.

Living away from my family for the first time helped me better appreciate my roots. Although I had expected to be away for two years, opportunity, necessity and chance extended my absence to nine years in the United States and in England. During those nine years I was fortunate to be exposed to a wide range of experiences, all of which afforded me a broader perspective on the world yet only increased my desire to return to Montreal. In particular, while I was a student employee at the Canadian Embassy in Washington in 1976, the U.S. bicentennial year, I saw an America weakened by and trying to recover from the deep divisions caused by the Watergate political scandals earlier in the decade. During that same period, on a trip to the Middle East, I was struck by the complexity of the political situation relative to the small size of the territories being fought over in that region. I quickly came to the conclusion that we, Quebecers and Canadians, for all our own divisive debates, were, with our huge territory and peaceable past, truly privileged.

The lessons I had drawn from my youthful experiences were confirmed years later during the Yugoslavian crisis, when I was invited to Vienna to take part in a conference on the future of Europe. The diplomats and politicians talked of their struggle to convince the members of the European Union to agree on a common position vis-à-vis Kosovo. During the conference there was also a great deal of discussion about the gaps in international law as it was applied to interventions in the Third World, where minority rights were so often and so permanently violated. One conclusion stood out: a country must be judged on its treatment of minorities. In this regard, Canada need not take a back seat to any nation.

In those long ago days, I had, like most young people, more opinions and solutions to offer than questions to ask about the great debates of the time. That is, of course, a natural expression of youthful arrogance. I now have four children, and thanks to them any remaining traces of that arrogance are gone. The society in which they will live is a major concern for me, and even though I entertain great hope for their future, I think we can still make improvements.

The Virtue of Compromise

From the time our ancestors settled on this continent, we have learned to compromise, particularly with regard to climate and geography, and on some occasions to history as well. Compromise is a reality essential to the civilized conduct of human affairs but it is often a reality that is difficult to accept. Canada itself is a compromise. In the 1850s, the Province of Canada, the union of Canada East and Canada West created out of the ill-conceived Durham Report, found itself deadlocked. The impasse flowed from a very complex problem: how to reconcile the idea of popular representation, supported by the predominantly Protestant, anglophone and more populous inhabitants of what would become the province of Ontario, with the religious, cultural and linguistic protection demanded by the mostly Catholic, francophone and less populous people of what would become the province of Quebec.

It was at that moment that creative visionaries such as John A. Macdonald, George-Étienne Cartier, George Brown, Hector-Louis Langevin, Samuel Tilley, Charles Tupper, Thomas McGee and others—men of diverse backgrounds, religions and opinions, but ready to make compromises for the common good—set to work. Together they found a solution to the deadlock: the principle of Confederation, and, in the process, they created a nation. Between 1864 and 1867, at the conferences of Charlottetown, Quebec and London as well as in their abundant correspondence, these men defended their differing visions for the northern part of the North American continent and yet worked out a compromise that has lasted 140 years. Their solution also launched a debate over the proper interpretation of the division of powers between the federal government and the provinces, a debate that has also lasted 140 years.

It is entirely natural for politicians to deliberate ideas. As a college and professional football player, I was accustomed to fighting for turf so I am not unfamiliar with the concept of competing interests. However, I am astonished at the ferocity demonstrated by politicians throughout the history of this country. They have fought for their beliefs with a resolve that my coaches would doubtless have appreciated. Such tenacity is, however, a basic characteristic of Canadian history. Were Louis Riel's actions treasonable or those of a great patriot? Was John A. Macdonald's National Policy a Central Canadian tool to dominate the West or the glue that assured Canadian sovereignty against a hostile and aggressive United States? Canadian historiography is replete with such seminal questions.

In my third year at Princeton University, a Montreal friend and I started a seminar on Canadian history. We persuaded Richard Challener, a well-known specialist in American foreign policy, to chair it. Both he and the American participants were stunned to learn that students from Atlantic Canada, from west of the Lakehead, from Quebec and from Ontario could hold such different points of view on these questions. During the two weeks we devoted to the place of Quebec in twentieth-century Canada, we invited two fellow Canadians of decidedly different views, historian Ramsay Cook and businessman Conrad Black, to give us their respective assessments of the Maurice Duplessis era. Sparks flew from the start. The vitality and passion demonstrated during the course of the discussion quickly put an end to any preconception among our American friends that—hockey aside—Canadians were politely calm, our politics dull. We also learned, to our dismay, the extent to which history can be rewritten and myths created.

Discussion can be a useful tool for looking at an issue from different perspectives and coming to a better understanding of it. Ultimately, however, I am unimpressed by the argument that we can find better ways to live together or improve our country by debating the intent of Canada's founders. I have never put much time or effort into arguing the relative merits of the competing claims between the federal and the provincial governments over the division of powers, for I have always believed federalism to be the most dynamic and sensible form of government ever invented. Although the balance of political power has swung back and forth between the provinces and the federal government throughout the history of Canada, it has invariably come to rest precisely in a place that has suited the vast majority of citizens. I tend to agree with Prime Minister Lester B. Pearson, who, in a speech in August 1963, said:

> Our federalism must be designed with enough flexibility to allow the existence of a Canadian Government that is strong within the limits of its jurisdiction so it can play its role fully among the great nations of the world, while also ensuring the progress and well-being of the Canadian population. We also want to give the provinces all the responsibilities and powers vested in them by the constitution, as well as the means to exercise these powers.[1]

It is precisely in the willingness to compromise that we can find the necessary flexibility spoken of so wisely by Mr. Pearson. I believe that as long as we aim for this kind of federal-provincial relationship, we will see there is no insurmountable obstacle to Canadian unity.

I am convinced that balanced federalism is possible because our constitution, which has been subjected to so much criticism, is a model of reasonableness. Our constitution, both written and unwritten, is not simply a noble formula, but, taken as a whole, is an accurate expression of who we are and the foundation upon which we can build what we hope to become. This is because democracy and the rule of law, which are at the heart of our political system, are of such extraordinary value that most of the world's nations have never experienced them, and their citizens have never benefited from the protections and the advantages these confer.

We are often given the impression that the quarrels over the distribution of powers between the federal and provincial governments are the private preserve of Quebec politicians. This is not the case. In fact, Oliver Mowat, the Confederation-era premier of Ontario, was so unwavering in his pursuit of provincial rights that it earned him the nickname "that little tyrant" from none other than Sir John A. Macdonald. It is true, however, that over time, Quebec politicians have led the way. It is, though, also fair to say that French Canadians have had the most to lose. Whether it was the Manitoba Schools Question of 1890, which created publicly funded separate schools for French and English students, or the Manitoba Language Question in the 1980s, which required all provincial laws and legislative documents to be translated into French, French Canadians generally, and French Quebecers in particular, have been wary of attempts by some of their fellow-citizens to shape Canada in their own image.

The Election that Changed Everything

Since Confederation, federal and provincial politicians have left the courts to decide disagreements over their differing interpretations of federalism. At no time, however, had the politicians questioned the foundation on which our political system is based. All that changed in 1970 when the sovereignist Parti Québécois contested its first election.

Since that Quebec provincial election, all debate has centred on the very underpinnings of our political system, effectively ending the natural constitutional development of our country. Instead of building consensus, we have held two referenda on Quebec independence and four major constitutional initiatives on the role of Quebec in Canada. Since that election, entire forests have been felled to provide the paper on which to publish the various constitutional positions. Oceans of ink have been spilled to write about the positives and negatives of federalism, sovereignty and any number of positions in between.

In 1970 we in Quebec decided that federal-provincial relations, or the Canada-Quebec debate, was not just an important issue in our political discourse; it was the only issue. Economic growth, prosperity, taxes, education, health care—all came to be viewed through the lens of Quebec versus Canada, as if Quebecers were somehow not Canadian or as if the view from Ottawa somehow always accurately reflected the national sentiment.

An objective reading of Canadian history teaches us a very different lesson: that, in fact, it has never been a question of Quebec versus Canada or Canada versus Quebec. For example, the showpiece of the pro-sovereignty Yes side during the referendum of 1995 was the defeat of the Meech Lake Accord, an arrangement that would have allowed Quebec to sign the Constitution Act, 1982 with, in the words of then–prime minister Brian Mulroney, "honour and enthusiasm." Jacques Parizeau (then premier of Quebec), Lucien Bouchard (then leader of the Bloc Québécois) and other sovereignists argued with great passion and skill that by failing to ratify the Accord, English Canada had ganged up on Quebec to deprive it of its legitimate demands. This fact, for the sovereignists, proved that Canada could never work to the benefit of Quebec, and they ably exploited the raw emotion that the defeat of the Accord provoked in Quebec. Ironically, during the lead-up to the referendum and the defeat of the Accord, the sovereignist movement had spared no effort and was in fact over-joyed to join with Newfoundland premier Clyde Wells and others to denounce the Accord precisely because it demonstrated that Canada could work in the interests of the people of Quebec.

The Meech Lake and post-Meech periods are over. The politi-cal scene in Canada has evolved, but has the political discourse in Quebec changed? The 2007 Quebec provincial election was described by pundits and politicians as a watershed election. But was it? Is there any discernible difference between the thread that ran through that election and every other one since 1970? The Parti Québécois campaigned on the issue of sovereignty; the Action démocratique du Québec ran on a platform of achieving autonomy; the Liberals asked for our vote to protect Quebec's interests against Ottawa. It was the same old theme, except that in this horse race there was no clear winner.

Since 1970, every provincial election has had sovereignty, autonomy or the defence of Quebec's interests as an overarching theme. For nearly forty years, the sovereignty debate has trumped all other subjects and sapped the energy of an entire generation of talented leaders, all the while diminishing the importance of the issues that interest citizens most: the economy, the envi-ronment, health care and education. In the past ten years, since the rise post-Meech of the Bloc Québécois, a similar situation in Ottawa has deprived Quebecers of the usual left-centre-right debates federally as well. This dialogue is at the heart of healthy discourse in other democratic countries. In France, for example, the election of Nicolas Sarkozy signalled an entirely new direc-tion for the country, but it came about only after a heated debate with Ségolène Royal of the Socialist Party that helped all French citizens to make an informed choice about their future president.

An Obese Government

In the meantime, we, in Quebec, have turned to the province to answer any and all of our problems. The Government of Quebec has 255 agencies, boards, bureaus, centres, commissions, committees, councils, Crown corporations, forums, foundations, institutes, offices, secretariats and societies, including, one suspects for the purposes of comic relief, the Allégement Réglementaire et Administratif (Regulatory and Administrative Streamlining) listed on its Web site. To its credit, Quebec has traditionally had a strong civil service, but the sheer size of the Quebec administration is mind-numbing. The Province of Quebec has, with five million fewer people than Ontario, more elected representatives. The City of Montreal has almost as many elected representatives as do the provincial governments of Alberta and Saskatchewan combined.

Do we really need so much government? Of course not. However, in the climate of present-day Quebec, it requires a very brave soul indeed to suggest the state could afford to skip the occasional lunch, let alone shed a few pounds. Its defenders are legion. Quebecers may have adopted the overarching welfare state later than most of our neighbours, but we have since embraced it with gusto. However, by accepting the status quo, we are sacrificing our future for an illusory security that will protect neither us nor our children. Our appetite for statism has become insatiable.

There was a time when we saw poverty, violence and hopelessness, and our first response was to ask what we as citizens could do. We now demand that the state fix everything. The obligations of citizenship have seemingly, over time, been reduced to the simple act of voting, and even the number of voters has declined greatly. Surrendering obligations in return for security would seem like a very favourable trade, but with each obligation we surrender we become more dependent on a state that is already overwhelmed. We have all become willing consumers of the Great Largesse. In fact, some of our largest corporations seem incapable of surviving without the protective umbrella of provincial subsidies and grants.

A great deal has changed since that long-ago election of 1970, and we have clearly not prepared ourselves to deal with this new reality. Technology has eliminated many traditional manufacturing jobs, as has global competition, particularly from low-wage countries such as China and India. Highly skilled, educated workers thrive whereas low-skilled jobs remain vulnerable to outsourcing. Quebec politicians of all parties fought to have employment training become a provincial responsibility. Now that we have this responsibility, should we not take positive charge of it?

Every day we are presented with more and more evidence of the growing disparity between our highest- and lowest-paid workers. What is far more disturbing is the widening gap between those at the top and those in the middle. With the increasing importance of technology in our manufacturing processes, we have to do a much better job of equipping Quebecers with the skills to take on these high-value jobs. This means an emphasis on education, training and lifelong learning.

We need a business environment that encourages innovation, the use of advanced technologies and entrepreneurship. To stay competitive, we need to train more engineers, doctors, scientists and entrepreneurs, and having trained them, we need to find ways to keep them here. We can no longer afford to have our best and brightest leave for greener pastures in other provinces or countries. And there is no denying they have been leaving.

Due to this unacceptable situation, dissatisfied citizens will continue to vote with their feet and leave Quebec until things improve, but that will only begin to happen when we demand more of our elected leaders and more of ourselves. The problems we face as a society will not be solved by a program here or a compromise there, and a quick patch job will not help. Not one of these difficulties was caused by Canadian federalism. Not one of these predicaments was caused by an absence of sovereignty, a lack of autonomy or an inadequate number of people prepared to defend Quebec against Ottawa. We have now explored innumerable iterations of what Canadian federalism should be. It is time to stop talking about what it should be and start living with what it is: an imperfect system that can be improved.

These issues will not be solved by further federal-provincial disputes or by additional arguments that, if only each level of government had more money, there would be less poverty, less violence, less hopelessness. Nor will they be solved by those in power congratulating themselves on having created additional programs—corporate and individual—or, not to be outdone, by those out of power claiming that if only they were in power, they would create more programs still.

Any move away from the political status quo will be difficult to accomplish. "There is," said an Italian philosopher, "nothing more difficult to take in hand, more perilous to conduct or more uncertain in its success than to take the lead in the introduction of a new order of things." Nonetheless it must be done to restore a harmonious balance between citizens and government, for this "new order of things" is perhaps best seen not as new but rather as a return to where we once were.

There are good reasons to believe that we may be suffering from collective amnesia. As is often the case with this particular affliction, the onset occurred so gradually that we no longer have any memory of where we began. In fact, so far removed are we from this past that it is now difficult to pinpoint the exact moment when we first chose this disastrous road. Although these situations are never cut and dried, we have been creating the conditions of our current predicament since that watershed election of 1970.

The brilliant American biographer Robert Caro made the point that "power does not always corrupt, but power always reveals." What has been revealed of our political leaders since the election of 1970? In Quebec, it is rare to find, irrespective of party, a solution to a problem that does not involve greater debt. Is there anything more revealing than a post-secondary education system that is chronically underfunded? Or a health care system that consumes almost fifty cents of every tax dollar and yet is broken? Or a high-school dropout rate of more than 30 per cent? Is there any more revealing metaphor of the state in which we find ourselves than the collapse of the overpass on Concorde Boulevard in Laval, a vivid example of our crumbling infrastructure? The choice between sovereignty and Canada may now be the status quo in this province, but those who aspire to leadership should not be afraid to question it.

Today's leaders have an obligation to succeeding generations to ensure that their road will be paved with as much opportunity as ours has been. We have hard choices to make, and these choices have nothing to do with the constitution or, for the most part, with the federal government. How do we increase our high-school graduation rates? How do we resolve the chronic underfunding of our universities and ensure they remain world-class institutions? Where will we find the funds desperately needed by our health care system? How do we reconcile our stated concern for the environment with our actual consumption of electricity— which is among the highest per capita in North America? Are we prepared to forgo the heavy subsidies that keep our electricity rates so low (and which benefit our biggest industrial consumers and our wealthiest citizens) and pay the true market rate? This one simple decision would provide the provincial treasury with billions of dollars, doing much more for the economy than the infamous "fiscal imbalance" debate that monopolized the federal and Quebec political scene for a decade. These funds could be invested in health care and education and they could be used to begin paying down our large public debt. This money would also bring lasting environmental benefits by providing the funding necessary for emerging green technologies.

Lost Time

Recent surveys consistently show Quebecers' major concerns to be the environment, health care and our presence in Afghanistan. None of these issues will be solved by another constitutional debate, though the decisions on these controversial subjects will be difficult to make. For example, in the early 1960s, U.S. President John F. Kennedy had to determine whether or not to send a civil rights bill to Congress. He knew the decision would be contentious, but he eventually chose to do so anyway. Later he remarked to a friend, "Sometimes when you think back on what you did, the only question that comes to mind is 'Why did it take so long?'"

In Quebec, too, we are going to have to make some tough choices. They will require courage, but I am convinced that, looking back, we will, like President Kennedy, ask ourselves: "Why did it take so long?" To those who think these difficult questions can be avoided, that everything will just work itself out, I would ask why, in L'Éloge de la Richesse (In Praise of Wealth) by journalist and economist Alain Dubuc, Quebec ranks consistently near the bottom compared with other provinces and states with respect to all major economic indicators.

Over the past few years, there has been a growing discussion in Quebec between those who believe the answer to our difficulties lies in more state intervention and those who believe in less. Over the next decade, I would much prefer to listen to that discussion than to waste more time on the worn-out ideas and the blunt threats of the pro-sovereignty Yes and the federalist No sides. The political parties, whether their end goal is to save Canada or to make Quebec independent, all seem keen that the wrangling continue—and why not? It is their raison d'être. What would the Parti Québécois be without this useless confrontation? It is safe to say that the increase in support for the Conservative Party in the 2006 federal election was due in part to its having distanced itself from this sempiternal debate.

The world is changing rapidly, and we are being forced to confront challenges we can no longer ignore. As citizens, we need to insist that our elected representatives and that we ourselves do more to address these issues. Consider education. There is an inverse relationship between education and poverty: the more of the former, the less of the latter. Education is the only real ticket to a better future, and though it is true that Quebec is not the only province to let down the next generation, we can find no comfort in the failure of others. We are not adequately preparing this next generation to meet the entrance requirements for the universities that will assure its future success. Education is the great equalizer, and it is the springboard to a better life for all human beings, irrespective of race, culture or religion.

The overall statistics reveal that Quebec's educational system is broken. What the figures do not show is the time lost to missed opportunities and all-too-numerous setbacks, and all the people whose lives could have been so productive but have gone off course because of the system's failure. Despite the great effort expended by so many in our schools and universities, we simply must do better to ensure Quebecers succeed in an increasingly competitive world.

A New Canada

In May 2005, I explained to my family that I was going to run for the Conservative Party in Outremont. My primary objective, to put it simply, was to demonstrate that an alternative kind of viable federalism could be offered to, among others, those who had for several elections voted for the sovereignist Bloc Québécois. I also hoped my candidacy would show that the Conservative Party could find support in Quebec. Like so many other Quebecers, I wished to see an end to the stale debates on sponsorship and sovereignty and redirect this interest towards more current matters, such as improving education and health care, as well as building more productive relations with the U.S. In short, I hoped for a dialogue promoting the healthy management of public affairs.

The very day I was chosen as a candidate, Conservative Party member Belinda Stronach crossed the floor to join the Liberals. As it turned out, the federal election was delayed for nine months. My plans and my timeframes obviously had to change, but because of this delay I came to know my constituency better and I also deepened my understanding of Canada. Although I had crossed the country many times for professional reasons, I had never had the occasion to meet with both small groups of citizens and with provincial politicians. The postponed election gave me the opportunity to take the pulse of Canadians right across the country.

During my travels, I found more national similarities than provincial differences. My unscientific poll allowed me to discern the existence of two common points among Canadians. The first was an overall dissatisfaction with the state of public affairs: the sense that federal, provincial and municipal governments no longer worked as well as they should. There was a feeling that the political establishment, frozen in partisan aspirations, had neglected to re-examine our post–Cold War assumptions in the context of a greatly changed society. The second was the optimism and pride that Canadians feel for their country. It is often said that Canadians are in search of an identity, but this idea could not be more mistaken. Although we have no monopoly on freedom and democracy, these fundamental human values are intimately linked to our national identity. They are the starting point for the optimism that Canadians share about the future of our country.

During these travels I also found a new Canada, a Canada that is very different from the one of the referenda years. I became aware that the country would not react as it had in 1980 and 1995 to either a new referendum or to the threat of a new referendum on the future of Quebec. Canadians have been living with the notion of Quebec sovereignty since 1970 and have accepted that this idea is part of our national debate. However, I found a new confidence across the country, due largely to the economic revolution that took place while Prime Minister Brian Mulroney was in office. The Canada that has emerged from this difficult but necessary transformation is a country changed from the one we knew a decade ago.

In fact, as I try to describe this new Canada, the words of the respected western Canadian historian W.L. Morton come to mind:

> It no longer matters to any what a man's origin is—English, French, German, Ukrainian, Scots, Irish, Welsh, Italian—any of all the multitudinous strains of Canadian nationality. There is no British Empire any more: there is no longer any adventitious advantage in being English, or disadvantage in not being English. Without any man having to turn his back on his past, without any fervor of conversion from one nationality to

another, we have all quietly become Canadians. This means that in the future any national majority will be a varying one, a majority of opinion and not of race.[2]

Mr. Morton, writing this in 1964, was ahead of his time. But his observation is now, in my view, a faithful description of the present situation in our country.

The Legacy of Mulroney and Lesage

The economic vision of deregulation, tax reform and free trade, which Mr. Mulroney courageously promoted, cost him dearly in terms of popularity, but Canada has emerged stronger from these economic policies. Mr. Mulroney's fall from favour reminds me of Jean Lesage, the father of the Quiet Revolution, the soul of modern Quebec, whose statue stands so proudly in front of the National Assembly in Quebec City. Elected in 1960 on the slogan "It's Time for a Change," he seemed unbeatable—which did not save him from defeat in the elections of 1966.

According to the historian Donald Creighton, Sir John A. Macdonald had an interesting perspective on the role of politicians. Mr. Macdonald believed that a politician could remain a competent craftsman or even become a great artist but should never aspire to the foreign roles of prophet, philosopher or engineer. In fact, the principles that have served Quebecers so well are not to be found in prophecy, philosophy or science. Instead, we need only look to the history and traditions of our province and our country to find these beliefs. 1) Ideas that work are more valuable than any ideology. 2) Governments are responsible for creating conditions that allow us to live a better life; they are not the moral arbiters of how we choose to live it.

No generation has either the wisdom or the time to create an ideal world. There is no genius among us who can solve all

our problems with some new policy or unheard-of social structure. This is why we must return to certain fundamental and
universal principles. Earlier I wrote that time has whittled away
the arrogance of my youth, when I thought I had all the answers.
Nevertheless, the intervening years have allowed me to develop
some ideas on the roles that governments should play.

These are not new principles, but they are principles that
have struck me because of their practical and universal nature.
We need progressive policies designed for people in need and
not for their self-proclaimed representatives, policies that protect individual liberties and promote success. We need policies
for families and for communities, the people who will build the
next generation. It is time to remember the lessons bequeathed to
us by Premier Lesage and Prime Minister Mulroney. It is time to
elect leaders who are willing to sacrifice their popularity for the
common good, and governments who do not fear defeat in the
pursuit of big ideas.

In 2005, the Parti Québécois platform promised that the
party would hold a referendum on sovereignty as soon as it was
elected. The referendum question would be absolutely clear and
would not contain the idea of a Quebec-Canada partnership. A
referendum victory, of whatever size, would lead to a unilateral
declaration of independence. Two years later, weakened as a
result of a third-place finish in the 2007 election—its worst performance since 1970—the Parti Québécois changed its mind...
again. That referendum has now been postponed indefinitely.
Meanwhile, the political uncertainty that makes up such a large
part of our present difficulties continues. This situation is clearly
unacceptable. Quebec society cannot allow itself to live through
another decade of hemorrhaging human capital, investment,
jobs and economic growth. It would simply be unfair to the next
generation for us to yield to this navel-gazing reflex.

It is vital that the French fact survive in North America and that this culture flourish. Bill 101 (the Charter of the French Language) and a declaration by the federal Parliament affirming that Quebec's people constitute a nation are not in themselves sufficient guarantees. If it is true that vibrant cultures flow from solid and dynamic economies, we have to face the fact that our future is in danger unless we are prepared to make very difficult decisions. To do this, our leaders will need to arm themselves with courage: either we make the choices ourselves, or they will be made by others in offices in New York, Beijing, Delhi or Toronto.

A better future is possible. We have only to put out a hand and grasp it. It is not a question of sacrificing anything but rather of seizing an opportunity to transform Quebec into a richer and more dynamic society. Most of the problems we face are not unique to our province. All the same, as Quebecers, we must remind ourselves that we occupy a special place in the political and cultural evolution of Canada. We are the inheritors and guardians of the French fact in North America, and we are responsible not only for its survival but also for its long-term significance in a rapidly changing world.

Towards the end of the First World War, Prime Minister Robert Borden, seeking to provide direction to Canadians, said:

> Above all let there be unity of purpose. I have spoken of waste; but unnecessary discord and unseemly controversy are the worst possible waste of the nation's effort. Discord arises chiefly through lack of mutual understanding; Canadians of different communities and provinces should know each other better, should strive for a wider vision of each other's purpose and aims. Upon that truer understanding the united national spirit of the future must be founded.[3]

Ninety years later these words are still relevant. How well do Canadians of different communities and provinces know each other? Have we gained a broader view of each other's goals and objectives? Have we, as Québécers, understood the significance of the rapid changes that have taken place in the rest of Canada, especially in the West, over the last decade?

A Dream

In May 1987 Prime Minister Mulroney and his provincial counterparts unanimously ratified the Meech Lake Accord. I remember the great feeling of pride I had as I got out of bed and read the news in *Le Devoir*. That newspaper, founded by the great French-Canadian nationalist Henri Bourassa, carried the headline in huge print: LE CANADA DIT OUI AU QUÉBEC! (Canada Says Yes to Quebec!) This pride was not mine alone; rather, I sensed deeply that it was shared by all my fellow-citizens. We all realized the ratification of the Meech Lake Accord was the result of hard work, imagination, real leadership and a generosity of spirit that is part of the Canadian character.

That, in the end, the Meech Lake Accord failed should in no way be seen as a condemnation of Canada or of the constitution. This setback in no way marks the end of the work to be done. The ancient Greeks believed that destiny is forged on the anvil of character. The many linguistic and regional battles that we have lived through in the 140 years of Canada's history do not define our national character and do not foretell our destiny. We have proved this over and over again in the course of our history. On each of these occasions, as Prime Minister Borden said, we had a common purpose in view.

There will always be regional frictions. They flow from the very nature of federalism and will always be resolved in the context of our democratic society and the rule of law. However, it is precisely because of that generosity of spirit that we will one day arrive at an understanding. I am convinced that one morning I will read on page one of *The Globe and Mail*—the newspaper founded by George Brown, the great English Canadian nationalist—a headline that declares: QUEBEC SAYS YES TO CANADA! However, as federalists we must understand that if we are to win over the vast majority of Quebecers to this goal, we are going to need something more than a "generous" sponsorship program. Sprinkling dollars around will never ensure Canadian unity. We do not need any more flags or the lazy rhetoric of fear to ensure that we subscribe to the idea of Canada. What we do need, what all Canadians need, is "good government," that practical promise of public competence that is written in our constitution.

In the coming years, Canadian citizens are going to have to make crucial decisions about their future. It is imperative that Quebecers take an active part in these debates. We must start proposing solutions, not just raising objections, and we must constantly be alert to take advantage of the good times and successfully weather the bad ones. We are blessed with abundant natural resources, and we are as creative and have the potential to be as productive as anyone else. We do not, however, have any divine right to prosperity. Our success is wholly dependent on making effective use of what we have. The federal compromise worked out by our ancestors compares favourably to the political system of any other country. It will never be a barrier to the pursuit of the ideals and dreams of Canadians, for our system of government is open to change and adjustment.

We are already seeing the proof of this change. In the past two years alone, a western Canadian has become prime minister, the fiscal imbalance has been recognized and corrected, and Quebec has been recognized as a nation and acquired a voice at the United Nations Educational, Scientific and Cultural Organization

(UNESCO). Do we understand how well federalism can serve us? As Quebecers, we have spent the last few decades "defending our interests" at the federal level and calling into question the very basis of a country that we ourselves helped to build. It is time now for us to engage in some healthy self-criticism, to face up to problems that have now become urgent and that are, for the most part, within our jurisdiction to solve. It is time to stop dwelling upon the injustices of the past, most of which have been dealt with since that long-ago election of 1970, and to contemplate the situation in which we would like to find ourselves ten years from now. For Quebec and for Canada, the time is right to define what that future will look like and start to create it.

DANIEL FOURNIER *is a businessman, the president of* ACNG *Capital Inc. and a member of several corporate boards. He has a degree in history from Princeton University and a degree in jurisprudence from the University of Oxford, where he was a Rhodes Scholar. He also played professional football for the Ottawa Rough Riders and was a Conservative candidate in the 2006 federal election.*

Notes

1. Lester B. Pearson, "Speech to the Congress of the Association des hebdomadaires de langue française du Canada, August 17, 1963. www.collectionscanada.gc.ca/primeministers/h4-4030-e.html#tphp (accessed May 27, 2008).

2. W.L. Morton quoted in Charles Taylor, *Radical Tories: The Conservative Tradition in Canada*, Toronto: House of Anansi Press, 1982, p. 68.

3. Robert Laird Borden, "Speech at the Directors' Luncheon, Central Canada Exhibition, Ottawa, September 9, 1918." www.collectionscanada.gc.ca/primeministers/h4-4063-e.html (accessed May 27, 2008).

2

JEAN LECLAIR

FORGING A TRUE FEDERAL SPIRIT

Refuting the Myth of Quebec's
"Radical Difference"

. . . il est plus commode de faire d'un principe une hérésie que de l'approfondir
par la discussion.[1]

MADAME DE STAËL,

Considérations sur la Révolution française, VIème Partie, Chapitre XI

IF THERE exists one recurrent theme in the Quebec, and indeed
the Canadian, political universe, it has to be the centralization of
powers by the federal government. However, only in Quebec is
this phenomenon referred to as the "implementation of a *unitary,*
not to say *imperial* political regime,"[2]—a regime which, if we are
not careful, could lead to the "*complete dissolution* of Quebec's cultural identity within the Canadian identity."[3] As for philosopher
Michel Seymour, he speaks of the "*total* invasion of [Quebec's]
jurisdictions."[4] And Joseph Facal, a former minister in the Parti
Québécois government, intones the same anthem when referring
to "the emergence of a political system increasingly *unitary,* in

an increasingly dominant government."[5] As for Henri Brun and Guy Tremblay, one can read the following enormity in their otherwise very interesting monograph on Canadian constitutional law: "It is only through [the central government's] generosity that the provinces still enjoy a measure of autonomy in Canada."[6]

The above-mentioned authors are both well known and respected scholars. They are in no way identified with the rancorous and bitter fringe of the nationalist movement. There would be reason to wring our hands should their apocalyptic conclusions in any way be right. However, reading these disturbed and disturbing comments brings to mind Prince of Talleyrand's observation that "all that is exaggerated is worthless."

Now, I recognize the generosity of the Supreme Court's interpretation of the powers conferred to the federal government by the constitution. I have said it myself.[7] That vigilance is required to ensure that the interests of the provinces are not ignored is no doubt necessary. But does that mean that such a liberal interpretation ineluctably leads to the "destruction" of provincial powers and to the implementation of a unitary Canadian state, that is, one where all power is held by the central government and where the provinces, especially Quebec, will have "to settle for small crumbs of power"[8]? Does this mean that the Supreme Court has forsaken the federal principle and condemned provincial autonomy to death? One only has to possess but a rudimentary knowledge of what constitutes a genuine unitary state, that of France, for instance, compared to Canada, to be torn between uncontrollable laughter and pure incredulity on reading these catastrophic premonitions.

By dint of always breathing in the same ideological incense, by dint of thinking that the Belgian federation (ah, what would we do without it!) is the only one to which Canada can be compared; by dint of hauling themselves up on one another's shoulders without knowing whether or not the initial argument is sound, some Quebec scholars have come to profess ideas that would make an expert in comparative federalism convulse with laughter. Now I hasten to say that there probably are entirely sound reasons to want independence for Quebec. But to suggest that Canada is "unitary" or, more hilarious still, "imperialist," is utterly ridiculous.

In the following pages I shall try to identify the foundation on which is based this paranoid understanding of Canadian federalism, and to explain why the Supreme Court's generous interpretation of federal powers will not lead to the forecasted apocalypse (A). I shall also demonstrate in this first part why the legitimate exercise of its powers by the federal government is not automatically synonymous with the "defeat" of Quebec, as certain influential Quebec nationalists think. In short, that the federal Hydra is perhaps possessed of fewer heads than is generally thought, and that the ones remaining are not all wearing a hostile expression.

I shall also examine what cultivating a "federal spirit" would really mean for Quebecers (B).[9] Keeping in mind that Quebecers twice rejected democratically the eventual separation from Canada, it behooves them, along with the rest of Canada, to reflect constructively upon the federal structure to which they are still committed. Indeed, in the land of "50 per cent + 1," the 1980 and 1995 referendum results should at least mean that, although not fully satisfied, Quebecers still have not entirely repudiated federalism as a political system. Of course, all political parties will seek a majority wherever they find it, but independence has heretofore not carried the day. I shall also take a look at what embracing a federal spirit would actually mean to Anglo-Canadians (C).

Finally, briefly comparing the Canadian federation to its American counterpart, which has incontestably moved towards a radical centralization, I shall identify the social, economic and institutional factors that have acted, and will continue to act, in Canada, as obstacles to the unbridled centralization of federal powers (D).

A. The Quebec Sovereignist Orthodoxy: Unrestrained Centralization of Federal Powers Destructive of Quebec's Cultural Specificity

Before giving the floor to the critics of Canadian federalism, a word about "sovereignty" and "federalism."

The sixteenth-century jurist Jean Bodin, desirous of placing the King of France above Catholic/Protestant conflicts, wrote a book arguing that the cohesion of the political community required the monarch be invested with a perpetual, absolute and indivisible sovereignty, that is, the power "to give and to break the law." For Jean Bodin, any sovereignty shared among more than one power centre would be synonymous with social disorder: "The marks of sovereignty are indivisible, for he who has the power to make laws for all, that is to command or to prohibit what he wishes, [is authorized to do it] without anyone being able to appeal his decisions or even less to oppose his commands."[10] The downfall of monarchs and the advent of nation-states shall in no way unsettle the centrality of this *indivisible* notion of sovereignty in modern political thought. Indeed, the contrary is true.

However, and as opposed to Jean Bodin's absolute and indivisible concept of sovereignty, there appeared, almost at the same moment, another political notion: federalism. This concept would evolve over time, of course, but remains rooted in the conviction that concentrating all power in a single hand is not the best form of government. Quite to the contrary, the idea of small states uniting to achieve certain goals, and choosing to remain autonomous in the achievement of others, appeared to federalist thinkers to be a route that was often more fruitful.

From this basic idea of an association of states, the concept has developed of a central government to which the member-states would each cede a measure of their own sovereignty. To offset this power loss, each of the federated states would have the right to take part in the governance of that central authority. This explains why the political institutions of the central government are composed of two chambers: the House of Commons, where sit the elected representatives of the people, and the Senate, which represents the interests of the federated states—or, more specifically in Canada, the four "regions" of the state: Atlantic Canada, Quebec, Ontario and the West. Added to this participation is the protection, recognized and guaranteed in writing by the country's constitution, of the federated states' autonomy (from the Greek *auto* and *nomos*, meaning "ruled by its own laws"). Indeed, there is no federation when one order of government is completely subjected to another. In Canada, sections 91 and 92 of the Constitution Act, 1867 enumerate the *mutually exclusive* powers attributed to the two orders of government, provincial and federal.

Why was this federal structure viewed as more promising? First, because it combines the strength of a small, local, more homogeneous community with the benefit of belonging to a greater whole, better guaranteeing the security and prosperity of all. Second, it avoids the "too small" of the local community and the "too big" of the national community that risks swallowing the former. In addition—and this is especially true of the Canadian federation—federalism enables, or tries to enable, the coexistence of multiple cultural identities.

But there is still more. Federalism was born of a long tradition of thought whose central assumption is that the freedom of the individual is best guaranteed when "power constrains power"; in other words, when sovereignty is divisible and shared.

French writer François Mauriac, when Germany was still divided, apparently said in jest: "I so love Germany that I rejoice at there being two of them." One could say that federalists so love liberty that they prefer to be governed by two authorities rather than one. Indeed, multiplying political communities means multiplying the democratic spaces where citizens can express their will. It also means empowering citizens to play one order of government against the other. Quebecers have long been experts at this game up until, after the setback of the Meech Lake Accord in 1990, they elevated sulking to the status of a political philosophy.

Of course—and herein lie both all its fragility and all its strength—a federal structure is based upon compromise and restraint; on the conviction that no one is cast in a single mould, and that individuals, while shaped in part by their cultural heritage, can still "think themselves" by themselves and can venture, without fear of death, well outside the narrow circle of the so-called "authentic culture" drawn by self-proclaimed High Priests of the "national question," be they Quebecers, *Canadians* or Aboriginals.

BY WAY of introduction, let us recall the conclusion of Eugénie Brouillet's book *La négation de la nation* (The Negation of the Nation), a work of some undeniable qualities, and which is becoming, in Quebec, the last word on the Supreme Court's interpretation of the division of powers in Canada:

> The [Canadian] federal system has followed a resolutely cen-tralist evolutionary path, to the point where *the entirety of Quebec's legislative powers,* in the name of the national interest, can be shrunken by the will of both the federal Parliament and the Supreme Court of Canada; and [Quebecers should

remember] that the ultimate result of such an evolution could consist of *the complete absorption of Quebec's cultural identity within that of Canada.*[11]

Before examining how the author's totalizing idea of Quebec's "culture" explains her point of view, I would like to analyze this thesis of unbridled centralism. The reader will forgive me for being a bit technical, but the inquisitive citizen is entitled to know whether it is accurate to claim that there is "something rotten" in the state of Canada.

First of all, and I want to repeat it, several of the central government's powers have indeed been generously interpreted by the Supreme Court since the start of the 1980s. It is equally true that the criterion of economic efficiency has served as a springboard for such interpretation. Finally, it must be admitted that this criterion is open to criticism, for its general tendency is to favour the interests of the national community without duly acknowledging the interests of the provincial communities.[12] Let us, however, note that, though unable to justify everything, the idea of functionalist criteria relative to economic efficiency should not systematically be discarded. Between flat-out economic functionalism and flat-out cultural identity concerns, there should be some room for balancing these competing values. Moreover, when comparing current Supreme Court decisions to those of the fifties, one must recognize that provincial fields of jurisdiction have also been generously interpreted. Indeed, since 1980 the Supreme Court has recognized the constitutional validity of a number of provincial laws having to do with morality and public order. And if the constitutional legality of these same statutes had been tested against the legal standards as they had been set by the court during the fifties, they would most probably have been considered unconstitutional, that is, as measures infringing upon the federal government's exclusive power to legislate over criminal law.

This being said, and acknowledging that the Supreme Court has certainly generously interpreted the federal fields of jurisdiction, should we fear that the central government will reduce the overall legislative powers of Quebec? Will the doors of Quebec's legislature have to close in a few years because Canada has become a unitary state? The answer is, of course, a resounding no.

Eugénie Brouillet's thesis of the massive destruction of provincial powers rests on the potentialities of six areas of federal jurisdiction: 1) The power to regulate matters of "national concern." 2) The power to intervene in cases of "national emergency." 3) The power to make laws for the "general regulation of trade." 4) The power (the recognition of which is entirely hypothetical at the present time) to implement international agreements signed by Canada even if they deal with matters falling within the exclusive purview of the provinces. 5) The power to make laws in the field of communications. 6) The power to spend in areas exclusively attributed to the provinces.

Let us quickly review each of these claims. The "national concern" doctrine was revived in 1988 in the *Crown Zellerbach* decision.[13] Based on that doctrine, the Supreme Court has conferred upon itself the power to declare that, if and when certain criteria are satisfied, a specific matter will from then on qualify as a matter of "national concern." As a result of that conclusion, the matter is thenceforth declared to fall under Parliament's *exclusive* jurisdiction. In addition, the court indicated that whether the matter in question had formerly been under provincial jurisdiction was of no import. In this particular case, the court concluded that the regulation of saltwater pollution qualified as a matter of national concern.

Had the constitutional clock been stopped in 1988, Eugénie Brouillet would be perfectly right to say that this power "constitutes one of the greatest threats to the balance of power between the two levels of government."[14] However, although Brouillet acknowledges that the decision was far from unanimous (three of the seven judges dissented), she scarcely said anything about the dissenting decision of Justice Gérard La Forest, which was one of the fiercest and most eloquent in Canada's constitutional history. Neither does she say that this same judge, in 1992, then speaking in the name of a unanimous court, refused to acknowledge that environmental protection was an exclusively federal matter, affirming instead that it came under the jurisdiction of both levels of government (*Oldman River*).[15] Neither does she say that the same judge, in 1997, in the *Hydro-Québec* decision, restated this point of view, recalling that, in light of the *Oldman River* decision, it was not possible to conclude that the Supreme Court was promoting "an enthusiastic adoption of the 'national dimensions' doctrine."[16] In both *Oldman River* and *Hydro-Québec*, the court chose an approach recognizing that both the federal *and* provincial levels of government have the authority to regulate matters concerning the protection of the environment. And if the court took pains to confine the recourse to the "national concern" theory to very exceptional circumstances, it was precisely because that theory could potentially disturb the federal equilibrium. Strangely enough, the *Oldman River* case is nowhere even alluded to in Eugénie Brouillet's work, and the important *Hydro-Québec* decision deserves only one line in a footnote.[17]

As for the federal emergency powers, they authorize the central government to pass laws in any field, regardless of the division of powers, whenever highly uncommon circumstances so justify. This was the case, for example, in both world wars, and in the "apprehended insurrection" of October 1970. Only temporary measures can be based on this power, an emergency being intrinsically limited in time. Therein resides the distinction between the emergency powers and the "national concern" doctrine, which endows Parliament with a *permanent* power to legislate over a new matter. Eugénie Brouillet rightly says that in 1976 the Supreme Court authorized the federal government to resort to its emergency powers in peacetime (*Anti-Inflation* case).[18] In that decision, a temporary federal statute intended to fight inflation was held to be constitutional, even though it encroached upon areas of provincial jurisdiction. Never has Parliament resorted to this power since then. Does it threaten provincial autonomy? Might it be invoked without rhyme or reason by the federal government? No. Emergency situations are, by definition, extremely rare. And Eugénie Brouillet would undoubtedly agree that Canada is not a police state, except perhaps in the minds of a couple of lunatics.

As for Parliament's power over matters of trade and commerce, it is confined to the regulation of international and interprovincial commerce. All matters relating to local trade and business—wholesale or retail—fall within the provincial sphere of jurisdiction. However, in 1989 in the *City National Leasing* case,[19] the Supreme Court recognized a new federal power over matters relating to the "general regulation of trade." Eugénie Brouillet's criticism of this decision is on the whole very fair, but she has it say things it simply does not. For example, she declares that the conditions that must be met to trigger the exercise of this power do not constitute "obstacles to the *virtually unlimited* expansion of the federal jurisdiction" over commerce.[20] She agrees with the militant sovereignist Vilaysoun Loungnarath, who says that the federal government can, under the terms of this new power, "through some artificial redactional detours,... *appropriate nearly any field of economic regulation*, and consequently adopt uniform rules for the whole country."[21]

The reader would be justified in saying "Hey! That is disquieting, that is!" Now, I agree that the court's reasoning does raise certain problems.[22] The range of this new power nevertheless remains very limited. It does not allow unrestricted federal intrusions in matters of local trade, as we are given to understand. Labour relations, wholesale and retail trade, local industry, the whole field of contracts—and I could go on—remain under provincial jurisdiction. The new federal power only authorizes the regulation of a matter "concerned with trade as a whole rather than with a particular industry" (*City National Leasing*). This prevents Ottawa from regulating a particular business or industry under the pretext that it is operating at the national level or because it is of national importance for the economy. As yet, this power has justified the enactment of a federal statute prohibiting unfair competition and of another having to do with trademarks. It could possibly be resorted to in order to authorize the adoption of federal securities legislation. Since 1979, Ottawa has been strongly pressed to do just this but has, for unknown reasons, held back. If the federal government's sole mission was the "decapitation" of provincial powers, why would it turn a deaf ear to these siren songs prodding it to wield the executioner's axe?

In a famous 1937 decision, the Judicial Committee of the Privy Council[23] decided that the power to implement international treaties signed by Canada should be entrusted to the level of government which, under the terms of sections 91 and 92 of the Constitution Act, 1867, was competent over the matters dealt with by the treaty in question (*Labour Conventions* case). In other words, contrary to the argument advanced at the time by the federal government, the judicial committee refused to vest in Parliament an exclusive power to legislate with respect to the implementation of treaties. To conclude otherwise, according to the committee, would have administered a fatal blow to the structure of Canadian federalism:

> It would be remarkable that while the Dominion [Federal Parliament] could not initiate legislation, however desirable, which would affect civil rights in the Provinces, yet its Government not responsible to the Provinces nor controlled by Provincial Parliaments need only agree with a foreign country to enact such legislation, and its Parliament would be forthwith clothed with authority to affect Provincial rights to the full extent of such agreement. Such a result would appear to undermine the constitutional safeguards of Provincial constitutional autonomy.[24]

Eugénie Brouillet rightly states that certain judges have questioned the validity of this reasoning. Still, these isolated opinions have never won the support of the court itself. For reasons I shall go into in section (D), and which have to do with the fact that our present parliamentary institutions are not very representative, there is a small likelihood that such a reform would seriously be considered by the Supreme Court.

As for the field of communications, I grant that the provinces could have been allowed more leeway. However, it is in my view an exaggeration—an understatement—to assert, as do several nationalist pundits (Eugénie Brouillet not being one of them), that the sole and unique purpose of federal involvement in the field of communications is systematic, total, absolute, integral and complete annihilation of Quebec culture. Listen carefully:

> Pan-Canadianism rages through the news bulletins of Radio-Canada and clashes head-on with the intellectual and cultural

life of Quebec. The transformation of *La chaîne culturelle* into *Espace musique* is founded on this logic. It reproduces at the radiophonic level what had already been launched on RDI [the Radio-Canada TV equivalent of *Newsworld*]. It consists of reflecting the entirety of the pan-Canadian francophonie, even if that means shrinking the space occupied by Quebec culture.[25]

Finally, by reason of its revenues being greater than those of the provinces, the central government has the power to spend not only in its designated fields of jurisdiction but also in provincial sectors such as health, post-secondary education and welfare. It can do this unconditionally. The majority of these unconditional federal transfers are in the form of equalization payments. These are meant to "ensure that provincial governments have sufficient revenues to provide reasonably comparable levels of public services at reasonably comparable levels of taxation."[26] The central government can also make these cash and/or tax transfers conditional, and these conditional grants are what provincial politicians generally refer to as the federal spending power.

No doubt, the federal spending power, to the extent that it is exercised in areas of provincial jurisdiction, does present serious problems, especially when transfers are conditional. This power disrupts the priorities set by the provinces in their day-to-day management of areas where they are better positioned than the federal bureaucrats to understand the ins and outs of ongoing problems: health, post-secondary education and welfare. As for equalization payments, clear, public and predictable rules of calculation will have to be adopted. The kind of unfairness inherent in negotiating on a one-on-one basis is prejudicial to all provinces, not just to Quebec. As political scientist Alain Noël rightly reminds us,[27] in the absence of such rules, suspicion and confrontation will prevail upon the kind of trust necessary to successful intergovernmental relations. I shall come back later to this question of the federal spending power.

Before concluding on this point, I wish to underline a dimension of the Canadian division of powers that nationalist scholars take great care to ignore. Let us recall that the unbridled centralization theory holds that the federal government is usurping provincial powers, and it conveys the idea that a federal intervention on a specific matter denies the provinces the ability to legislate over it. In other words, because the constitution declares the federal and provincial powers to be mutually "exclusive," Canadian federalism is held to be a zero-sum game: matters falling within the provinces' fields of jurisdiction can never be the subject of a federal intervention, and vice versa. This is only partly true. There are indeed matters that are the exclusive preserve of one or the other level of government. Thus, the federal parliament is the only one that can enact the Criminal Code, because of its exclusive power to regulate criminal law. Neither Quebec nor any other province could do this. Quebec has, however, enacted the Civil Code of Quebec, since jurisdiction over "property and civil rights" has been granted exclusively to the provinces. And all things being equal, the power subsumed under "property and civil rights" is vastly more important on the scale of society as a whole than is the power to suppress deviance. The average reader would never suspect just how vast is the area of jurisdiction that allows for the adoption, among other things, of a civil code. The federal parliament is not endowed with the power to adopt a civil code. It is not, however, always that simple. As we will now see, the concept of exclusivity is no obstacle to an overlapping regulation of the very same matter.

Take, for example, the protection of the environment, to which I have already referred. Canada's federal constitution, written in 1867, makes no mention of the environment. Consequently, it is not a subject matter exclusively assigned to either order of government. Therefore the following question has arisen: does the protection of the environment fall under either the provinces' or the central government's exclusive authority? As I have pointed out earlier, the Supreme Court twice in recent years refused to recognize an exclusive and exhaustive federal jurisdiction over such a matter: "The subject of environmental protection [is] all-pervasive, and if accepted as falling within the general legislative domain of Parliament..., could radically alter the division of legislative power in Canada."[28] Conversely, the court has also refused to vest in the provinces an exclusive power to legislate with respect to this subject matter, because this would "[have] prevented Parliament from exercising the leadership role expected of it by the international community and its role in protecting the basic values of Canadians regarding the environment through the instrumentality of the criminal law power."[29] The court has instead envisaged the environment as a "diffuse subject" over which legislative power is concurrent.

In other words, we must examine the powers spelled out in the constitution and analyze "how they may be employed to meet or avoid environmental concerns" (*Oldman River*). And the court further adds, "[w]hen viewed in this manner it will be seen that in exercising their respective legislative powers, both levels of government may affect the environment, either by acting or not acting."[30]

Interestingly, the provinces come out winners under this approach. Indeed, the specific and detailed character of the federal fields of jurisdiction allows for only relatively limited environmental intervention: navigation, fisheries, Indian and federal property, to mention only a few. Only the federal legislative power over criminal law authorizes more extensive action in environmental protection. However, once again, this power is not unlimited. Any such federal intervention can only justify the regulation of matters or activities threatening the environment or health to the point of provoking a dangerous situation. Without such demonstrable danger, federal involvement based on Parliament's jurisdiction over criminal law is unconstitutional. As for the provinces, they possess a much wider arsenal of intervention, holding as they do the power to regulate industrial and business activities as well as all activities related to the exploitation of natural resources. They also have sway over agriculture and municipal activities. In short, the provinces are invested with the power to restrict, if they so wish, activities well known to be the most polluting.

Furthermore, even though in cases of inconsistent provincial and federal environmental statutes, the latter will prevail—that is, the provincial law will be held inoperative to the extent of the inconsistency—for the paramountcy doctrine to be triggered, the existence of an inconsistency must first be established. Now, in order to guarantee the provinces the greatest possible latitude, the Supreme Court usually resorts to a very narrow definition of inconsistency. It can be summarized thus: a conflict between a provincial and a federal statute will be established "where one enactment says 'yes' and the other says 'no'" (*Rio Hotel*).[31] Consistent with this logic, the court recently had occasion to repeat that a provincial law more stringent than its federal counterpart is not, in fact, inconsistent with the latter (*Rothmans, Benson & Hedges Inc.*).[32] Indeed, if the provincial law is more stringent, then it not only meets but it goes beyond the threshold established by the federal statute. In other words, the central government can establish minimal environmental standards beyond which, in exercising their own powers, the provinces are authorized to go.

Should a large majority of Quebecers choose to vote for a national party with both an environmental platform and the possibility of acceding to power, they could then participate in the adoption of effective federal environmental legislation. Furthermore, they could demand the same kind of environmental courage from their own provincial government. As I have tried to demonstrate, the power of one level of government does not necessarily impair the power of the other. Quite the opposite.

On several occasions in recent years, Andrée Lajoie, a well-known constitutionalist, convinced sovereignist and member among other things of the Commission on Fiscal Imbalance, has denounced the federal "invasion" of Quebec's fields of jurisdiction.[33] In her analysis of the Supreme Court's decisions on the division of powers, she distinguishes between what she dubs Quebec "victories" and "defeats." Now, oddly enough, in light of what I have just been explaining, the *Oldman River* and *Hydro-Québec* decisions are treated as "defeats" for Quebec, on the grounds, among others, that the Supreme Court has interpreted Ottawa's jurisdiction over criminal law much too generously. But how can our right to demand effective environmental action from *both* levels of government somehow amount to an attack on what Andrée Lajoie refers to as Quebec's "values." Would an all-powerful provincial government be a better guarantor of a healthy environment? Have Quebec governments, either Péquiste or Liberal, really used all their constitutional manoeuvring room to vigorously tackle environmental problems? The very asking answers the question.

It is also interesting to note that a sovereign Quebec, where environmental matters are concerned, would bear a striking resemblance to the Quebec that presently exists. Forever languishing in the Opposition, the majority of Quebec's federal members of Parliament do not hold the reins of power and cannot effectively influence Canadian environmental policy. That at present is amply demonstrated. They have no way of forcing the

Cabinet to adopt a "greener" stance. And the situation would be exactly the same in an independent Quebec; Quebecers would inherit transborder Canadian pollution (which would not have the courtesy to respect the frontiers of an independent Quebec) and they would have no way of participating in the establishment of minimal norms, as they could, should they so desire, within the framework of the Canadian federal system as it now exists.

Andrée Lajoie has exercised, and continues to exercise, a considerable influence in certain Quebec intellectual and governmental circles. I believe that it is thus necessary to stress the extremely exaggerated character of her conclusions. Considering the very restrictive conditions of application of "the general regulation of trade" power, keeping in mind that almost all public property belongs to the provinces, keeping in mind that the Supreme Court has denounced what it calls the "enthusiastic adoption of the 'national dimensions' doctrine" and that it has systematically refused to resort to it since 1988, keeping in mind that labour relations are essentially a provincial matter and bearing in mind that the Supreme Court has recently refused to generously interpret the federal government's jurisdiction over banking (*Canadian Western Bank v. Alberta*),[34] and finally considering that she does not say a word about the federalizing potential of a simultaneous application of the double aspect theory and of a restrictive theory of inconsistency (the approach taken by the court in environmental matters, as described above), one is flabbergasted, nonplussed, at the following conclusion by Andrée Lajoie: "Not only fields of jurisdiction fundamental to development, such as the economy, communications, regional development, environment and natural resources, but also the more traditional fields of labour relations, transportation and even matrimonial law *have been almost completely federalized [by the Supreme Court].*"[35] One would think this was a critique of American federalism by a Texan!

Finally, while acknowledging that the federal spending power raises serious problems, and, similarly, granting that the Supreme Court has generously interpreted the federal fields of jurisdiction and, hence, that vigilance is always the price of safety, claiming that Canada has become a unitary state or that the federal parliament has completely invaded the provinces' powers is simply ludicrous.

One last word on the role of the Supreme Court in the interpretation of the division of powers. Premier Maurice Duplessis bequeathed a saying to those who despair of ever being witty: "The Supreme Court of Canada is like the Tower of Pisa: it always leans on the same side." Some take pride in cheerfully repeating this, a knowing and goofy smile on their lips, forgetting that some events and sayings are best left hidden under the veil of oblivion. Yes, Duplessis was chastened several times by the Supreme Court. It condemned him *personally* to pay damages to a Jehovah's Witness for having, when he was premier of the province, *illegally* ordered the cancellation of the claimant's business licence because he disliked the latter's religious creed (*Roncarelli v. Duplessis*).[36] In the middle of the Cold War, the court had the courage to declare unconstitutional the Act to Protect the Province against Communistic Propaganda—the so-called Padlock Law, whose sections 12 and 13 authorized the imprisonment of anyone publishing, printing or distributing "any newspaper, periodical, pamphlet, circular, document or writing whatsoever propagating or tending to propagate communism or bolshevism" (*Switzman v. Elbing*).[37] I say this: lucky for us that during this period the Supreme Court did always lean on the same side.

THOSE WHO have not by now given up reading this essay will perhaps be saying to themselves: "This is all very nice, but this division of powers is really pretty complicated, since, while providing for mutually exclusive fields of jurisdiction, it none-theless does not prevent concurrent actions by both levels of government." And in that they would be quite right. The very famous nineteenth-century intellectual Alexis de Tocqueville affirmed that federal systems all suffer from "inherent evils" of which "most prominent... is the very complex nature of the means they employ." Indeed, he says, there is no escaping the difficulties arising from the clash and the overlap of two sover-eignties. And, he adds, "the federal system, therefore, rests upon a theory which is complicated at the best, and which demands the daily exercise of a considerable share of discretion on the part of those it governs."[38] How then, does one tackle a complex idea? Tocqueville says, by proposing a simple idea offering all the appearances of truth:

> A proposition must be plain, to be adopted by the understand-ing of a people. A false notion which is clear and precise will always have more power in the world than a true principle which is obscure or involved. Thus it happens that parties, which are like small communities in the heart of the nation, invariably adopt some principle or name as a symbol, which very inadequately represents the end they have in view and the means that they employ, but without which they could neither act nor exist. The governments that are founded upon a single principle or a single feeling which is easily defined are perhaps not the best, but they are unquestionably the strongest and the most durable in the world.[39]

Those who cling to the thesis of unbridled centralism all share this one simple and exceptionally effective idea: an exclu-sive Quebec nationalism based upon a totalizing and univocal understanding of Quebec's culture.

Whether it is the vengeful and hatred-driven nationalism of a Pierre Falardeau[40] or the incontestably democratic and inclusive nationalism fuelling the works of Michel Seymour, Eugénie Brouillet and others, it remains true that, within this nationalist perspective, there is *but one* nation to which citizens can adhere. The nation is a whole, to which citizens "belong" and from which they can detach themselves only by leaving it completely. As the saying goes, "A door must either be open... or closed."

I do not doubt that Quebec nationalism is civic and open to differences. But it remains no less indivisible and exclusive. It holds that one's loyalty to the nation, although voluntary, centres only on *one* nation: that of Quebec. Outside of it, there is no salvation. Citizens who, without renouncing their love of French or of Quebec, prefer their right to freely choose their allegiances to "authenticities" in which others would wrap them—and who prefer a double allegiance to a single one—these citizens become heretics. Because the nation feeds on unanimity, it is allergic to plural belongings.

Federalism and nationalism, the reader will surmise, do not get on well together. The first presumes that citizens of a same state are entitled to claim allegiance to more than one political community; the second excludes that possibility.

This first idea—that one can claim membership solely in a *single* nation—is inseparable from another: everything, absolutely everything, is cultural. From the regulation of ventilation ducts to pencil erasers, everything bears the indelible stamp of the distinctive culture of the nation. Even so-called universal values are reduced to the level of historically contingent cultural facts. Nothing is shared with people outside of the nation's cultural perimeter.

In addition to being intrinsically problematic, this totalizing notion of culture is also incompatible with any federal logic.

The latter is clearly premised upon the idea that certain values can indeed be shared and that there is a sphere of civic life that is impervious to radical cultural differences.

For instance, the nation is, in the eyes of Eugénie Brouillet, the principal means by which a people can flourish and develop. She defines a nation as a "particular historical community, institutionally more or less complete, occupying a given territory, and whose members share a common culture." In this perspective, a people can have but *one* common culture. And she goes on, stating that the "culture," or more specifically the "cultural identity" of a people, "encompasses all the elements of human activity, be they social, religious, political or economic."[41] In short, only the nation has the required legitimacy to pronounce on these issues.

It is in light of this monistic idea of nationalism and culture that Brouillet envisages the function of federalism. Basically, the latter would, in essence, be "a legal and political response to this desire for political autonomy to which nations aspire."[42] Eugénie Brouillet admits that federalism presupposes dual allegiances, but within her totalizing nationalist logic this can mean only one thing: within the Canadian federal state, Quebecers have the right to belong to the Quebec Nation, just as Anglo-Canadians have the right to belong to the Canadian nation. The categorical imperative of nationalism forbids one from claiming an allegiance to more than one political community.

For Andrée Lajoie, the coexistence of multiple allegiances in the same individual is equally impossible. In her analysis of federalism, the "Québécois" are a minority group distinct from "the wielders of the powers necessary to exercise political domination, such powers having been initially exercised by the Canadian bourgeoisie that grew out of colonization... [A] dominant power that was subsequently transferred by means of the neoliberal globalization, into the hands of the more extended group now running the North American economy."[43] But who are these "dominant groups at once economic and nationalistic" if not the Anglo-Canadians? In fact, in her view, Quebecers are cast in the mould of a single identity, and the National Assembly of Quebec retains the exclusive right and power to exercise the sovereignty of Quebec's political community. Thus, the only common ground possible between peoples is that which can be negotiated around their radical differences.

The idea that several loyalties can be blended within a single person, and that some might be of greater importance than others, is just irreconcilable with the nationalist logic.

When pushed to its limit, this logic delegitimizes all federal activity, the Quebec nation-state being the only one entitled to speak in the name of its citizens. The central government is presumed never to speak in the name of Quebecers. Worse still, every initiative taken by Ottawa is seen as having no other purpose than the pursuit of "Canadian nation-building." This said, all is said. The federal monster—slimy, insatiable—is staring at Quebecers with bulging eyes.

Reading Michel Seymour, Andrée Lajoie, Joseph Facal and their consorts, this arrogance and presumption are striking, assuming as they do that the rest of Canada has no concern other than that of trampling on and crushing Quebec, or that federal politicians wake up in the night, the days being too short, to think up new, "shifty and hypocritical"[44] ways to enslave and humiliate us. I strongly doubt that Quebec should be the sole pre-occupation of Anglo-Canadians; however, I am convinced that the federal government is absolutely necessary to these nationalist thinkers. It may not be the source of all our troubles; it is certainly the source of all their thoughts. Although execrated, its existence to them is indispensable. It offers a perfectly coherent structure to their thinking. It not only spares them from doing a mite of comparative federalism (except, of course, for their enthusiastic embrace of Belgian federalism)[45]; it also prevents them from inquiring as to whether or not the other provinces may play any particular role in the political construction of the Canadian state. The federal government, being the source of all of Quebec's problems, is thus the obvious excuse that saves Quebecers the trouble of examining themselves critically.

Ironically, several of these scholars are self-proclaimed pluralists fervently favouring a "dialogue between nations." But if we are up to our necks in our distinctive culture, and ontologically incapable of understanding the other's differences, because that other is not us, and since we share absolutely no values with our neighbours, could someone please tell me what in the world will incite us to discuss anything with them?

From that perspective of both a totalizing preconception of cultural identity and an indivisible understanding of political sovereignty, Canadian federalism can never amount to anything more than a failure in the eyes of nationalist scholars. Their Jacobin notion of the nation-state holds that a political community can never have but a single centre. And this ideological posture forces the citizen to choose one community and only one. Added to that is a teleological and eschatological view of the future of nations whose "natural destiny" will invariably be independence.

As I read these authors' works, I often ask myself: what about all these Quebecers voting and taking part in federal elections, those with a seat in Parliament, those working in the federal public sector, what about that majority that chose not to break with the rest of Canada in both 1980 and 1995? If they are all taking part in this despicable "Canadian nation-building" enterprise, must we conclude that their only choice is to be traitors, sellouts or idiots?

To think about federalism requires a certain number of premises. 1) Differences do exist among humans, but a human being per se is the locus of the coexistence of multiple allegiances: to be human is to be plural. There is nothing ignoble about feeling a dual (or for that matter a triple) allegiance. Think, for example, of all those Quebec sovereignists holding French passports. 2) All is not cultural. 3) The very nature of federalism is both to limit state power and to ensure the peaceful management of relationships among different political communities. 4) Federalism, of course, entails respect for the autonomy of the federated entities, but it also requires the cultivation of a certain form of solidarity, hence the recognition of the legitimacy of all fellow confederates—including the central government. 5) A climate of tension is consubstantial with the federal idea, indeed, with politics in general and democracy in particular. If Quebec sovereignty was anything but a fantasy, had it been subjected to the same reality test that federalism has faced since 1867, it would not be free of tensions either. 6) Federalism is not a zero-sum game: federal "victories" have not been losses for Quebecers, unless one assumes that the federal system excludes them. 7) Like it or not, a majority of Quebecers, for reasons as mysterious as those which tie the *indépendantistes* to their cause, do remain attached to Canada, while at the same time feeling a stronger attachment to their province.

I would not presume to claim that the nationalist perspective deprives the above-mentioned authors of their right to criticize the work of the Supreme Court, or federalism in general. I say that this perspective does not generally permit them to do justice to the work of the court or to the federal principle. I say "generally" because some committed nationalist authors are also models of intellectual rigour.

The driving force of this kind of nationalist thought remains the myth of the Conquest: federalism would, in truth, be just another form of colonialism by the "English." As proof, the abuse of the word "imperialism." Constitutionally speaking, the impression is at times that the Quiet Revolution never occurred: Quebecers would still be today only bearers of water and hewers of wood for anglophone capitalists. It could be said of some nationalists what was said of the French aristocrats after the Restoration: They have learned nothing, and forgotten nothing.

B. The Cultivation of a Federal Spirit in Quebec

The cultivation of a federal spirit requires, above all, that we extricate ourselves from the quagmire of cultural essentialism, which holds that, everything being cultural, there is really only one way of doing things: the Quebec way. First of all, this idea quite wrongly presumes that Quebecers are unanimous about everything, all bathing as they are in the azure-tinted waters of their "common culture." Secondly, it breeds a discourse where Quebecers share absolutely nothing with their Anglo-Canadian neighbours.

Furthermore, as I have emphasized above, this essentialist approach misrepresents every federal intervention as not only unconstitutional but, even worse, as an imperialist invasion. By way of illustrating this false logic, take, for example, the federal spending power. The federal government has adopted some programs that fall within provincial areas of jurisdiction: the Canada Child Tax Benefit, the Millennium Scholarships, the Canada Research Chairs, the Canadian Foundation for Innovation, among others. There are excellent reasons to be critical of these interventions. After all, if federalism—which includes the founding principle of provincial autonomy guaranteed by the notion of exclusivity—is more than a mere system of decentralization, then we have to admit that, in their exclusive fields of jurisdiction, the provinces should have the upper hand.

However, from the problematic character of such interventions, can it be inferred that there is indeed a federal will to eradicate the culture of Quebec? We can certainly disapprove of such federal interventions, but should we conclude that Quebecers are completely oblivious to the "values" underlying them? Of course Quebec culture differs from the culture of other provinces, but Ontario is not Turkmenistan, Alberta is not Togo, and Canada is not Russia. What is more, are these federal interventions designed to promote a *substantive Canadian* cultural *content*—whatever that might be? Do all university students holding Millennium Scholarships go around singing the praises of the federal state? Do all incumbents of Canada Research Chairs dedicate their works to the memory of Pierre Elliott Trudeau? Have the federal research grants awarded to Quebec scholars prevented them from saying exactly what they think? In truth, we are light-years away from any Soviet-style crushing of Quebec's identity. Having rid ourselves of this navel-gazing posture for a second, could we not conclude that the use of the spending power is, instead of a vast program of cultural cleansing, actually aimed at something much more banal, namely the attempt by politicians (federal ones in this case) to try to please the entire electorate at whatever cost?

Cultivating a federal spirit would also necessitate the admission that a federal structure has virtues other than just recognizing a measure of autonomy for the provinces. If it is true that federalism, recognizing cultural diversity, contributes to the peaceful coexistence of different groups,[46] in return it also prevents the advent of radical forms of nationalism by institutionalizing solidarity relationships between these same groups. If it is true that federalism recognizes and encourages a closer-knit social solidarity among provincial communities—such solidarity stemming from the greater homogeneity of the local population[47]—in return it also provides an institutional framework for the moral obligations woven by time among diverse human groups brought together by history. It also allows the overcoming of the kind of egoism that nationalism can generate.

Indeed, a community can sometimes find cohesion in its will not to help its neighbour.

On this theme of federal solidarity, I underline that the cultivation of a federal spirit imposes the obligation to consider problems of governance other than from a strictly narcissistic viewpoint. Canada's social union initiative is a case in point. "Social union" is a catch-all name that refers to a whole bundle of federal initiatives in the field of social policy, initiatives that are based, for the most part, on the federal spending power—including equalization payments. For several Quebec scholars, the exercise of the federal spending power—and thus Canada's social union itself—has only one object: "the complete invasion of Quebec's jurisdictions."[48] They would therefore have no other purpose than to promote the dreaded "Canadian nation-building" enterprise. Right off the bat, we can state with confidence that this assessment is certainly wrong in the case of equalization payments.

The mechanism of equalization payments aims at redistributing wealth in the Canadian state from the richest to the poorest provinces. It may well be managed awkwardly, even incompetently, but this is its objective. In Quebec, it has been declared that the answer to fiscal imbalance does not lie in more generous federal cash transfers but rather in a reduction of Ottawa's fiscal reach in favour of the provinces. In other words, the latter should be given "tax points" presently monopolized by the federal government. Such a solution would enable a province such as Ontario to garner some very substantial fiscal revenues; I strongly doubt it in the case of Quebec. However, it would be of little benefit to the less populous provinces, the insufficiency of the revenue generated by the transfer of tax points preventing them from funding public services of equivalent value. In short, for those provinces, the preservation of both the central government's power to tax and its power to redistribute wealth is essential. As Sarah Fortin[49] reminds us:

> The social union is not just an abstract concept, or some idea elaborated in times of crisis in order to try to bolster... a feeling of national cohesion... it touches on much more concrete stakes, such as the ability of several provinces to garner the fiscal revenues needed to provide their population with similar social programs of high quality. This is certainly true of the poorest provinces. By way of illustration, remember that in 2004–2005 the share of provincial revenues made up of federal transfers ranged from 16% in Alberta, to 42% in Nova Scotia.

Solutions offered by Quebec cannot ignore this reality. By the way, let us insist on the fact that a federal spirit, or rather the most basic intellectual honesty, requires us to remember that presently Quebec is a "poor province," that is, receiving equalization payments. So—and here I am borrowing some rhetoric from nationalist Lucien Bouchard—we have to have "the courage, the honesty, the political and moral robustness"[50] to acknowledge that taxpayers in Ontario and Alberta are presently funding part of Quebec's social programs.[51]

To take into consideration the point of view of the other provinces is also to stop imagining that all Anglo-Canadians are clones of Pierre Elliott Trudeau. Yes, the Canadian Charter of Rights and Freedoms did contribute to the development of a pan-Canadian identity. But in no way did it totally rub off the feeling of belonging of Canadians to their regional and provincial communities.[52] To consider the point of view of others is also to admit that Quebec public policies are far from being unique in the world and that they bear some striking similarities to those of other provinces, especially those of Ontario and Alberta.[53] Finally, it is also to admit that the Canadian federal regime must aim to satisfy the needs of all the members of the federation, not simply those of Quebec.

Cultivating a federal spirit is to be wary of the solutions advocated by Mario Dumont. Consistent with his opportunism but inconsistent with his principles, this leader of the Action démocratique du Québec (ADQ) is now offering us a new bauble: "autonomism." By his own admission, he is neither federalist nor separatist and has therefore accomplished the feat of being half-virgin. He is now offering Quebecers "autonomy without constraint." This political concept, a "sovereignism" of sorts, deprived of its veil of "dignity" and of "natural destiny of the nation" is in reality nothing but a fierce will seeking more power (the province recuperating all federal jurisdictions) and more money (the province levying all taxes). It is, in fact, a quest for a federalism in which Quebec would hold all the rights and the other partners would bear all the responsibilities.

The constitutional position of the ADQ perfectly incarnates the unavowed desire of several Quebecers to form an independent state within a Canada whose nature is none of their concern. Truth be told, the three major components of the party's constitutional platform, that is, the autonomy of Quebec understood as a one-on-one negotiation with Ottawa, the withdrawal of Quebec from the Council of the Federation and, above all, the collection of all taxes—including federal taxes—just amounts to delirium. It is the attitude of sulking children that feel all their whims should be indulged. Behind this mask, cowards can boast all they want, for this ideology is handy: they can embrace it without committing to anything. Once they have "courageously" hammered out Quebec's "traditional" demands—a concept that can be extended infinitely because the realm of Quebec culture knows no bounds—they can vociferously denounce Canada for failing to satisfy them.

Within a federal context, provincial autonomy is not solely a matter of one's rights opposed to the rights of others. In true federal logic, such autonomy must be counterbalanced by the participation of all citizens in that part of political life falling under the aegis of the central government. And this obligation to participate is all the more true where Quebecers are concerned because, as I have said before, they have twice democratically refused to reject the Canadian federal system.

This "thirst for independence within a united Canada" also has a perverse effect. It goes a long way towards explaining the many messiahs who have succeeded one another in Quebec over the last few years. Indeed, one would have to be a god to have Canada recognize Quebec, *within our present federal structure*, with the status proposed either by the Allaire Report[54] or the ADQ's "autonomistic" platform, or again by "sovereignism" which, like the first two and contrary to *"indépendantisme,"* has never really been anything other than a variation on the theme of renewed federalism.[55] The main trait of messiahs is to be crucified. To this, Lucien Bouchard can bear witness. As long as we Quebecers fail to admit that there are limits to provincial powers and as long as we fail to recognize the legitimacy of the central government, we will keep on sending off our provincial politicians—armed as they are with their "autonomism"—to a certain death. And we condemn ourselves to eternal disappointment. If, however, we assess the situation from a federal perspective, which is not exclusively Quebec-centrist, we can see that while Quebec's culture may not have succeeded in lighting up the world, it is doing very well for itself, thank you very much.

One could say of federalism what Tocqueville said of democracy:

If your object is not to stimulate the virtues of heroism, but the habits of peace; [...] if, instead of living in the midst of a brilliant society, you are contented to have prosperity around you; if, in short, you are of the opinion that the principal object of a government is not to confer the greatest possible power and glory upon the body of the nation, but to ensure the greatest enjoyment and to avoid the most misery to each of the individuals who compose it—if such be your desire, then equalize the conditions of men and establish democratic institutions.[56]

The francophone majority making up the specificity of Quebec's political community has, in spite of having suffered undeniable injustices, succeeded in prospering within Canada. It is certainly not subjected to an imperialist regime, and, importantly, there is nothing vile or base about the attachment of Quebecers to Canada, as mysterious as it may seem to some.[57]

To go on enjoying these advantages, Quebecers should play the federal game to the hilt. A first step would be to stop snubbing their noses at the idea of having their say in the exercise of federal political power. This is, though, precisely what they are doing when electing and re-electing the Bloc Québécois, this apparently permanent fixture of the Opposition. This party whose raison d'être is the quest for a Yes vote on sovereignty yet, ironically, is eternally condemned to say no.

But, you ask, "What of English Canada in all this?"

C. Cultivating a Federal Spirit in English Canada

I often reflect that, if for many Quebecers the history of Quebec ended in 1760, for many Anglo-Canadians Canada's history only began in 1982 with the advent of the Canadian Charter of Rights and Freedoms.

No doubt, for many Anglo-Canadians, the Canadian Charter has become a national icon that has provided the missing foundation for a pan-Canadian identity. Nor do I question the conclusion according to which the Canadian Charter has rendered more difficult a *historical* definition of Canada, a state understood as the space of coexistence of distinct political communities, each deeply rooted in its own French, British and Aboriginal cultural soil. Abstract notions of equality and multiculturalism tend to marginalize history. Nowadays, it seems less and less important when determining whether or not one is Canadian to know one's origins, historically speaking, than to know whether one is for or against gay marriage or for or against abortion.

Is that to say that this Anglo-Canadian identity would be more civic and open than would a "Québécois" identity? No. Just try to suggest to Anglo-Canadians that we make Turkish, rather than English, the national language of instruction, and substitute the history of Bangladesh for that of Canada, and it will soon become evident that the Anglo-Canadian identity is as firmly anchored, culturally and historically, as that of Quebec.

However, the advent of the Canadian Charter has in no way blotted out all provincial or regional loyalties. At most, we can draw the following conclusion: while Quebecers' attachment to their province is stronger than to Canada, the feeling of belonging is, among Anglo-Canadians, most probably much stronger for Canada than for their province.[58]

Cultivating a federal spirit requires Anglo-Canadians to recognize that problems of diversity affect all societies, but that federalism assumes that a deliberate choice is exercised to institutionalize *a certain form* of political and territorial diversity. All federations are as different as are their historical circumstances. The kind of diversity initially chosen, which could have been different but was not, necessarily brings about political and normative consequences that must be kept in mind if the stability of the state is not to be jeopardized. True, the nature of diversities may evolve, but as political scientist Michael Burgess has correctly pointed out, that fact "does not prevent contemporaneous diversities from being essentially historical phenomena."[59]

It is then unnecessary to prove the existence of a formal "pact" between the "two nations" in order to demonstrate that the object, among others, of the Canadian federation was to guarantee to Lower Canada's political community, in its majority francophone, a sphere of political autonomy. One would have to be at once a dunce in addition to an idiot to deny the fact that the object of the 1867 federation was the institutionalization of a particular form of political pluralism in which a francophone majority in Quebec would play a fundamental and incontrovertible role.

We too often forget that the Canadian federation is the child of a secession. The United Province of Canada created by the 1840 Act of Union was severed in two in 1867 in order to create Ontario and Quebec. The Fathers of Confederation were perfectly conscious that they were concentrating a francophone majority on the Quebec territory. By doing so, they recognized a certain kind of political pluralism that was inevitably going to bring about consequences in the future.

Now this asymmetry, based on language and territory, institutionalized in 1867, is still growing today—Quebec is becoming more and more francophone. If the Canadian state's stability demanded that it be respected then, the same goes today.

One more word about the Canadian Charter: a number of scholars, after the fashion of Eugénie Brouillet, have described it as an instrument purported "to undermine Quebec's cultural identity while reinforcing the Canadian identity."[60] No doubt allowing for the nullification of certain sections of the Charter of the French Language, the Canadian Charter limited the province's latitude to regulate language issues. At the political and symbolic levels, the effect was disastrous. But will a closer look show that the provincial power to legislate over linguistic matters has indeed been emasculated and that Quebec's specificity has been flouted?

Take, for example, the *Ford* decision, which has certainly had the greatest reverberations. In that case, the Supreme Court declared unconstitutional sections of the Charter of the French Language requiring public signs, commercial advertising and firm names to be in French only. However, the court did not disavow the objective of the Charter of the French Language. Rather, it explicitly acknowledged that there was a rational connection "between protecting the French language and assuring that the reality of Quebec society is communicated through the 'visage linguistique' [(linguistic face) of Quebec]." Further, whereas it concluded that requiring the exclusive use of French did not constitute a reasonable limit to the claimant's freedom of expression, it nonetheless made it clear that "requiring the predominant display of the French language, even its marked predominance, would be proportional to the goal of promoting and maintaining a French 'visage linguistique' in Quebec [and would therefore satisfy the requirements of both charters]."[61] Unless we deny that Quebec's anglophone minority is part of the provincial political community, this approach seems to me an entirely acceptable compromise.

Two important features of the *Ford* debate are often suppressed by nationalist scholars. First, despite what is constantly repeated in Quebec,[62] the most controversial section in the *Ford* decision, that is, section 58 of the Charter of the French Language which states that "public signs and posters and commercial advertising shall be solely in the official language [French]," was invalidated—not, I wish to stress, under the terms of the *Canadian* Charter but because it infringed upon the freedom of expression guaranteed by the Quebec Charter of human rights and freedoms.

Indeed, for technical reasons, the Canadian Charter did not apply to section 58.[63] As for section 69 regarding firm names, it was invalidated as infringing upon both charters. Secondly, and even more importantly, the Supreme Court decision was approved by the Human Rights Committee of the United Nations,[64] the said committee having judged that the imposition of French unilingualism applied to commercial signs and advertising violated the freedom of expression guaranteed by the United Nations' International Covenant on Civil and Political Rights. Would an independent Quebec refuse to comply with the standards of international law?

SOME WILL object that the rest of Canada will never explicitly recognize Quebec's specificity in the constitution! This is probably true. All the same, most Quebecers, I am convinced, would in any case never be entirely satisfied, always being among the first to disparage the very symbols they clamour for. For example, in 1987 when it was proposed that Quebec be recognized as a "distinct society," how many voices were raised—and not only among sovereignists—saying that this was nothing more than tokenism. But, more seriously, why should our collective existence depend *entirely* on our being recognized through the eyes of the other—"if not recognized we are humiliated, scorned, colonized, etc."? And if the federal structure, *as it now exists,* renders impossible the forecasted cultural cleansing and guarantees, on the contrary, a special status to Quebec and a peaceful existence to its citizens, could we not mute the ethnocide megaphone?

I now intend to address this last issue.

D. Why Canada Is Not Yet a Unitary State

Reading the above-mentioned sovereignist scholars leaves one with the impression that they are describing the American, not the Canadian, federation. In the United States, since the end of the Second World War, the Supreme Court has interpreted Congress's powers with extraordinary generosity. To such an extent that some American academics refer to "the death of federalism." How is it, then, that the Canadian Supreme Court has, by comparison, been so timid in allowing federal intrusions upon provincial powers? A court which, we are led to believe, is diabolically inclined to eradicate Quebec's culture?

The Supreme Court justices are instinctively aware of the truth of Tocqueville's saying which, in his analysis of American judges, underlines that they are "all-powerful as long as the people respect the law; but [that] they would be impotent against popular neglect or contempt of the law."[65]

There exist in Canada socioeconomic and institutional factors upon which the people's opinion and that of its elected representatives has built itself and goes on doing it. These factors form the basis of the people's respect for the law. The absence of their equivalents in the United States explains, I believe, why the catastrophe predicted by nationalists has not yet happened and probably never will happen.[66]

The territorial distribution of cultural minorities can be counted among these socioeconomic factors. In the United States, no minority group constitutes a majority in any given state. On the contrary, Americans have knowingly avoided any such territorial concentration. Thus, there has never been any serious challenge to building a predominant national identity. However, in Canada, as we have seen, the Fathers of Confederation were perfectly conscious that they were creating a political space in Quebec that was principally francophone. Today, this asymmetry is growing ever stronger. In addition, thinking of the linguistic and territorial asymmetry generated by the creation of First Nations territories such as Nunavut and Nunavik, can we go on speaking of a simple "duality"? Canada's linguistic and territorial duality is therefore an extremely powerful centrifugal force.

The importance of natural resources in provincial economies constitutes another important centrifugal factor. The provinces own their natural resources, which play a major role in their economy. The nature and importance of such natural resources vary from one region to another: wheat on the Prairies; forestry in British Columbia; fisheries in Nova Scotia, Newfoundland and British Columbia; oil and gas in Alberta; potash in Saskatchewan; hydroelectric power in Quebec. The manufacturing sector predominates in Ontario and Quebec. The provinces profit hugely from these resources. That is why, in 1982, their consent to the constitution's repatriation was made conditional on adopting a constitutional amendment guaranteeing their continuing control over these resources (section 92A of the Constitution Act, 1867). According to Andrée Lajoie, as we have seen, Parliament is vested with the power to regulate Quebec's natural resources. If that were so, which it is not, it would logically follow that Parliament would be endowed with an equivalent power to legislate over the resources of *all* provinces.[67] Could anyone seriously think that Albertans would joyfully welcome the central government's appropriation of the power to manage the province's petroleum resources?

Another decentralizing factor lies in the demographic difference between the provinces. If Canada were a unitary state, as sovereignists claim it already is, how could the specific interests of citizens of Prince Edward Island, Saskatchewan and Newfoundland—less populous provinces—be voiced? Notwithstanding what Quebecers think, all Anglo-Canadians do not desperately aspire to become Ontarians...

Of all institutional factors, the relatively unrepresentative character of the federal parliament is certainly the most important.

For Parliament to legitimately claim the power to intervene in local matters, its ability to adequately represent regional interests would have to be demonstrated. But, as opposed to the German Bundesrat, for example, the Canadian Senate does not at all represent regional and provincial interests as it should. In addition, our British-style parliamentary system, combined with the custom of "party discipline," concentrates power in the hands of the federal Cabinet. Members of Parliament, therefore, are unable to voice their constituents' worries or preferences without their party leader's endorsement. Consequently, at the federal level, neither the House of Commons nor the Senate possesses the required legitimacy to deal with local matters.

Furthermore, the very same parliamentary principles and party discipline operate at the provincial level, so that premiers—when their party forms a majority in the legislature—also wield an enormous amount of power. We observe every day how jealously the provincial premiers guard their powers. Would they give them up without a struggle, should Ottawa lift its finger to request it? This institutional element constitutes a substantial obstacle to unbounded centralism.

In sum, the Supreme Court justices are well aware of all these centrifugal factors. To ignore them would be to imperil the stability of the state. Failing to admit that Canada's federal system requires the recognition of provincial differences would lead to disaster. The Supreme Court justices understand that very well. It may be sad for some people to ascertain, but the justices are not servile sycophants of the federal government.

THE CANADIAN federal system has its shortcomings. But it is not an imperial regime, and it would be quite wrong to speak of an unbridled centralization endangering Quebec's identity. The federal government is not the source of all our trials.

Quebecers can and must take part, with deserved pride, in this federal state they so fully helped to build and to govern. If they wish to abandon it, let them choose the road of pure and simple independence, the road that severs all political connections, the road that ends all obligations of reciprocity. However, should they wish to remain in Canada, let them leave behind the rhetoric of "radical differences," the endless demands embodied for now in so-called "autonomism." Let them embrace the fact that if federalism implies rights, it also entails responsibilities. Autonomy is not egoism disguised as national pride.

JEAN LECLAIR *is a professor of constitutional law at the Université de Montréal.*

Notes

1. "Making a heresy out of a principle is easier than clarifying it through discussion." (my translation)

2. François Rocher, "La dynamique Québec-Canada ou le refus de l'idéal fédéral" in Alain-G. Gagnon (ed.), *Le fédéralisme contemporain—Fondements, traditions, institutions,* Montreal: Les Presses de l'Université de Montréal, 2006, pp. 93–146, at p. 120 (my translation and my emphasis).

3. Eugénie Brouillet, *La négation de la nation—L'identité culturelle québécoise et le fédéralisme canadien,* Quebec: Septentrion, 2005, p. 384 (my translation and my emphasis).

4. Michel Seymour, "La proie pour l'ombre. Les illusions d'une réforme de la fédération canadienne" in A.-G. Gagnon, *supra,* pp. 211–236, at p. 230 (my translation and my emphasis).

5. Joseph Facal, "Mondialisation, identités nationales et fédéralisme. À propos de la mutation en cours du système politique canadien" in A.-G. Gagnon, *supra,* pp. 237–250, at p. 237 (my translation and my emphasis).

6. Henri Brun and Guy Tremblay, *Droit constitutionnel,* 4th ed., Cowansville: Yvon Blais Inc., 2002, p. 437 (my translation and my emphasis). They also add the following (*ibid.*): "[Decentralization] is not guaranteed by the Constitution of Canada. It survives only on sufferance of the Central

government. The latter possesses the means to invade, at will, most provincial fields of jurisdiction."

7. Jean Leclair, "The Supreme Court's Understanding of Federalism: Efficiency at the Expense of Diversity" in *Queen's Law Journal*, vol. 28 (2003), pp. 411–453 and Jean Leclair, "The Elusive Quest for the Quintessential 'National Interest,'" in *The University of British Columbia Law Review*, vol. 38 (2005), pp. 355–374.

8. Michel Seymour, *supra*, p. 230.

9. On the very same question, see Éric Montpetit's interesting essay: *Le fédéralisme d'ouverture—La recherche d'une légitimité canadienne au Québec*, Quebec: Septentrion, 2007.

10. Quoted by Jean-Jacques Chevallier, *Les grandes œuvres politiques de Machiavel à nos jours*, Paris: Armand Colin, 1996, p. 40. (my translation)

11. Eugenie Brouillet, *supra*, p. 384. (my translation and my emphasis)

12. Leclair, *supra*, 2003 and 2005.

13. *R. v. Crown Zellerbach Canada Ltd.* [1988] 1 SCR 401. Available online at http://scc.lexum.umontreal.ca/en/1988/1988rcs1-401/1988rcs1-401.html (accessed May 27, 2008).

14. Eugénie Brouillet, *supra*, p. 292. (my translation)

15. *Friends of the Oldman River Society v. Canada (Minister of Transport)*, [1992] 1 SCR 3. Available online at http://scc.lexum.umontreal.ca/en/1992/1992rcs1-3/1992rcs1-3.html (accessed May 27, 2008).

16. *R. v. Hydro-Québec*, [1997] 3 SCR 213, par. 116. Available online at http://scc.lexum.umontreal.ca/en/1997/1997rcs3-213/1997rcs3-213.html (accessed May 27, 2008).

17. She also relegates to a footnote the following information: in the 1995 RJR-MacDonald case (*RJR-MacDonald Inc. v. Canada (Attorney General)*, [1995] 3 SCR 199), the Supreme Court recognized the constitutional validity of a federal statute prohibiting, with a few exceptions, the advertisement of tobacco products and any other form of activity designed to encourage their sale. In so doing, and contrary to the Quebec Court of Appeal in the very same case, the court refused to rest its argument on the "national concern" doctrine.

18. *Reference re Anti-Inflation Act*, [1976] 2 SCR 373. Available online at http://scc.lexum.umontreal.ca/en/1976/1976rcs2-373/1976rcs2-373.html (accessed May 27, 2008).

19. *General Motors of Canada Ltd. v. City National Leasing*, [1989] 1 SCR 641. Available online at http://scc.lexum.umontreal.ca/en/1989/1989rcs1-641/ 1989rcs1-641.html (accessed May 27, 2008).

20. Eugénie Brouillet, *supra*, p. 303. (my translation and my emphasis)

21. *Ibid.*, p. 305. (my translation and my emphasis)

22. Leclair, *supra*, 2003.

23. Canada's court of last resort until 1949; established in London, it heard the appeals of the Supreme Court's decisions.

24. *Canada (Attorney General) v. Ontario (Attorney General)*, [1937] A.C. 326 at p. 352 [*Labour Conventions*].

25. Michel Seymour, *supra*, p. 230. (my translation)

26. See Constitution Act, 1982, section 36(2). See online at http://laws.justice. gc.ca/en/const/annex_e.html#I (accessed May 27, 2008).

27. Alain Noël, "Équilibres et déséquilibres dans le partage des ressources financières" in A.-G. Gagnon, *supra*, pp. 305–338.

28. *R. v. Hydro-Québec*, par. 115. Available online at http://scc.lexum.umontreal. ca/en/1997/1997rcs3-213/1997rcs3-213.html (accessed May 27, 2008).

29. *Ibid.*, par. 154.

30. *Friends of the Oldman River Society v. Canada (Minister of Transport)*, *supra*.

31. *Rio Hotel Ltd. v. New Brunswick (Liquor Licensing Board)*, [1987] 2 SCR 59, par. 5. Available online at http://scc.lexum.umontreal.ca/en/1987/ 1987rcs2-59/1987rcs2-59.html (accessed May 27, 2008).

32. *Rothmans, Benson & Hedges Inc. v. Saskatchewan*, 2005 SCC 13, [2005] 1 SCR 188. Available online at http://scc.lexum.umontreal.ca/ en/2005/2005scc13/2005scc13.html (accessed May 27, 2008).

33. Andrée Lajoie, "Le fédéralisme au Canada: provinces et minorités, même combat" in A.-G. Gagnon, *supra*, pp. 183–210 (hereinafter 'Lajoie 2005'); Andrée Lajoie, "Garantir l'intégration des valeurs minoritaires dans le droit: une entreprise irréalisable par la voie structurelle" in Jean-François Gaudreault-Desbiens and Fabien Gélinas (eds.), *Le fédéralisme dans tous ses états—Gouvernance, identité et méthodologie*, Montreal/Brussels: Yvon Blais/ Bruylant, 2005, pp. 365–381 and *Quand les minorités font la loi*, Coll. "les voies du droit," Paris: Les Presses universitaires de France, 2002.

34. *Canadian Western Bank v. Alberta*, 2007 SCC 22. Available online at http://scc.lexum.umontreal.ca/en/2007/2007scc22/2007scc22.html (accessed May 27, 2008).

35. Lajoie 2005, p. 195. (my translation and my emphasis)

36. *Roncarelli v. Duplessis*, [1959] SCR 121. Available online at http://scc.lexum. umontreal.ca/en/1959/1959rcs0-121/1959rcs0-121.html (accessed May 27, 2008).

37. *Switzman v. Elbing and A.G. of Quebec*, [1957] SCR 285, p. 288. Available online at http://scc.lexum.umontreal.ca/en/1957/1957rcs0-285/1957rcs0-285.html (accessed May 27, 2008).

38. See *Democracy in America*, (Book I, Chapter 8), translation by Henry Reeve, revised and corrected, 1899, available online at http://xroads.virginia. edu/~HYPER/DETOC/toc_indx.html (accessed May 27, 2008).

39. *Ibid.*

40. Pierre Falardeau is a well-known filmmaker, director, *indépendantiste* and, more particularly, mud-slinging pamphleteer.

41. Eugénie Brouillet, *supra*, pp. 71, 64, 289. (my translations) See also pp. 65, 143–144, 155 and 237.

42. *Ibid.*, p. 73. (my translation)

43. Lajoie 2005, p. 205. (my translation)

44. Michel Seymour, *supra*, p. 224. (my translation)

45. The future of the Belgian federation may well be a split rather than the claimed joyful brotherhood of the Walloons and the Flemish. Hugues Dumont, an expert—a real one this time—on the issue of the Belgian federation, has already predicted today's political turmoil: "[Democracy] assumes... a will to deliberate together to arrive at a common action... [Now,] the danger threatening the Belgian state over the next few years is not hard to guess at. It resides in the erosion of this will, and, along with that, in a continual diminution of what underlies meaningful federal citizenship and a living experience of constitutional patriotism. The only major decisions this state would still be capable of making will have to do with new transfers of jurisdiction to its component parts. Always moving in this direction, it would be bound to vanish for want of nourishment for those controversies that have heretofore kept it alive. 'Where would the danger be?' some might ask, 'Isn't every state mortal?' Maybe, but let us acknowledge that this particular state had met a wonderful challenge at the ethical level, a challenge worthy of our interest in these days of growing and destructive nationalisms: that of showing the possibility for two increasingly distinctive nations to live under the same political roof." The quote is from

"La mobilisation du droit comme instrument de changement du cadre national en Belgique," in Pierre Noreau and José Woehrling, *Appartenances, institutions et citoyenneté*, Montreal: Wilson & Lafleur, 2005, pp. 89–107, at p. 106. (my translation)

46. Eugénie Brouillet, *supra*, p. 74.

47. *Ibid.*, pp. 75–76.

48. Michel Seymour, *supra*, p. 230. (my translation)

49. Sarah Fortin, "De l'union sociale canadienne à l'union sociale fédérale du Canada" in A.-G. Gagnon, *supra.*, pp. 339–370, at p. 361. (my translation)

50. Rémi Maillard, *Lucien Bouchard: Mot à Mot*, Montreal: Stanké, 1996, p. 31. (my translation)

51. Like all provincial governments, Alberta receives its share of federal financial transfers to meet the costs of certain specified sectors such as health, post-secondary education and welfare. However, it does not benefit from equalization payments. Equalization is a separate program that, unlike other federal programs, is not calculated according to the number of citizens per province, but rather according to the fiscal capacity and thus the wealth of each province. That is why Alberta and Ontario are usually—some years there are exceptions—the only "suppliers" in the equalization program, that is to say that part of the taxes raised by the federal government in these provinces is redirected to the poorer provinces. So, it is true that the federal government sends money to the Alberta government, about 16 per cent of the revenues of this province in 2004–2005, for example. However, the net amount that Alberta taxpayers send to the federal government in income tax and other taxes is more than what they receive in payments to their provincial government or in direct payments.

52. See, for example, David E. Smith, "Prairie Political Culture and Canadian Federalism" in C. Lloyd Brown-John (ed.), *Centralizing and Decentralizing Trends in Federal States*, Boston: University Press of America, 1988.

53. Christian Rouillard, Éric Montpetit, Isabelle Fortier and Alain-G. Gagnon, *La réingénierie de l'État: vers un appauvrissement de la gouvernance québécoise*, Quebec: Les Presses de l'Université Laval, 2004.

54. Parti liberal du Québec, *Un Québec libre de ses choix. Rapport du comité constitutionnel*, January 28, 1991.

55. As Laurent-Michel Vacher so rightly said in *Une triste histoire et autres petits écrits politiques*, Montreal: Liber, 2001, p. 54: "Sovereignism can be solved

within constitutional negotiations... If we must remain associated in a sort of federative manner with the rest of Canada, our elected representatives will be amply mandated to negotiate and to conclude this type of arrangement which is by nature neither assured, nor radical, nor irreversible." (my translation)

56. Alexis de Tocqueville, *supra* (Book 1, Chapter 14).

57. For several nationalists there is something demeaning about being a federalist. But what about a political option which exposes its *pays*—its "country"—to the point of indecency, all year long and, again and again, on June 24, but which, when the time comes to courageously assert itself in the form of a referendum question, desperately tries to cover this same *pays* as it would its private parts? The reader is aware that I am referring to the refusal of the Parti Québécois to include, as demanded by the Liberal opposition, the word *pays* before the term "souverain" in the 1995 referendum question. See the unedifying attempts by Jacques Parizeau—this king of the dodge—to again dodge the issue in *Le Journal des débats* of the National Assembly for Thursday, September 7, 1995. The same Parizeau who three years later will affirm: "We are often told that the 1995 question was unclear. It is true, as I have often stressed, that the question I would have preferred was the following: 'Do you want Quebec to become a sovereign country [*un pays souverain*] on the (date)...?'" (J. Parizeau, "Lettre ouverte aux juges de la Cour suprême," *Le Devoir*, September 3, 1998, p. A9). (my translation) Ironically, that is *exactly* the question Daniel Johnson put to him on September 7, 1995. Lucien Bouchard himself said later he would be disposed to "study ways of formulating a clearer question," as reported by Michel Venne in "Bouchard promet une question plus claire," *Le Devoir*, Friday, August 28, 1998, p. A1. (my translation) Has grovelling become a dignified process of achieving independence?

Other nationalists, such as Joseph Facal, *supra*, p. 246, think that "the fact that so many Quebecers do not see this, [the federal move to negate the Quebec nation] proves the ravages that forgetfulness and ignorance can generate." (my translation) Oddly enough, and contrary to Facal's opinion, a serious analysis of the views of French-speaking "Québécois" students on the history of Quebec demonstrates that the vast majority of them share a Falardesque understanding of Quebec history. See Jocelyn Létourneau and Sabrina Moisan, "Mémoire et récit de l'aventure historique du Québec chez les jeunes Québécois d'héritage canadien-français: coup de sonde, amorce d'analyse des résultats, questionnements," *The Canadian Historical Review,* vol. 85, 2004, pp. 325–356. Joseph Facal does not have to worry. And we could have been spared the publication of Gérald Larose's utterly ridiculous *Parlons de souveraineté à l'école,* Montreal: Éditions les Intouchables, 2006.

58. With perhaps the exception of Newfoundland...I would add that we should be wary of this claimed unanimity among all Canadians regarding the Canadian Charter. Indeed, we should be very mindful not to confuse the opinion of the Canadian majority with that of the chic intellectual left of metro Toronto...

59. Michael Burgess, "Gérer la diversité dans les États fédéraux: approches conceptuelles et perspectives comparatives" in A.-G. Gagnon, *supra,* pp. 487–502, at p. 501. (my translation)

60. Eugénie Brouillet, *supra,* p. 329. (my translation)

61. *Ford v. Quebec (Attorney General),* [1988] 2 SCR 712, par. 73. Available online at http://scc.lexum.umontreal.ca/en/1988/1988rcs2-712/1988rcs2-712.html (accessed May 27, 2008).

62. Eugénie Brouillet, *supra,* p. 334.

63. *Ford v. Quebec (Attorney General),* [1988] 2 SCR 712, par. 34.

64. *Ballantyne, Davidson et McIntyre v. Canada,* Communication 359/1989 and 385/1989, CCPR/A/47/D/359/1989, May 5, 1993.

65. Alexis de Tocqueville, *supra* (Book 1, Chapter 8).

66. Most of the ideas expressed here are borrowed from Ronald Watts, "The American Constitution in Comparative Perspective: A Comparison of Federalism in the United States and Canada," *The Journal of American History,* vol. 74, The Constitution and American Life: A Special Issue, 1987, pp. 769–792.

67. Ironically, the works of sovereignist constitutional scholars such as Andrée Lajoie are a storehouse of arguments for advocates of a highly centralized federation! These authors read the Supreme Court's decisions with a mind to find in them even the tiniest springboard for greater federal power.

3

BENOÎT PELLETIER

RECLAIMING CANADA

The Affirmation of Quebec's Identity within the Canadian Federation

WHEN I decided to enter politics in 1998 by joining the Quebec Liberal Party, I knew I was taking a substantial risk. Indeed, it is not an easy task in Quebec to associate oneself with an avowed federalist party. In a sense, it is an open invitation to be branded as a traitor, a collaborator or a colonial subject.[1] Despite this, I made the leap into politics precisely because of my love for Quebec and my desire to contribute, in my own way and to the best of my abilities, to the advancement of this society into which I was born. I chose Quebec with as much affection, sincerity and conviction as do many of the sovereignists I know. Now I live my political life at the Quebec National Assembly but reside in Gatineau, some five hundred kilometres away. I am a staunch defender of Quebec's interests. I want what is best for the North American French-speaking minority of which I am a proud member.

What sets me apart from the sovereignists has nothing to do with my degree of attachment to Quebec. I simply believe that Quebec has the best chance of achieving its destiny and its full potential by participating wholeheartedly in the Canadian experience. The very foundation of my political involvement is Quebec and my ardent desire to participate in reinforcing its special identity. It is my belief that Quebec may find a place of its own in Canada, one that is "first class" and well respected.

If the deep-seated motivation for my political involvement is Quebec itself, the context that I have chosen is the vibrant atmosphere of Quebec politics; Canadian federalism is the inherent force guiding my personal experience. Henceforth, my main objective is to foster a stronger Quebec within Canada. I know very well that it *is* possible to favour a fruitful relationship with Canada while having a profound devotion to Quebec. Many federalists bear witness to this fact day after day.

I do not believe that solely financial or other material reasons are sufficient for justifying the bond that exists between Quebec and Canada. On the contrary, in addition to the obvious economic motives for choosing Canadian federalism, our attachment to Canada as Quebecers is also based on other vital interests, namely culture and language, the two driving forces of our identity.

The Essential Affirmation of Quebec's Identity within the Canadian Family

A society's identity, whatever it may be, is the lifeblood that endows it with its own uniqueness, its individuality. This is the very essence of its being. This is what sets it apart from all others.

Quebec's identity is rooted in a number of indigenous characteristics: the French language, Quebec culture, civil law, the province's distinctive institutions and way of life in general. Its history and geography have also contributed to shaping Quebec's unique physiognomy and, as such, cannot be overlooked.

We, the inhabitants of Quebec, are not French-speaking Americans, nor are we French men and women living in America. We are quite simply... Quebecers! We share a uniquely blended culture that grew from our French roots, was seasoned by an aboriginal substratum, then influenced by the British as well as our American neighbours and, not least of all, by a myriad of immigrants from all parts of the world.

Quebec's characteristics are so outstanding that it constitutes a veritable nation in its own right. This fact has even been recently acknowledged by the House of Commons.[2]

A nation consists of the strong union of its members within one and the same community. It is, in a sense, a widespread and extended family in which individuals have come to be united, either de facto or by some manifest desire to do so. The nation is composed of relatively objective factors, such as recognized territory, language(s), culture, religious assemblies and traditions. There are also a host of subjective aspects, such as observable influences of the past or present, the citizens' will to make their own decisions, their awareness of their unity, and their wish to live and face the future together. Hence, the nation postulates a form of "self-representation" in that it defines itself according to the image portrayed by its very own citizens.[3] It has its spiritual components but could never subsist on mere subjective elements; it must have as its basis more tangible workings. In a nutshell, "it is both body and soul."[4]

We, Quebecers, constitute a nation because we are a group of humans located in a precise territory, because we share a common past and enjoy communal traditions, because we are motivated by the will to live together and mainly because we dream the same dreams in terms of what we want to become. Quebec's identity is based upon uniquely defining features that clearly differentiate it from all other groups. Owing to its ethnocultural characteristics,

Quebec qualifies sociologically as a nation. It also does so politically because of its institutions and its solid internal structures and organization.

Obviously, any identity that has a national character is fundamentally an evolving concept. It remains in perpetual motion. Religion is a prime example. Today, organized religion occupies a far smaller place in the definition of Quebec's identity than it did many generations ago.

From the Canadians we were in the eighteenth century, to the French Canadians we became in the nineteenth century and remained until the last quarter of the twentieth century, to the Quebecers we now are, it has been a long path we have trod together since our sometimes wearying journey began. In his writings, political scientist Léon Dion has traced the many forms that Quebec's nationalist consciousness has taken over the years. From conservative nationalism to the more social-democratic and socialist forms, and via liberal nationalism, we have endured numerous mutations and collectively survived these changes.[5]

Throughout this long journey, there has remained one unshakable constant, namely Quebec's identity and its citizens' continuing desire and need to ensure its permanence.

Identity has always been the driving political and governmental force of all Quebecers. When Quebecers speak out so loudly in defence of social justice, it is because we know that our society's cohesiveness depends on safeguarding our identity. If economic development is so important (or at least it should be) to us, it is because without it, Quebec has no influence, either politically or culturally, nor may it even reap the moral wealth of its identity. Our efficiency as a nation and our capacity to adapt to the ever-changing world we live in rest upon our will and our ability to quickly reorganize and modernize our state apparatus and its institutions. Our very survival depends upon it.

It is frequently heard among media commentators that Quebec would do well to set aside the identity debate and move on to what they designate as the "true priorities," that is, such issues as health, education, economy and the environment. They seem to forget that all of these concerns are intricately related and that Quebec nationalism is the product of the interaction among economic, social, political, institutional and cultural considerations. Dissecting identity into piecemeal bits of society means depriving Quebec of the cement that ensures unity, coherence and development. Forgive me for insisting, but identity is the bedrock upon which all political actions and deliberations in Quebec and Canada exist. Quebec could never be what it is without this essence that guarantees its momentum, unity and perseverance.

Seen from this perspective, it is clear, then, that those who refuse to join in Quebec's quest for identification, because they choose to focus only on the economy, social equity or strict management of public policies and finances, commit a fundamental error. They overlook the fact that identity is the key to understanding why we, Quebecers, make decisions that differ from those of our neighbours and generally go about our business as a distinct society.

Did I say "distinct society"? Those words are loaded! In fact, they have been virtually taboo since the failed Meech Lake Accord.[6] In a report approved by the Quebec Liberal Party in 2001, I proposed replacing this phrase with the term "specificity."[7] This initiative was met with approval, since nowadays most politicians, political scientists and pundits refer to Quebec's specificity rather than to the aforementioned Meech Lake concept. In my mind, specificity brings together the characteristics I have mentioned above, which sum up Quebec's national identity. Now this specificity must be heralded, made known and emphasized throughout Canada and internationally.

Likewise, the federative approach, which I hold dear, must be rooted in strengthening Quebec's own consciousness within Canada and abroad. It is based upon Quebec standing on its own throughout Canada and fearlessly welcoming the most demanding and inspiring challenges.

Far from being an obstacle to Quebec's development, Canadian federalism is in fact an incredible springboard for advancing Quebec society. Contrary to what some may think, most Quebecers willingly identify themselves with Canada[8] and display a unique sense of pride in belonging to this somewhat successful experience in human organization. They embrace Canada's outstanding values such as official bilingualism and cultural diversity as well as the protection of rights and freedoms. They are even proud of their Canadian citizenship. Furthermore, the majority of Quebecers are devoted federalists, even if they find this hard to acknowledge. Just consider the following: far more than they would care to admit, most Quebecers do espouse a belief in the Canadian federative system through which power is shared between two orders of government and which offers them numerous places and means for expressing their democratic convictions, whether it only be within the federal and provincial parliaments. Many Quebecers are also adamant defenders of the constitution and the inherent division of powers, federal-provincial equilibrium and the federative spirit. As strange as this may sound, I would hardly be surprised to find that Quebecers are the most federalist of all Canadians. At the very least, we likely have less ingrained unitary reflexes than some of our fellow Canadians.

On this issue, Quebecers are clear-sighted, since federalism is a marvellous way to structure power and political relationships within a country. It allows for the pooling of resources, values and ideals among citizens through central (or federal) institutions, and the expression of community voices and other particular realities—as in Quebec—by means of local (or provincial)[9] bodies. In this manner, a federal structure makes it possible to encompass the diverse and exclusive components within a unified whole, entailing both a sharing and an awareness of exclusivity.

Federalism, as a basis for casting the foundations of state powers, is, in my opinion, the most complete form of decentralization known to us today. Federated entities (provinces, townships, cantons, communities, regions, Länder, states, etc.) are sovereign in exercising the jurisdictions granted to them under a binding covenant or constitution. They are not legally subject to the central institutions, nor does the federal ideal want them to be politically or financially subject thereto.

In federations of any kind, tense situations among partners are inevitable, whether between two orders of government or among the federated entities (provinces) themselves. Nonetheless, most of the time these situations are fruitful and inspired by healthy competition between players with divergent interests. In some cases, they even lead to honourable compromises. Most important, however, they should not be avoided or feared but rather skillfully managed.[10]

Being a federalist means believing in individuality and the right to be different. It also means being self-determining in spirit, since federalism cannot be seriously considered without a deep respect for voluntary self-rule and the abilities of each partner, whether federal or provincial, to tender to its own responsibilities.

Historically, in Quebec, the principle of autonomy took root to politically affirm those who seek to increase Quebec's autonomy within Canada. These federalists who profess autonomy are in search of a more flexible and decentralized form of federalism.

Other than the search for more autonomy within Canada and outright sovereignty for Quebec, there is nothing. For this reason, the hypothetical third option set forth by the Action démocratique du Québec simply does not exist.

Occasionally, some political theorists dwell on the idea of a confederation, an association of sovereign states bound together by an international treaty but which maintain all the attributes of their individual sovereignty. A true confederation is unthinkable between Canada and Quebec unless the latter becomes independent and forms a sovereign country in its own right. As for the European model, a formula that stands halfway between a federation and a confederation, it also bases itself upon the sovereignty of each member-state. If this model were to be applied to Canada, it would also imply the independence of Quebec.

The 1980 and 1995 sovereignty-association and sovereignty-partnership projects were largely inspired by the idea of a confederation. The 1991 Allaire Report[11] leaned heavily in the same direction, since it favoured gutting federal institutions, which over the short term would have caused considerable harm to the proper functioning of Canadian federalism.

I am a staunch federalist and have no reservations about this philosophy. Although it is true that defending Quebec autonomy and promoting the province's specific identity remain part and parcel of my political involvement, it is no less true that I consider these two causes well within the Canadian federative framework and the constitutional powers granted to Quebec by it.

Indeed, the Quebec autonomy that I defend is the one provided in the constitution of Canada and which formed the basis for Quebecers' adherence to the federative compromise in 1867. It is this very agreement that allowed the Quebec Nation to survive and develop on the northern reaches of this continent. As for the identity of Quebec that I enthusiastically promote, I want it to be appealing and welcoming.

Obviously, I am well aware of the fact that historians, political scientists and sociologists make a distinction between ethnic nationalism (also known as ethnonationalism) and civic (or civil) nationalism. The first is a nationalistic form wherein the *nation* is essentially defined in terms of *ethnicity*, whereas the second rests upon the concept of territory and the active participation of its *citizens* via their values, institutions and shared social behaviours.

Quebec nationalism, as in the case of many nationalisms worldwide, takes its inspiration from both of these sources. Indeed, ethnocultural traits, more precisely language and culture, are essential for its existence. Nonetheless, these characteristics alone are insufficient to properly describe the Quebec Nation. The purely ethnic concept of Quebec nationalism underestimates, even blocks out, the priceless contribution of the Aboriginals and of the English-speaking and allophonic communities in the making of contemporary Quebec.

As such, I prefer rallying to the call of civil, rather than ethnic, nationalism when describing the Quebec Nation. Civil nationalism includes everyone. Moreover, this form of nationalism impresses me as being more democratic than the other, as being more equitable and compatible with liberal ideals. Indeed, thanks to the civil concept, all citizens are called upon to participate in the life and livelihood of the nation. The civic concept of Quebec nationalism, as contrasted with the ethnic one, also empowers Quebec to lay claim to greater political legitimacy and to take its rightful place and promote its initiatives on both continental and international scenes.

I am an avid believer in our society's power of consensus. I feel that the politician's mission must be to seek the common good, namely the well-being and security of all individuals in society, and the overall well-being of society itself. Yet, only a civil concept of nationalism gives access to these fundamental objectives. This concept alone also makes it possible to consider Quebec as a "global society"—as expressed so aptly by sociologist Simon Langlois[12]—that is, as a well-rounded nation replete with a multiplicity of interests and realities. Have we sufficiently matured to attain a "global nationalism"? I genuinely think so. In this global nationalism,[13] my wish is for everyone to feel at ease.

Hence, I do not and cannot subscribe to a purely ethnocentric concept of Quebec identity. We, Quebecers, have absolutely nothing to gain collectively by shutting ourselves off from the outside world and essentially becoming a ghetto. We risk losing everything. As a society, we need a strong breath of fresh air to continuously revitalize our existence. Therefore, it is in our best interest to open our hearts and arms to all those who wish to build Quebec.

The extent to which the current debates on reasonable accommodations and immigration have generated public interest demonstrates that we, Quebecers, are still searching for identity. Deep in our soul, we fret at the thought of what lies in store for our society. Obviously, the Quebec government and its institutions have a central role to play in order to ensure Quebec's steadfast existence and identity. Likewise, citizens have the duty to rise to its defence (and to its support), in a spirit of open-mindedness, tolerance and compassion. The challenge that lies before us, collectively and individually, regardless of origin, religion or language, is to make contemporary Quebec that very special place in which we have chosen to live and shape our destiny.

This does not mean turning away from our duty to welcome immigrants, make them feel at home in our French language and ensure their successful integration in our society. On the contrary, this is an absolute necessity if we want Quebec to be a flourishing community.

This also does not mean turning our backs on the economic problems generated by excessive or precipitated immigration.

Rather than turning immigrants away, we must foster economic prosperity in order to welcome even more of them. This means offering immigrants training and assistance in accessing the labour market. How else may we face our future?

Among these numerous challenges, Quebecers must meet pluralism and diversity head-on. Indeed, our claim to the right to be different within the vast Canadian community must also extend to the minorities in Quebec who make their homes among us.

The Quebec that I cherish is a modern, pluralistic and open-minded society based upon shared values, whose pivotal language is French and whose widespread culture is the Quebec culture, in itself defined as generous, outgoing and comprehensive.[14]

Quebec Must Start Anew

Quebec must start anew, must lay its foundations upon a new base. Although it is true that Quebecers have a duty to remember—as in the motto "*Je me souviens*" (I remember)—and that the iniquities that have marked our history are still alive in the collective subconscious, we must not continuously live in the past and take comfort in negativism. After standing firm in *l'hiver de la survivance*[15] (the winter of survival), will Quebec awaken to the blooming of a spring renaissance? It is to be hoped.

It is my earnest desire that everyone, regardless of their ethnic origin or political allegiance, may come to identify themselves with Quebec. This raises, however, the question as to whether or not we will succeed in depoliticizing our national debate. Admittedly, this appears to be an ominous task since the sovereignist movement has, over the years, monopolized national symbols and points of reference. Such depoliticizing is to be encouraged because Quebec's national identity belongs to everyone. It is for this reason that in 2001 I made a very strong plea for Quebec federalists to reappropriate the terms and symbols that belong to the national movement, including Quebec's flag, which is also a birthright for all Quebecers.[16]

Within the Canadian federation, Quebec enjoys considerable leeway in self-governance. Its powers, which devolve from the constitution or administrative agreements, are quite substantial and encompass economics, education, culture, language, communications and even immigration. They have, over time, made it possible for Quebec to develop its national identity, and they continue to do so today. It should never be forgotten that the Quebec Nation that we are presently promoting has grown and blossomed within the Canadian federation. This means that Canadian federalism, far from being an impediment, has in fact greatly contributed to Quebec as it exists today.

Now it is up to Quebecers to seek once again to exercise healthy leadership in Canada, as we have done time and again since its creation. We must endeavour to leave our mark on the future of this country as we have done in the past. This means striking up new alliances with our fellow provinces. Quebec also needs to have a clear vision as to the part it is playing—and the role of its partners—in this Canada of tomorrow.

When I served as a Member of the National Assembly in the Official Opposition, I delved into the creation of this vision. This led to the report I mentioned previously.[17] It set forth the following two-step approach: 1) The Quebec government would explore all administrative (non-constitutional) reforms that could enable Quebec to move forward in Canada. 2) A longer-term project would encompass all constitutional reforms, whether limited or far-reaching. I still think this approach is valid for Quebec, despite the fact that the time for making constitutional reforms is still premature. The first step involving non-constitutional (administrative) changes must be carried on. That being said, I sincerely believe that Quebecers must persevere on the path to constitutional changes and that reforming the Canadian constitution, far from being frivolous, remains a necessity although not an immediate priority.

I am fully aware that Canada's constitutional issues are of great complexity, as I have spent years studying the subject of constitutional amendment. As it stands, the National Assembly and the Government of Quebec still have not signed the Constitution Act, 1982,[18] for reasons that, in my view, remain relevant. No amendments or corrections have been made as regards Quebec since this act came into effect, notwithstanding the highly limited 1997 constitutional amendment pertaining to the abolition of denominational school boards in Quebec.[19] One day, it will become imperative to reform the constitution such that it may present Canadian reality in its entirety, including Quebec's specificity.

Since we, Quebecers, are a minority in Canada, we attach great importance to the constitution. We are aware, perhaps more by instinct than by hard facts, that by its very nature the constitution is likely to provide us with a certain type of protection and the means for counterbalancing, to a limited extent, the will of the majority regarding the orientation of the Canadian federal system.

A country's constitution, regardless of the country, is a contract binding all its constituents, and dare I say, all its citizens.[20] Every person must find sufficient reasons for voluntarily participating in the life of that country. Each individual must be able to find his or her place in that constitution. In other societies, such as the United States, the constitution is a sacred document, a genuine object of veneration. In Canada, the constitution is still an unfinished work since Quebec refused to sign the document, and also because of what was simply not discussed by the politicians during the deliberations of 1981–1982.

With the intention of fuelling the debate and mapping out avenues of solution, I have promoted the idea of drafting a federalist charter.[21] In doing so, my goal was not to propose a new round of constitutional negotiations; quite the contrary. As a matter of fact, no one says that this document must be strictly constitutional in nature. The form and content of the charter could be varied and all-encompassing. To begin with, a simple declaration of political intent could outline the basis of what should become a constitutional precept.

No matter what its form, the charter would make it possible to confirm the very essence of the federal principle in Canada and to emphasize respect for the federative model and the jurisdictions of each order of government. It could, as an example, include a code of conduct applicable to all partners (that is, the provinces, the territories and the Canadian government), similar in style to what is found in other federations, where the principle of federal courtesy and loyalty governs relations among the federated entities (provinces) themselves or between them and the federal government.[22] In a nutshell, it could contain the principles and values at the core of contemporary Canada, including Quebec's specificity.

Since 2003, the Quebec government has concentrated on exploring non-constitutional avenues for making Quebec progress in Canada and for improving Canadian federalism. This approach has proven its worth and must be continued. However, this should not prevent us from looking further into the future and developing projects, whether they are constitutional in essence or otherwise.

I do not share the opinion of those fearful individuals who think that Quebecers should renounce their constitutional objectives owing to the risks of another failure in doing so. According to these timid souls, it would be wrong for Quebecers to seek recognition for their specificity in the Canadian federation: the latter need only to assert their identity and to fully use what they already have within Canada.

According to the proponents of this view, it would be enough for Quebecers to act as if they were good and strong in order to assume such qualities, without considering what others may think and, most of all, without making any effort to influence the country's political and constitutional future. In my view, this is a mistake. I maintain that Quebecers must speak out regarding Canada's evolution and insist that the Canadian constitution takes their unique reality into account. It is one thing to affirm ourselves for who we are or claim to be; it is another thing to be recognized as such. If affirmation is self-instilled, recognition is the work of another person. We, Quebecers, do have the legitimate need to see our identity recognized within Canada. As stated by the Catalan author Montserrat Guibernau: "The struggle for recognition entails the desire to be regarded and treated as an equal, as someone who has a voice and is able to participate in the political processes affecting his or her future."[23]

Although constitutional reform is not merely desirable but remains a pressing issue for me, this in no way is meant to diminish the value of Canadian federalism in its current form. On the contrary, not only is Canada, as it stands, an economic and financial success for Quebec, more importantly it is also a formidable human experience. Our country, the envy of many people around the world, is a viable experiment in the harmonious cohabitation of cultures. In this context, Quebec's specificity must be seen as a source of enrichment rather than a hindrance to the unity or integrity of Canada. Practically speaking, I believe that Quebec's specificity constitutes one of Canada's great values that must be solemnly recognized as such.[24] If it is true that Quebec is enhanced by belonging to Canada, then the same holds true that Quebec enriches Canada.

In the past, the saying "Canada is the source of our strength" circulated widely; this still stands as a truth today. It may be out of date and a tad audacious to say that we, Quebecers, must reclaim Canada, as the title of this essay suggests, but let us, at the very least, reaffirm ourselves in this country with conviction and resolve. We will come out of this experience as winners.

Everywhere we look, great political and economic unions are developing. The European Union—a one-of-a-kind supranational system—provides us with an example of audacity and determination. All these unifying movements gravitate towards a form of interdependency, namely the organized management of relations between countries, nations of various types and other collectivities. This tendency makes federalism in general, and Canadian federalism in particular, all the more relevant.

This is a time of collaboration between states and other types of societies, whenever such cooperation is possible and productive. This explains why it is not unusual for a nation, in the sociological or political meaning of the word, to choose to develop within a larger framework that envelops and transcends it. This is in fact the case of many nations.[25] Hence, it is no small wonder that Quebec, as a nation, makes its home within the comfort of a greater national entity that is Canada. By itself, Canada is a nation not only within the sociological and political sense of the word, but also a full-fledged country. There can be no denying that the nation of Quebec belongs to the Canadian nation.

This has been said by many others before me, but it is worth repeating in this context: a nation and a state (country) are not necessarily equivalent. One state may be plurinational, whereas another may be made up almost exclusively of a single nation or ethnic nationality.[26] Indeed, a "sociological" nation can coincide with the territorial limits of a country. Nonetheless, even in such a case, the nation in question is never totally homogeneous. Invariably, there are various groups or ethnic communities contained therein. It also happens that a state may precede the nation, in that once the former is created, little by little, it develops its own national characteristics, which most often encompass the unique national realities that exist within it. This is the case of Canada.[27]

For this reason, being a Quebecer is in no way incompatible with being a Canadian. These allegiances can be very nicely blended together. In fact, Quebecers have only to gain with a dual sense of belonging. Many Quebecers feel they are Canadian, but they wish to be Canadian in their own manner. And that is it!

As such, Canada is not a foreign country for Quebecers. It is our home, the belonging that we have toiled to build. Canada neither alienates Quebecers nor makes us subservient. Again, on the contrary, it offers us among other benefits a high standard of living, a strong potential for economic development, an interesting internal market, support via equalization payments, natural and other resources, a multitude of values, international recognition and acceptance. In addition, in Canada, the French language is not just a regional language among others but has the stature of one of two official languages from coast to coast. This empowers the French language, giving it significant leverage to meet the challenges of globalization.

Globalization, this rampant phenomenon on everyone's lips, is first and foremost a global network of exchanges and communication that links individuals, groups and collectivities. International events, trends or influences now have a direct impact on localities, no matter how remote. Reciprocally, an isolated locality may affect the international scene for any number of reasons.[28] It seems as though international borders no longer exist and that even the acts of an individual may provoke worldwide consequences. In this context, even nations that do not have full state sovereignty may legitimately aspire to play a political or economic role internationally.[29]

Globalization has thus given birth to two opposing forces. On the one hand, political and economic superstructures have flourished. On the other hand, regions have aggressively risen to the fore. In either case, it is the state and its sovereignty that have paid the price.[30] Indeed, in some of these supranational or transnational structures, most states have had to abdicate parts of their sovereignty or, at the very least, facets of their sovereignty's attributes.[31] As regards internal governance, owing to regional pressures, states have had to deal with new demands regarding subsidiarity, decentralization, deconcentration and political autonomy, including federalization.

If the first trend, which moves towards the creation of large entities, makes the sovereignist concept more unstable and unpredictable (which does not work to the advantage of Quebec sovereignists), the second one, typified by the expansion of regions, confirms nonetheless that countries must be sufficiently flexible to take into full account national or other realities expressed by their citizens (which creates quite a challenge today for Canadian federalists).

In order to more precisely favour taking these trends into consideration and to create a more hospitable environment for Quebec's identity in Canada, I have promoted flexibility and a certain type of asymmetry in the application of federalism. However, such asymmetry has limits that I believe are inherent in the federal principle.[32] Consequently, it should never be of such breadth and scope that it might endanger our own Canadian cohesion.

Asymmetry is a synonym of flexibility. It is a way to respond both to Quebec's specific aspirations and to those of our other federative partners in Canada. There is no need to emphasize that the formal acknowledgement of asymmetric federalism by the first ministers of Canada in September 2004 constitutes an achievement that the current Quebec government is particularly proud of. Yet, this is not all, for in addition to this recognition enshrined in two health care agreements, the government of which I am a member has many other praiseworthy achievements.[33] This government has achieved, in the entire history of

Quebec, the greatest number of intergovernmental agreements in one term of office.

In addition to the acceptance of asymmetric federalism by the first ministers and to the House of Commons' own acknowledgement that the Québécois form a nation, we have obtained a seat for Quebec at the United Nations Educational, Scientific and Cultural Organization (UNESCO) and formalized the province's international role, which is without precedent. All these agreements that we have concluded with the Canadian government come with no strings attached, and the most important of them are worth billions of dollars for Quebec, a sum that does not include the partial settlement of the fiscal imbalance announced in the March 2007 federal budget. Once again, these are important gains for Quebec.

These accomplishments eloquently demonstrate that it is possible to change the course of Canadian federalism and advance the cause of Quebec without touching the Canadian constitution.

By adopting a non-constitutional approach, the government to which I belong has transformed a defeatist attitude into a genuine winner's mindset. Indeed, since 2003, this is the government that has given true meaning to Quebec's autonomy and has endowed it with a solid foundation. This is all the more important for us since we believed that Quebecers desperately needed to restore their self-confidence in intergovernmental policies, especially since the episodes involving the 1981–1982 repatriation, the failed 1987–1990 Meech Lake Accord and the rebuffed 1991–1992 Charlottetown Accord.

From now on, we, Quebecers, know that we can once more exercise a real influence over the course of events in Canada. To do so, we must bank on our successes, continue to explore non-constitutional agreements for reinforcing Quebec within the Canadian federation and pursue purely constitutional reforms over the long term. We must also give ourselves a project that unites us. This presupposes that we take stock of our shared values, regardless of the form this exercise may take.

Action démocratique du Québec leader Mario Dumont believes that reasonable accommodations are in harsh contradiction to our general values. As I see things, they show tolerance and respect for our neighbours, insofar as these accommodations in no way impose on our society constraints that are excessive.

Particularly in North America, as in many other places, individual rights and liberties take precedence, to the detriment of collective rights. Some proponents push their ideas with such deceivingly egalitarian thinking that they want to level and harmonize everything in sight, thereby eliminating all forms of difference. Once again, I maintain that diversity must be shared rather than destroyed. We must avoid crushing collectivities or atypical realities by pushing them into a uniform mould, as they form our civilization's originality.

Globalization has in many ways espoused bits and pieces of individualistic ideology, favouring efficiencies over innovation and uniformity over particularities, which indicates that this trend is far from perfect. It carries in its wake effects that homogenize, blend and dehumanize. It also encourages anglicization and acculturation, especially the disproportionate and widespread dominance of one local culture, that of the United States of America.

Seen in this light, globalization can be a threat to individual societies, which risk being engulfed in a nameless melting pot. I see nationalism as a likely counterbalance, up to a point, to the most negative aspects of unremitting globalization.[34] Yet, for nationalism to operate this way, it must be generous and inviting, because too much xenophobic ethnocentric nationalism is worse than the dangers of a globalized world.

Quebec's quest for identity must, on the one hand, offer sufficiently impenetrable protection from threats to its integrity associated with the globalizing phenomenon; on the other hand, it must remain open enough to welcome the beneficial effects of modernization. Indeed, nationalism must neither be a rampart against the modern world nor a barrier to universality; it must include both. It must avoid narrow-mindedness and be part and parcel of humanity's grandiose objectives.

In light of this precarious balance, Quebec's new start must be grounded upon an affirmation of its identity, upon renewed leadership within the fold of Canada and abroad and upon a reformulation of values shared by Quebecers. It also implies a sense of responsibility for all involved and a profound commitment to the common cause of building our social project.

The current government is proposing such an all-inclusive project to Quebecers. It is centred on streamlining public finances, reinforcing economic recovery, reining in public debt and tax burdens, making government more efficient, and furthering decentralization and regionalization, sustainable development, environmental protection and new energy initiatives. This ambitious undertaking also includes consolidating the health care system and Quebec's public education network, fostering improved relations with Aboriginal peoples and maintaining the momentum that Quebec has reinstated in intergovernmental relations. It would be hard to imagine a project better adapted to Quebec's present needs and Quebecers' newly evolving agenda.

With this new awareness, we have, in my opinion, a vested interest in reasserting our ties with Canada and strengthening them rather than allowing other forces to dissolve them and isolate Quebecers. Indeed, at the same time that I am seeking with other federalists to make our Canadian journey evermore interesting, the other movement, the sovereignist option, is pulling in the opposite direction. The sovereignists' premises are grounded upon faulty foundations that crumble under analysis.[35] They stem from the mistaken belief that Quebec, by simply acquiring full sovereignty, would enjoy total social solidarity, renewed economic strength and unfettered influence abroad. Sovereignists have voluntarily turned a blind eye to the fact that Quebec's full sovereignty could unleash social disorder, economic decline and a weakening influence everywhere, while a disinterested international community would blandly take note.

The accession of Quebec to complete sovereignty or independence remains a haphazard and difficult undertaking. Anyone who thinks that such a project would move quickly and involve few disturbances would do well to reconsider. Along with economic upheavals would come,[36] to mention a few difficulties, long and complex negotiations with the rest of Canada,[37] the hurdle of the Clarity Act,[38] the labyrinth leading to international recognition, and not least of all, various consequences resulting from a possible unilateral declaration of independence.

I instantly recognize Quebecers' right to choose their destiny and I fully realize that their partisanship in Canadian federalism could never be unconditional. Nonetheless, my message to Quebecers is not to become ensnared by the din and drone of the sovereignist sirens.

It is worth recalling the inspiring image described by French philosopher Ernest Renan in which Canada, as all nations, is a daily plebiscite.[39] This country should never be imposed upon Quebecers; we must never be enclosed and forced to live in it. We must be presented with a stimulating image of Canada, one that allows us to see ourselves in both our country and its constitution. My goal in politics is not to offer Quebecers a Canada that is their only option, but rather to portray it as their best option!

AUTONOMY? NATIONALISM? Sovereignty? Federalism? Few countries on Earth must deal with so many concepts. In Quebec, the political debate is an old song often revamped and repeated.

That so many Quebecers may be tired of hearing it is more than comprehensible. None of these preceding outcomes is inevitable, and resignation will solve nothing.

Indeed, as a very small minority population in the Americas, Quebecers cannot enjoy the luxury of passivity and lack of involvement. We must not be indifferent to what will become of us in the Canada of tomorrow, nor casually take the path leading to secession. Lucidity must be the guiding light for our collective efforts. Intrepid and sufficiently down-to-earth we must remain, so as not to be seduced by inaccessible visions.

We, Quebecers, are sentenced to life for Excellence! What a heavy burden to bear... and how captivating! More than ever before, we must lay out plans and construct dreams for a Quebec that eschews apathetic victimization: plans that will channel the pride it cultivates from within to see the future with optimism, and dreams that will inspire ambitions to pursue those plans. Canada is one of these plans, one of these dreams, that I believe Quebecers must embrace and pursue. It is certainly demanding, and it will require us to be proactive and visionary in all that concerns relations with our federative partners.

In fact, though, all Canadians must pull together boldly and creatively. At a time when many countries around the world are witnessing substantial changes in their political and constitutional structures in order to meet the momentous challenges of this new century head on, Canada must also adapt and innovate the federative institutions and relations that give it life.

Ultimately, Canada's identity must include Quebec, and we, Quebecers, must embrace Canada in our own national character; only once this happens can federalism fully succeed.

BENOÎT PELLETIER *is Full Professor at the University of Ottawa's Faculty of Law. He has been Minister for Intergovernmental Affairs in the Quebec government since 2003.*

Notes

1. For example, see Hélène Ruel, "Il faut qu'on mène l'ultime bataille: Bernard Landry poursuit sa marche vers la souveraineté," *La Nouvelle Union*, November 15, 2006, p. 2. It is reported in this article that Bernard Landry said of me during a public meeting that at heart I was a colonial subject.

2. Canada. *House of Commons Debates*, Official Report (Hansard), vol. 141, no. 084, 1st Session, 39th Parliament, Wednesday, November 22, 2006: "That this House recognize that the Québécois form a nation within a united Canada."

3. Michel Seymour, *La nation en question*, Montreal: L'Hexagone, 1999, p. 98: "The national identity of an individual or of a group is almost always a matter of self-representation... To speak of nationhood is to identify the way in which a group conceives of itself. Populations may have self-representations sufficiently specialized that they go to the point of affecting the different concepts of nationhood." (my translation) See also Geneviève Mathieu, *Qui est Québécois? Synthèse du débat sur la redéfinition de la nation*, Montreal: VLB Éditeur, 2001, pp. 75, 80: "The definition of a nation must therefore respect the conceptual pluralism needed to make an adequate analysis of the reality and at the same time respect the nature of self-representation essential to the building of a national identity." (my translation)

4. Ernest Renan, "Qu'est-ce qu'une nation?" in Michel SarraBournet and Jocelyn Saint-Pierre (eds.), *Les nationalismes au Québec du XIXᵉ au XXIᵉ siècle*, Quebec: Les Presses de l'Université Laval, 2001, p. 359.

5. Léon Dion, *Nationalismes et politique au Québec*, Montreal: Hurtubise HMH, 1975.

6. The Meech Lake Accord would have inserted in the Canadian constitution an interpretative clause providing, in part, that Quebec constitutes within Canada a distinct society and that the legislature and government of Quebec shall preserve this characteristic.

7. Benoît Pelletier (ed.), *A Project for Quebec: Affirmation, Autonomy and Leadership*, Final Report of the Special Committee of the Quebec Liberal Party on the Political and Constitutional Future of Quebec Society, Montreal, 2001.

8. Hugo de Grandpré, "L'option souverainiste stagne ou régresse, plus de huit Québécois sur dix le croient, selon un sondage," *La Voix de l'Est*, June 23, 2007, p. 2: "Thus 91% of those surveyed said they were very or fairly proud of being Quebecers. The proportion is 93.3% among francophones, compared with

83.4% among non-francophones. Eighty-six per cent said the same thing regarding their pride in being Canadian (85% for francophones, 87% for anglophones and allophones.)" (my translation)

9. On this point see Daniel J. Elazar, *Exploring Federalism*, Tuscaloosa: The University of Alabama Press, 1987, p. 12, where the author tells us that in its very simplest form federalism comes to this: *self-rule plus shared rule*. See also Montserrat Guibernau, *Nations Without States, Political Communities in a Global Age*, Cambridge & Oxford & Malden: Polity Press, in association with Blackwell Publishers Ltd., 1999, p. 51: "At the centre of the federalist idea lies the assumption of the worth and validity of diversity. For this reason, federations have often proved highly useful political tools in protecting national minorities concentrated in particular territorial areas within the federal state. For instance, Quebec, the only French enclave in North America, is one of the most active nations without a state in struggling to secure its linguistic and cultural development, in principle, within the Canadian federation."

10. *Ibid.*, p. 53: "Federation does not eliminate conflict. To a certain extent it could be argued that the acknowledgement of diversity is in itself a source of conflict, but as Burgess stresses, this 'does not have to be conceived as a weakness.' The success of federal systems is not to be measured in terms of the elimination of social conflicts but instead, in their capacity to regulate and manage such conflicts."

Let us note here that it is precisely the need to manage conflict well, among the federal partners, that partly explains the creation of the Council of the Federation in 2003 on the initiative of the Quebec government. This institution is intended to favour dialogue and mutual understanding between the Canadian provinces and territories.

11. Quebec Liberal Party, *A Quebec Free to Choose*. Report of the Constitutional Committee of the Quebec Liberal Party (chaired by Jean Allaire), Montreal, 1991.

12. Simon Langlois, "Le choc de deux sociétés globales," in Louis Balthazar, Guy Laforest and Vincent Lemieux (eds.), *Le Québec et la restructuration du Canada, 1980–1992: Enjeux et perspectives*, Sillery: Septentrion, 1992, pp. 95–108.

13. I referred earlier (*supra*), to a work of Léon Dion in which he analyzes the different kinds of nationalism that have characterized the history of Quebec. This study was completed in 1975, with the social-democratic and socialist

forms of nationalism. I propose the following question: would we not now be in the presence of a new form of nationalism in the making: *global nationalism?* In this regard, the Quebec Nation would be seen as a large, open and multiple community, an identity made up of numerous components.

14. Language is the ideal communication tool. It allows individuals and human groups to communicate their values and to be in touch with their surroundings, indeed with humanity. In Quebec, French is the official public language. It should be seen as an instrument of integration, not of exclusion. As for culture, this is an imaginary entity within which anything at all can be recognized, no matter what its origins. It is made up of sounds, objects and images, but also of customs, usage, manifestations of every kind, convictions, ways of seeing and doing that all contribute to giving a group its distinctiveness. The Quebec culture is the society's central component: it defines the common culture.

15. Fernand Dumont, *Genèse de la société québécoise*, Montreal: Boréal, 1993, p. 330.

16. This was during a speech I gave at the General Council of the Quebec Liberal Party, in Trois-Rivières, March 10, 2001.

17. See Benoît Pelletier, *supra*.

18. *The Constitution Act, 1982*, being Schedule B to the *Canada Act 1982* (U.K.), 1982, c. 11.

19. *Constitution Amendment, 1997 (Quebec)*, s. 1./97-141, C. Gaz. 1997.II.1 (published as an extra on December 22, 1997).

20. I subscribe to the philosophy that maintains it is free consent, voluntary belonging, that constitutes the basis of social existence. That is the philosophy underlying the principle of the sovereignty of the people, a principle that is in turn the basis of democracy. That is why I think that a nation's existence comes, in some real measure, from the will of its people, that federalism should not be considered as a straitjacket restraining the entities that make up a country, and that the constitution is...a contract among individuals, groups and the elements that make up a state.

21. The federalist charter was among the electoral promises Stephen Harper put forward in a speech in Quebec City on December 19, 2005: "We will also collaborate with the Council of the Federation in order to improve the functioning of our federal system. We will adopt a federalist charter to begin with, to solidify our commitment to a federalism that is more effective and better balanced." (my translation)

22. See Benoît Pelletier, *supra*, pp. 78–82.

23. Montserrat Guibernau, *supra*, p. 26.

24. This idea touches in a way on what Montserrat Guibernau said *ibidem*, p. 35: "In this context, internal differences do not pose a threat to the state's integrity, rather, they are incorporated into the state's culture and are considered part of it."

25. See Montserrat Guibernau, *supra*, pp. 27–28: "My argument is that while some nations without states may secede, most of them are likely to achieve greater political autonomy within the political institutions which are currently being developed."

26. See Michael Keating, *Nations Against the State: The New Politics of Nationalism in Quebec, Catalonia and Scotland*, 2nd edition, New York: Palgrave, 2001, p. 3: "The whole world is parceled up into discrete units, either by aligning states with ethnically defined nations, or by assimilating nations into larger states. My argument is that these... are analytically quite distinct categories, which empirically may or may not coincide."

27. See James S. Colman, "Rights, Rationality and Nationality," in Albert Breton et al. (eds.), *Nationalism and Rationality*, Cambridge: Cambridge University Press, 1995, p. 11: "Walter Connor (1991, 6) defines a nation as 'a group of people who believe they are ancestrally related. It is the largest grouping that shares that belief.' This definition, however, excludes those groups, such as 'Americans' or 'Canadians' which have been created as national groups by the existence of a state."

28. See Anthony Giddens, *The Consequences of Modernity*, Stanford: Stanford University Press, 1990, p. 64: "Globalization can thus be defined as the intensification of worldwide social relations which link distant localities in such a way that local happenings are shaped by events occurring many miles away and vice versa."

29. See Montserrat Guibernau, *supra*, p. 21: "From a financial perspective, globalization has broken up the classic nation-state's monopoly of the economy. Interdependence and the proliferation of multinational firms cutting across state boundaries permit nations without states to be considered as economic players. To succeed, they have to compete for foreign investment and encourage the production of high-quality and specialized products. Economic viability and the capacity to provide a sense of identity to its members are the two key issues which are likely to determine the relevance of nations without states in the near future."

30. *Ibid.*, pp. 18–20: "The increasing number of international organizations, multinational companies, supranational social movements and the technical sophistication of modern warfare are currently challenging this classic concept of state sovereignty. The state is exposed to pressure from above while at the same time it lays itself open to increasing internal strain to modify its traditional centralist nature and acknowledge the existence of territorially circumscribed cultural communities within itself which show a varying degree of national self-consciousness and put forward different socio-political demands... The rise of sub-state forms of nationalism in Europe and elsewhere can be interpreted as a product of the dialectic nature of globalization which consists in mutually opposed tendencies. Thus the globalization of the economy and social relations which contributed to the weakening of the nation-state also seems to have contributed to the intensification of regional forms of nationalism... The re-emergence of nationalism in nations without states is directly related to the intensification of global processes which have proven capable of altering the political, economic and cultural structures of current societies."

31. It is the case with the European Union, whose member-states have abdicated part of their sovereignty or, at least, attributes of their sovereignty.

32. See Benoît Pelletier, "L'asymétrie dans les États fédéraux: le cas du Canada," speech given during the Third International Conference on Federalism held by the Forum of Federations in Brussels, March 3, 2005. I there declared the following: "Asymmetrical federalism needs, among other things, to be careful of the coherence and cohesion of the whole. Without calling into question the federal principle, one cannot economize on basic federal responsibilities such as solidarity, the sharing of social and economic risks and opportunities, or the participation in common projects. So asymmetrical federalism must have some limits if it wants to still be 'federalism.'" (my translation) Also see, in the same context, *ibidem*, "Asymmetrical Federalism: A Win-Win Formula!" a piece appearing on the Web site of the School of Policy Studies, Queen's University, June 21, 2005: www.queensu.ca/iigr/working/archive/Asymmetric/papers/15a.pdf (accessed May 27, 2008).

33. The Canada-Quebec Agreement on Health Care: Asymmetrical Federalism that Respects Quebec's Jurisdiction, September 16, 2004. Federal-Provincial-Territorial Agreement on Health Care: A 10-Year Plan to Strengthen Health Care, September 16, 2004.

34. See Montserrat Guibernau, *supra*, p. 21: "The perceived threat of cultural homogenization is one of the factors contributing to the revitalization of minority cultures struggling to find a niche in the global net."

35. See André Pratte, *Aux pays des merveilles: essai sur les mythes politiques québécois*, Montreal: VLB Éditeur, 2006.

36. Michel Hébert, "Cinq ans de perturbations après un Oui," *Journal de Québec*, October 19, 2005, p. 7.

37. Regarding negotiations about the secession of Quebec, see: *Reference re Secession of Quebec*, [1998] 2 SCR 217.

38. *Clarity Act*, S.C. 2000, c. 26.

39. Ernest Renan, *supra*, p. 361. Renan discusses the existence of the nation that was, as he said, "an everyday plebiscite."

4

MARIE BERNARD-MEUNIER

LEARNING TO PLAY THE GAME

The Challenge of Quebec within Canada

FEDERALISM IS too complex and, on balance, too unstable a political system to adopt without being compelled to do so. There are geographical pressures, such as when the size of the territory makes a centralized management system difficult or even impossible. This is the case in Russia, the United States and Brazil. There are also historical pressures, as in the case of Germany, which came together as a country out of numerous kingdoms and principalities and which has always maintained an operating system that respects local particularities. Finally, a country can be "forced into federalism" by the cultural and linguistic diversity of its population. This is what has happened in Switzerland and in Belgium. In Canada, we have the combination of all three factors: the impact of geography, of history and of diversity. It would therefore have been very difficult for us to escape federalism!

The intention of this essay is not so much to defend the virtues of Canadian federalism as it operates now, but rather to invite readers to reflect upon the federal idea itself. To do this, I will use two examples: Germany, a fully mature federation, and the European Union (EU), which is still in gestation. Better understanding the resilience of German federalism and the ongoing vicissitudes of the EU should give us a different perspective from which to understand our own form of federalism.

Not wanting to carry out a comparative study of constitutional law, I will not spend any time on what likens German or European federalism with, or distinguishes it from, the Canadian experience. There are as many federalisms as there are federations, which is why comparisons are usually of limited interest. We can always find a federalism more centralized or less centralized than our own. So what I will focus on is not the practice of federalism, here or elsewhere, but rather the concept, the idea, the logic behind the institutions: because the work required to grasp the vision of federalism conveyed by a system foreign to us can renew and enrich our own thinking on the subject.

And so I propose to take a practical little detour through Germany and Europe before tackling the question of federalism in Canada. My goal is to show that examples from elsewhere will help us to better assess the strengths and weaknesses of our political system. These examples can also help us to draw some very pertinent conclusions about the true nature of federalism, especially that federations are always marriages of convenience, not marriages for love, and that they always entail a dual membership and a dual allegiance.

My words are meant primarily for those who are committed to staying within Canada. It is them whom I invite to more effectively take the measure of what belonging to a federation really means. All the same, whether one is sovereignist, autonomist or federalist; whether one wants to defend or to oppose the federal system; whether one wants to leave it, change it or promote it, we all have good reasons to deepen our understanding of what federalism is. And I would not hesitate to conclude that, among all of our political discourses, the federal one is the most in need of renewal.

German Federalism: Its Origins, Its Evolution and Its Present Problems

At the time of the Peace of Westphalia in 1648, the Holy Roman Empire of the German Nation consisted of 350 kingdoms, principalities and free cities, all of which had only one common purpose: to limit and to contain the central power. After the Napoleonic Wars, which signalled the end of the Holy Roman Empire of the German Nation, all these autonomous Germanic territories regrouped as thirty-nine sovereign states. The Congress of Vienna, in 1815, brought them together again within a loose Germanic confederation, as vast as it was various. Then, in 1870, Chancellor Otto von Bismarck was able to use the political influence and the military power of Prussia to unite Germany and make the King of Prussia the new emperor. The political system thereby created was halfway between a federation and a confederation. Most of the federated states (twenty-one out of twenty-five) remained monarchies and they jealously guarded their own sovereignty.

The First World War would signal the brutal and definitive collapse of this empire along with all its monarchies. The Weimar Republic that followed set up a political regime that was more like halfway between a federation and a unitary state. But Adolf Hitler undertook to rapidly destroy whatever was left of the federation. The regime became unitary and centralized. The concentration of power was absolute. The federated states lost all autonomy and would not recover it until 1945.

Indeed, right after the Second World War, the German Länder resumed their existence even before the new constitution was adopted or a federal government selected. The Allied Powers, which were occupying the territory, needed the Länder to quickly begin rebuilding Germany. And they hoped to endow the Länder with great responsibilities in order to head off the re-emergence of too strong a central power. When this latter came into being, starting in 1949, it immediately had to work with the Länder, which were by then very much in control of their own prerogatives.

And yet for all that, the Länder were not always able to fend off pressure from the new central power. In administrative matters and the operation of the law, they were able to hold on to a predominant position, but the central power progressively enlarged its hold on the legislative. To achieve this, the central power was able to use areas both of exclusive and of shared jurisdiction, but most of all it took advantage of article 72 of the new constitution, which gave it the right to legislate whenever the development of equivalent living conditions throughout the country rendered federal legislation necessary. For somewhat different reasons, we have experienced a similar evolution in Canada.

The Länder did not stand by passively while their legislative powers were being eroded. They compensated for the relative reduction of their jurisdictions by obtaining the right to take part in developing federal law within the Bundesrat (the federal council, a kind of upper house). And that is one of the essential attributes of German federalism. Through the Bundesrat, where each is represented by a member of its respective government, the Länder in fact have the use of an effective instrument of participation in any federal decisions that concern them.

And in their areas of exclusive jurisdiction, the Länder have also developed some effective mechanisms of horizontal cooperation, sometimes to harmonize their respective policies, sometimes to defend their common interests against the central power. These mechanisms of co-operation most often take the form of permanent conferences that bring together sometimes the minister-presidents (the equivalent of our provincial premiers), and sometimes the ministers responsible for particular portfolios such as education, culture or European affairs.

The truth is that the operation of the German federal system does not lead to very much confrontation between the different levels of government. There is frequent reference to the "co-operative" character of German federalism. Both at the federal and at the state level, Germans recognize the difficulty—indeed the impossibility—of separating powers rigidly and absolutely. The best solutions frequently require the intervention of both levels of government, and it should also be noted that some problems that theoretically concern only one or another of the different levels of government are often in fact closely linked and require joint effort to resolve.

The relative harmony that one can see in the operation of German federalism should not hide the fact that it too faces some tough challenges. We will look at three examples: the implementation of institutional reforms, the effect of European integration and the impact of German reunification.

The practice of co-operative federalism as I have described it led to a growing overlap of jurisdictions, to the point where more than 60 per cent of laws passed by the Bundestag (the legislative assembly) were being resubmitted to the Bundesrat because they supposedly infringed on Länder jurisdiction. And at times when the majorities in the Bundestag and the Bundesrat were not of the same political stripe, which was the case during most of Chancellor Gerhard Schroeder's mandate, this arrangement led to excessive delays and even to actual logjams. To alleviate this kind of problem, it was decided to spell out the jurisdictions of the different levels of government, also taking into account the transfer of some jurisdictions to the EU level, so that citizens could more clearly see who was responsible for what. The number of laws needing approval by the Bundestag and the Bundesrat was also reduced significantly. To work out this new division of jurisdictions, Germans were inspired by the principle of subsidiarity, meaning that areas of responsibility were assigned to the level of government best able to take them on.

This reform took place in 2005. Others have been in the works for years, such as a motion to reduce the number of Länder (some having been judged too small to fully take on their responsibilities, especially financial) and another to link the Länder's legislative assemblies to the Bundesrat (at the moment, it is Länder government representatives who sit in the Bundesrat). The other reform, which several Länder are hoping for, is a different tax-equalization system. I will come back to that idea when I deal with the challenges that reunification has brought to German federalism.

As in every country in the EU, European integration has had a visible impact on the working of German institutions. The Länder have adopted the same attitude towards Brussels they have towards their own federal state: if they cannot actually stop the transfer of jurisdictions, they want at least some say in the decision-making. For a long time, it had been accepted that the German government had to seek the advice of the Bundesrat and take it into account whenever a Brussels-originated draft directive had an impact on the Länder. But the states wanted still more authority, and in the Maastricht Treaty, in 1992, they received recognition of their sovereign rights and of their right to participate in European affairs. The Länder must, however, first come to an understanding among themselves and with the federal state before they can intervene at the European level. This is why the Länder have, since 1992, put in place a permanent conference of their ministers of European affairs.

The Länder's machinery for taking part in European affairs is neither simple nor swift, but that is the price of harmony and cohesiveness. Some of the states, such as Bavaria, are still quicker than others to denounce Brussels' intrusions into their jurisdictional fields, but the existing mechanisms also allow the management of such disputes.

The tax-equalization system in Germany has two characteristics that distinguish it from the tax-equalization system in Canada. First, the intention is not just to help out the poorer regions but to create equal living conditions across the whole territory. Second, there are two types of transfers: those from the federal government to those Länder that are eligible, and those from the richer Länder. Of course, the system has always been criticized, especially by those Länder that are called upon to give rather than to receive. However, reunification has brought about an unprecedented state of affairs. As long as Germany was only West Germany, the gaps to bridge were "manageable." The arrival of the new Länder with substantial economic problems created a genuine shock to the system. The combined transfer payments of the federal government and the richer Länder rose to seventy-five billion euros a year and will be maintained at this level until 2015. More than 85 per cent of these transfers go to the Länder of the former East Germany. And in the western part of the country, Länder that once received payments are now net contributors. Calls for a reform of the whole equalization system are starting to become urgent.

It is interesting to note that the Länder that benefited most from the equalization system to attain the enviable economic situation they are in now are the first in line to demand an overhaul of the system and to promote what they call "competitive federalism." With this reform, only Länder that could demonstrate clear effort and convincing results to improve their economic situation would be eligible for payments under the equalization system. It would assume that all Länder are starting on a more or less equal equal footing, which is far from the case. Several Länder (and not all of them in eastern Germany) are either too small or too poor to even think about coming into the race as equals. The introduction of competitive federalism seems quite unlikely, but it is just as improbable that the present system can continue as it is. The basic question is to what extent the principle of solidarity that requires governments to guarantee equal conditions for the whole territory can actually be maintained. As always, the Germans are trying to work out a new consensus.

This study of the origins, the evolution and the present challenges of German federalism shows us that while the Länder remain very strongly attached to their jurisdictional rights and prerogatives, they also demonstrate an unquestionable willingness to co-operate in order to bring about the workability of a system that they understand must serve not only their own interests but those of the whole country. It is clear that before reunification everything was easier because the developmental gaps were not nearly so great, but this culture of compromise and the diligent search for consensus, which have always characterized the operation of German federalism, should allow the country to meet the challenges it now faces.

European Federalism: The Dream and the Reality

To begin with, let me be clear that the European Union, properly speaking, is not really a federation, at least not in the generally accepted sense of the word. If I have chosen to speak here of the "European example," it is for two reasons. First, "the federal intention" has been always part of European institutions, either explicitly or implicitly. Second, and this is the most important aspect, the EU already operates in many respects as though it were in fact a federation. The transfer of jurisdictions from the member-states to Brussels is very real. Directives from Brussels apply directly to individuals and companies all across Europe. The European Commission is incontestably a supranational instrument. Even the European Council, since the progressive extension of majority rule (and the corresponding withdrawal of the rule on unanimity), no longer expresses the sovereignty of its member-states the way it once did. We are already in a world of shared sovereignties, common jurisdictions and multiple allegiances, but the EU is still an incomplete federation, an original and unprecedented model, a political enterprise that is still in the making.

In the minds of its founding fathers, Jean Monnet and Robert Schuman, Europe was destined to become a federation. Even the first European community, the European Coal and Steel Community (ECSC), was, to them, an initial step towards a European federation. The communities that followed, the European Atomic Energy Community (Euratom) and the European Economic Community (EEC), as well as the first common policies like the agricultural policy were all borne of the same logic: favour the sectoral approach, introduce the member-states to the joint management of concrete matters, develop a "communitarian approach" and thus build a reserve of mutual trust that would, bit by bit, lay the groundwork for the gradual emergence of a genuine European federation.

For its partisans, the federalist ambition is at the very heart of the whole European enterprise. Without it, the EU would be just an international organization like all the others. This is a vision that has been restated and defended by every president of the European Commission. Jacques Delors, a former president of the commission, liked to speak of Europe as a federation of nation-states. He thought that the very principle of federalism was the preservation of the autonomy and diversity of the federated states, and, therefore, that the member-states had nothing to fear in the idea of a European federation.

However, this vision was never widely shared. At the beginning, the idea of federalism was almost taboo. One might subscribe to it, but one would not try to impose it on those who were not yet convinced that it was the way of the future for Europe. Hostility to the idea of federalism ran deep. Its opponents simply did not see any need or any use in transferring to Brussels any jurisdictions that the states were capable of taking on. They also thought that, though federalism theoretically brought power closer to individual citizens, in Europe it would actually have the opposite effect. They felt that European federalism would be centralizing; it would distance citizens a bit more from the reins of power and, thus, it would be a backward step for democracy. It is worth remembering that for a very long time Germany was the only federation in Europe, and so very few Europeans had any direct experience of a federal regime and all that it implies in terms of shared sovereignty.

The division between the European federalists and their opponents goes back to the very beginning of the European adventure. The federalists always favoured the idea of a supranational Europe, a deeper integration, an extension of shared jurisdictions, a stronger role for the European Commission and for the European Parliament. Their opponents, however, always preferred a "Europe of homelands," a Europe that was intergovernmental rather than communitarian, in which the member-states through the European Council effectively controlled the institution and in which the European Commission was downgraded to the status of a technical body. If this alignment has always existed and still exists today, we can nonetheless distinguish two significant periods: one that begins with the creation of Europe in the 1950s and continues through to 1990, and another that runs from 1990 to the present. Without much exaggeration, one could say that the first was the period of communitarian Europe; the second, of intergovernmental Europe.

The first period saw the building of all the institutional machinery and the adoption of all the key common policies. What is curious is that the first jurisdictions transferred to Brussels were not at all those usually associated with the central power of a federation, namely defence, foreign affairs, currency. The success of the ECSC and the failure of the European Defence Community, which was first proposed by France and then irremediably compromised by that country in 1954, account for the fact that it appeared preferable to set aside the traditional prerogatives of central power and to focus on sectors that were less sensitive and more specific.

In the economic and commercial sphere, Europe at the time was quickly becoming a major player on the international scene. Its influence is nearly comparable to that of the United States. Through its common agricultural, regional development and industrial policies as well as through its institutions and standards in almost every sector, Europe is also having an increasingly direct and visible effect on the daily life of citizens in all of its member-states. The European Commission is becoming increasingly important, not just because of the rapid growth in the number of European officials but also through the political leadership exercised by its successive presidents. The abolition of borders and the adoption of a common passport have also contributed to Europeans' sense of belonging to the same political entity.

One could say that, until 1990, the forces favouring broader and deeper European integration were on a roll. They won all the battles, provided they were modest about their success and, especially, discreet. There was no question of celebrating the progress of federalism, since the word continued to evoke fear.

Beginning in the early nineties, the trend reversed. The international context changed. It was the era in which we discovered the impact of globalization and its resultant fears, in which the neo-liberal ideas of British Prime Minister Margaret Thatcher and United States President Ronald Reagan were on the rise (with all they implied about the disengagement, or diminishing role, of the state), in which the technological revolution radically transformed relations with authority and provoked an ongoing demand for more transparency and more democracy. Europe was changing too. The reunification of Germany revived, among its neighbours, some old concerns, and the fall of the Iron Curtain raised the question of expanding the EU to accommodate the Eastern and Central European countries. Assaulted by all these changes, Europe froze.

The Euro-skeptics (a new word that makes quite an impact) cheerfully greeted the end of this period, in which Europe had been uniting too rapidly for their tastes. Great Britain and the Scandinavian countries saw in this European enlargement an opportunity to dilute the communitarian and integrationist Europe and return it to a more intergovernmental Europe. In the new Central and Eastern European recruits, they saw some potential allies. Indeed, one can easily imagine that these countries were not much inclined to give up any of the sovereignty they had only just recovered.

If some saw in this enlargement the probable end of the federal dream, others believed it would be the moment of truth. Europe was going to have to choose between federalism and paralysis. And several voices were raised just then, notably in Germany, proposing a new agenda for a federated Europe.

In 1994, two leaders of Germany's Christian Democratic Union party, Karl Lamers and Wolfgang Schäuble, published *Reflections on European Policy*. Responding to the threats posed to the further integration of Europe, not just by the enlargement but also the rise of nationalism and regionalism, they proposed that before the EU consider any increase in its territory to the east, it strengthen relations among its existing members. Specifically, they proposed intensifying the Franco-German relationship and building a solid core in the heart of Europe that would be both the symbol of European integration and its propelling force. For them, this internal consolidation was a prerequisite for the enlargement, or, at the very least, would have to occur in parallel with it.

This idea would be brought forward again in 2000 by the German foreign minister Joschka Fischer, at the Humboldt University of Berlin in a speech often referred to as the most recent and most ambitious expression of European federalism. Mr. Fischer, like Mr. Lamers and Mr. Schäuble, raised the idea of a centre of gravity, a sort of European avant-garde. Like them, he also promoted the development of a genuine European foreign policy. Knowing that the political climate was even less receptive to the idea of federation than it had been in 1994, he sought to develop a discourse adapted to this new reality. He was also trying to appease the fears generated by German reunification, by insisting heavily on the fact that Germany had no other interests than those of Europe. Despite this, his speech did not have the impact he had hoped for. No one picked up the ball, and France showed itself especially cautious. In a way, the debate over federalism had become virtually academic, disconnected as it was from the everyday realities.

During the negotiation of the Maastricht Treaty, Prime Minister John Major had, on behalf of Great Britain, opposed even referring to Europe as a federation. The treaties that followed, Amsterdam (1997) and Nice (2001), only formalized the retreat from the federal idea and the triumph of the intergovernmental approach.

Suddenly, the European Commission no longer enjoyed the prestige it once had. Its role was considered too invasive; its attitude, too authoritarian; its culture, too bureaucratic. So it became the perfect scapegoat. The member-states held it responsible for everything that went wrong in their countries, yet took the credit for everything that went well. After each European summit, the heads of state and government returned to their respective capitals boasting of having once more defended the national interest.

And yet, during that entire period, there were undeniable European advances, such as setting up the Schengen free travel area,[1] adopting a single currency and developing the Third Pillar, which opened up a new area of co-operation among the European nations, the area of internal security, justice and criminal matters. But, and this is a crucial point, some of these advances (the Schengen travel area and the euro) did not involve all of the member-states. Did allowing some member-states to integrate farther than others bring about the "solid core" that some were calling for so passionately? Or did it, in fact, entrench the principle of a Europe "à la carte," in which each member-state could pick and choose how much integration it wanted? The answer depends largely on which point of view one favours.

Some federalists will certainly see the emergence of a group of countries that are ready to declare a stronger European will and assume a leadership role. They would argue that if they cannot persuade all member-states of the merits of federalism, then they will build it, bit by bit, with those who are interested. This a pragmatic response in a context not very favourable to their ideal of a federated Europe. Other federalists will argue that a Europe that allows member-states to pick and choose the parts they like signals the death of the federal idea. They cannot see how a monetary union would necessarily lead to a political union, and even less how the union of a few can bring about the union of the whole.

For these federalists, the subsidiarity principle also constitutes a serious threat to the European federal ideal. Designed to clearly spell out the jurisdictions of the respective levels of government and to resist the so-called Brussels "invasion," the subsidiarity principle, which allotted jurisdictions to the level of government best able to assume them, has become one of the major stakes itself and the subject of numerous confrontations. Whereas the more pragmatic federalists could live with it, the more dogmatic federalists feel that subsidiarity is a denial of shared sovereignties. Now, these shared sovereignties lie at the heart of the federal project. At the other end of the political spectrum, those who defend the absolute sovereignty of the states invoke the same subsidiarity principle to argue that the EU has yet to demonstrate that it is more capable than the member-states of taking on any responsibility whatsoever.

When one looks at the diversity and divergence of the points of view, it is hard to believe that, under those same circumstances and with those same member-states, anyone would even think of developing a European constitution. And yet... between 2001 and 2004, under the presidency of Valéry Giscard d'Estaing, a commission bringing together not only representatives of the member-states, but also those of future member-states, succeeded in working out a new constitutional document.

The constitutional project had high ambitions. It wanted Europe to take a new step on the road to political integration by electing a president and appointing a minister of foreign affairs. Although it had become an economic giant, Europe was still a political dwarf (to use an expression that was applied to Germany for some time). The new constitutional document was supposed to remedy this situation and, at least, begin to solve the problem. It was also intended to give juridical value to the Charter of Fundamental Rights, which had been adopted in Nice in 2001. And finally, and perhaps especially, it was designed to give Europe decision-making mechanisms that would allow it to function with twenty-five members, or even twenty-seven. It was an opportunity to review all the tools and internal treaties that the European Commission had developed over the years and to merge them into one document. The final result was an extraordinarily complicated piece of legislation containing more than 450 articles. The product of innumerable compromises, the document fully satisfied no one. Nonetheless it was deemed the best possible agreement under the circumstances, which is why it was sent to the member-states for ratification.

The outcome is well known. About two thirds of the member-states ratified the proposed constitution, more by parliamentary vote than by referendum. Two countries, France and The Netherlands, rejected it, and others, among them the United Kingdom, Poland and the Czech Republic—where the ratification process was expected to be very difficult—were very happy to find themselves freed from the need to "sell" their people or their Parliaments on the constitution they had signed. The reasons for the failure of the constitutional agreement are numerous and contradictory. It was too liberal for some, not liberal enough for others, but especially too "integrationist" for many Europeans. That, at least, is what one is tempted to conclude after reading the "mini treaty," or "simplified treaty," that was passed in 2007 to lead Europe out of the crisis generated by the French and the Dutch rejecting the original document.

It can be said of the new version that it is shorter because, essentially, it picks up only the chapter on institutional mechanisms. One cannot say, however, that it is any simpler, because the compromises are built upon some often very ambiguous formulations. Nonetheless, certain matters appear to be settled. There will indeed be a European president, who will be elected for a term of thirty months. There will no longer be a presidency that rotates every six months. There will not be a European minister of foreign affairs but rather a "high-level representative" with similar responsibilities. Double-majority voting (in which 55 per cent of the member-states representing 65 per cent of the European population is required for a motion to pass) will be maintained but will not be brought into force until 2014, or maybe even 2017 if Poland continues to be difficult. The number of European commissioners will be reduced to fifteen from twenty-seven. Majority decision will replace the rule of unanimity in many new areas, including the areas of justice and security, in which member-states have traditionally been very protective of their sovereignty. Finally, the Charter of Fundamental Rights will have legal value all over Europe, except in the United Kingdom, which has sought and obtained an exemption on this point and on several others. Just to be complete, it must also be noted that the elements of the treaty that gave official status to the flag and to the European anthem have been eliminated.

So what should one make of this latest chapter in the European saga? Some will say that the "federalist" ambitions have been downgraded yet again. Certainly, denying official status to the European anthem and the European flag clearly expresses a wish to disallow Europe anything that might resemble the attributes of a central power. But those who want to think that Europe's march towards a federal structure remains inescapable, despite all its ups and downs, will see indications of this approach in the election of a European president, the naming of an almost–foreign affairs minister and the increase in the number of areas of jurisdiction that will henceforth be decided by majority instead of unanimity. Perhaps it is in this last element that the ultimate test of European integration lies: the progressive transformation of the rule of unanimity into the rule of the majority. The former effectively gives member-states an effective right of veto, which often slows down and sometimes paralyzes decision-making. The latter, however, forces them towards collaboration. It speeds decision-making and facilitates agreements that go well beyond the lowest common denominator.

The struggle between those for and against a federal Europe, between those who want more Europe and those who want less, goes on. The final outcome is still uncertain. An eventual "unravelling" of Europe is not out of the question. In the relatively short term, that would bring Europe back to a free-trade zone. This scenario, however, does not seem the most probable. As the architects of the European Union were hoping, Europe has developed habits of co-operation that are now deeply ingrained, and the central power of Brussels, though it has been contested from time to time, has now become part of the European political tradition. In the face of present-day challenges, whether globalization, international security or global warming, it would be a rare European country that continued to think it best to go into battle alone. Only joint action and converging policies will allow Europe to have a real impact on the history of this century. All the European countries know that, even if some have been slow to acknowledge it.

Federalism at Home: Canadian Realities and the Quebec Perspective

Canada, clearly, is neither Germany nor the European Union. Germany, despite its local specificities, is a much more homogeneous country socially, culturally and linguistically. The EU brings together independent countries, and even though its present operation looks like a federation in many ways, one could hardly compare a member-state in the EU with a Canadian province. This having been said, we can still draw from our analysis of German and European federalism some pertinent lessons and useful perspectives for looking at the nature of federalism, relationships between the federated states and a central power, and relations among federated entities.

On the Nature of Federalism

One can identify four essential components:

First, *the balance point of a federation is always unstable.* It is unstable in the sense that it is never definitive. The phases of centralization and decentralization, which are always relative, follow one another, but whether in Germany or in Europe or in Canada, the tendency of the central power is always to increase its reach. Only resistance from the federated entities can counter this inclination, contain it and, in some cases, reverse it. In Canada, the Second World War led the federal government to move towards a centralization of power that the country had never known before and that more or less continues to this day. It is still too soon to say whether the "open federalism" practised by Prime Minister Stephen Harper's Conservative government will set off a search for a new equilibrium within the Canadian federation.

Second, *the strength of a federation depends upon its ability to reconcile two equally fundamental needs: the need to retain individuality and the need to unite.* The German federation works well because the Länder feel no threat to their identities and because they believe they are well served by their membership in a greater whole. In contrast, European integration is moving forward slowly and with difficulty because some member-states are still afraid of losing their identity (even if after fifty years of union one can readily distinguish a German from a French citizen or an Italian!) and because others (sometimes the same ones) are not yet ready to recognize that the EU allows for better management of problems, whether domestic or international. Similarly, many Quebecers believe that their identity is threatened within Canada and think that they would handle their own problems more effectively and have more influence internationally, if they were independent. The debate that sets European federalists and nationalists against each other is not fundamentally different from the one that pits federalists and sovereignists against each other in Canada.

Third, *federations are marriages of convenience and reason, never marriages for love*. Federalism does not have any emotional well-springs. Bavarians do not feel well loved by the rest of Germany (and that is an understatement!). Few Europeans are overflowing with admiration or affection for their neighbours; in fact, their European Union is made up of ancient enemies, whose differences have long been considered irreconcilable. Quebecers have a compulsive need for recognition. They easily feel humiliated or despised, and the constant affirmation of their difference betrays a profound insecurity. If Quebecers and federalism are to be reconciled, there must, above all, be no more "love-ins" like the one that took place in 1995. It would be far better to find a way to release Quebecers from their crippling need to be loved.

Fourth, *a federation implies a dual membership and a dual allegiance*. There can be no federation without a common project, without an ongoing commitment to consensus and without mutual trust. Loyalties and feelings of belonging can accumulate. One can be German and Bavarian, French and European. One can even be Bavarian, German *and* European. And all in whichever order one prefers. It is also possible, then, to be a Quebecer and a Canadian (or the reverse). What is not possible is to claim to want to stay in Canada while looking out only for one's own interests. If loyalties are going to accrue, there must be at least two of them and they must both be real.

On Relations with the Central Power

The German and European examples highlight a serious gap in the Canadian federal system, that is, the absence of provincial representation at the central level. In a federation, the legitimation of the federal power generally comes from the people, who elect the members of Parliament and choose the government, and from the member-states, who send representatives to the upper house, whether it be the Senate in Washington, the Bundesrat in Berlin or the Council of the European Union in Brussels. In Canada, the provinces do not have this institutional role at the federal level, and that fact is not inconsequential. In Germany, the Bundesrat allows the Länder to take part in developing and executing the federal laws that concern them, and this mechanism has also compensated them for some loss of local legislative jurisdiction. It is easy to imagine the political benefit the Canadian provinces could draw from a Senate that belonged to them. Instead of seeing this approach as a potential threat to the federal power as we do now, we should perhaps see it as a way to improve the functioning and the cohesion of the Canadian federation.

As to the division of jurisdictions and the subsidiarity principle, it is interesting to consider whether a more rigorous sharing of jurisdictions is possible, desirable or even necessary. Is the best model for Canada a German-style co-operative federalism, in which responsibilities are given to the level of government best able to take them on, and excessive overlapping is avoided while accepting that complex problems often require the joint intervention of both levels of government? Is a better model a European-style federalism, in which—theoretically—responsibilities are left to the most appropriate level of government but in reality jurisdictions are shared and the definition of shared objectives is emphasized over the definition of fields of jurisdiction? Or is the best model a kind of frontier federalism, in which each level of government tries for, and achieves, the clear definition of its exclusive territory? In any case, there seem to be at least two ways of protecting the federated states from intrusions by the central power: one being watertight jurisdictions; the other, the participation of the federated entities in central decision-making. We might very well expect that, lacking their own chamber in Ottawa, the Canadian provinces in general and Quebec in particular would continue to zealously guard their own areas of jurisdiction.

As for the often-expressed desire for a Quebec that would deal with the central power on an equal footing, it is important to recognize just how incongruous that idea is, as long as Quebec is part of the Canadian federation. Even the recently acquired recognition of Quebec as a nation does not change in any way the fundamental relationship that exists between a central power and its federated states. To demand a dialogue of equals is akin to starting down the road to independence since it confirms, from the beginning, an intent to negotiate a new union, not of ten but of two. It is a political option that we might want to consider, but we cannot go down that road and pretend that it will not lead to a rift with the rest of Canada. Although a federation may choose to treat its federated states differently to respond to special circumstances (our asymmetrical federalism), it cannot allow one of them to act as though it has the same status as the central power. To do so is to call into question the entire structure of the federation.

On Relations with Other Federated Entities

Once again, the German and European examples reveal a break in the Canadian federation: the weakness of interprovincial co-operation. Whereas the German Länder continually work together within the commissions that cover their exclusive jurisdictions and also within a commission of European affairs to define their positions and articulate them to the central power, and whereas the member-states of the European Union also interact constantly at every level, Canadian provinces are more likely to act alone and to negotiate separately with the central power. Co-operative mechanisms exist but they are used at only a fraction of their potential. The idea of creating a Council of the Federation, whose aim is to strengthen interprovincial and interterritorial relations, is probably the best initiative we have developed in a long time, but it remains to be seen how it will be used. In Quebec, even though the idea for the council owes a great deal to the present premier, support for it is fairly limited. There are even some Quebecers who claim to want to stay in Canada but wish to abolish the council.

If the Senate were a genuine chamber of the provinces, the dynamic would be quite different. And in the meantime, the provinces ought to evaluate the virtues of closer collaboration, which might not only help them share solutions to common problems but also change their relationship with the central power over the long term. For example, if one accepts the idea that the country needs a national policy to manage foreign investment in the natural resources sector, one can only hope that the provinces would be directly involved in developing such a policy. To do so suggests a way of working together that is very different from the one that exists now. In another example, if the provinces want to play a more important role at the international level, especially within organizations such as the World Trade Organization, they will have to talk among themselves and develop a joint strategy vis-à-vis the federal government. Quebec is proud of having acquired special treatment at the United Nations Educational, Scientific and Cultural Organization (UNESCO), but the stakes that accompany provincial participation in international affairs are of a different magnitude altogether. It remains to be seen whether Canadian provinces would be prepared to put up with the kinds of constraints the German Länder face in having to agree among themselves—and with the federal government—before they can be heard in Brussels.

It is only with great difficulty that Quebec ever sees the other provinces as strategic partners and potential allies. We are often satisfied just to restate our traditional demands (and always to the central power), and if one of these is met, another requirement is quickly added to the list. A more strategic view of these interests would allow Quebec to understand that demands from the other provinces can also be legitimate and that helping to satisfy those demands would create better conditions in which to achieve our own. And we might well set for ourselves more inspiring objectives than the simple satisfaction of raising our traditional demands. For example, listening to Newfoundland's premier, exasperated by the new rules for equalization payments, declare that from now on his province wants financial autonomy vis-à-vis Ottawa, we dream of hearing the same words in Quebec, especially since financial autonomy is the only true autonomy. The rest is only talk.

Over and above the specific lessons we can learn from the German and European examples that I have just outlined, there is another more general and more fundamental one, upon which it is worth reflecting. For a federal system to work, it is necessary that all its components—the central power and the local governments—subscribe to the same vision and share the same conviction that together they have more power to act than they could have separately. It is exactly this characteristic that gives the German federation its strength and that accounts for the vicissitudes of European federalism.

If the German Länder are still profoundly attached to their own identities and demand the right to be involved in any decision that affects them, they also have a true willingness to make the system work to the benefit of all and to recognize that the federal entity that is Germany does more for them than they would be able to accomplish individually. At the level of the EU, although it is less obvious that the member-states share a common vision, it is clear the idea that they can achieve more together than they would individually is making some real headway. It is for this reason that the European example seems somewhat paradoxical, in that the federal discourse remains widely unpopular (some member-states even seeking to eliminate any suggestion of a central power) but the European countries are accepting a progressive erosion of their sovereignty because solving their present problems requires it. All of us recognize that neither the challenges of globalization, nor climate change, nor international terrorism lend themselves to unilateral responses. If Europe wants to solve its own problems and have some influence in working out international solutions, its countries must unite. Although it has long been propelled by the ambitious vision of its founding fathers, the European Union is now driven by the need to better respond to ever greater challenges. Some of its member-states will need more time to accept the idea that even greater integration is unavoidable. Others have not yet given up on trying to reverse the trend. European federalism will, therefore, probably continue to evolve bit by bit, taking a few steps forward, then a few steps back and many more to the side.

In Canada, a common vision is far from manifest, and the conviction that we are better off together is not all it could be. Complicating this reality is the tendency to think that each province or territory is only out for itself and that, consequently, meeting our common goals is just too difficult. The challenge to federalists, especially to Quebec federalists, is enormous.

It is said that to win, one has to play the game. Quebec federalists will have little chance of persuading their fellow citizens about the merits of federalism if they are obsessed with being as nationalistic as the Parti Québécois or as autonomist as the Action démocratique, or, indeed, even more nationalist or autonomist than they are. There is nothing comfortable about being a federalist. To practise federalism is difficult enough; wanting to reform it demands much courage and much patience and, some say, borders on recklessness.

For Quebec federalists, the first and most important step is to shed their negative image. Federalists do not shatter dreams. Their aim is not to deprive Quebecers of a country. Their goal is to promote a political system that has value for millions of citizens around the world. To be convincing, the federalists will need to develop a new and inspiring plan of action. The weakness of the discourse until now has often been painful. The inspiration in this regard, as in everything, could well come from elsewhere. Which is what I have been trying to show.

A former student at L'École Nationale d'Administration in Paris with a master's degree in political science from the University of Montreal, MARIE BERNARD-MEUNIER *has spent her career in the Canadian diplomatic service, notably as Canadian Ambassador to Germany, to The Netherlands and to the United Nations Educational, Scientific and Cultural Organization (*UNESCO*).*

Note

1. The borderless union of almost all members of the European Union except the United Kingdom, Ireland, Cyprus, Bulgaria and Romania.

5

PATRICE RYAN AND FRÉDÉRIC BÉRARD

THE THREE SOLITUDES

The authors are co-founders of L'Institut du Canada Moderne, a think tank whose mission is to contribute, through ideas and research, to the renewal of the Canadian federation, its institutions and policies, giving an important place to Quebec in this process. The two following pieces are letters, one to a Toronto anglophone and one to a Quebec separatist.

LETTER TO AN ENGLISH CANADIAN FRIEND

DEAR PETER:

From time to time I think back to that long talk we had about Canada's future, one night in Toronto, over a few beers in a trendy bar on Queen Street West. As I said to you that evening, I still believe in the Canadian idea, that crazy dream of a great continental, bilingual, modern, secular, educated, entrepreneurial, courageous, multinational country that's active on the world stage. But you know what I think about that country. It doesn't exist anywhere but in our dreams. We should be building it, but nobody is working on that because we're afraid of failing. And I'm feeling a bit impatient because on the one hand I live in a Quebec that's often preoccupied with itself, but on the other hand some English Canadians have developed a feeling of superiority that I think is completely uncalled for.

Canadians can boast of having built a multicultural society. However, you find cosmopolitan cities like Toronto in all developed countries today. Canadians compare themselves with people in the United States and see themselves as progressive and open, but can they realistically make this same comparison with Scandinavians? Canada is also said to have found the path to compromise and moderation. But what future lies in store for our First Nations peoples, whose needs are consistently ignored in this rich country?

I want to thank you for that conversation all the same. I hope one day we can pick it up again. Every time there is a political event in Quebec, I'm tempted to compare it with what is going on elsewhere in Canada. Unfortunately, my friends in Quebec are not much interested in this kind of discussion. The recent rise of the Action démocratique, for example, is really nothing more than the Quebec version of a populist anti-state movement that has existed in Canada for a long time, namely among the Reformers in the West. I'd like to talk about this some more. But who with? Quebecers aren't particularly interested in Canada anymore.

I was thinking about our evening a while back while listening to Bill Clinton when he was in Quebec City to give a speech in June 2007. He said then that, in his opinion, in every community— Canada, for example—there are three minimum conditions for success: 1) all members have to be able to participate fully, and to the best of their abilities, in the life of the community; 2) the responsibility for the community's success has to be shared by all its members; 3) all members of the community have to feel a sense of belonging. It goes without saying that Quebecers participate fully in community life, but the last two conditions, I have to admit, worry me a bit when we talk about Canada.

What struck me most that evening in Toronto was just how rare it is in Montreal, when in conversation with friends or clients or people I meet on the street, that we discuss our country and what we would like to make of it. Fifteen or twenty-five years ago in Quebec, we talked constantly about the country's future, but that's no longer the case. You could say that in Quebec the culture is secure and that what we've come to call the "nation" is peacefully building itself without having to bring up all those existential questions we've been asking ourselves for forty years.

Beyond the superficial and sensational debates over "reasonable accommodations" for immigrants, almost no one in Quebec talks about the kind of country we want to live in. You no longer hear the federalists talking about modernizing the Canadian structure ("the time is not ripe," claim the ones who say they want to change the constitution some day). Likewise, except in the opinion pages of *Le Devoir,* no one seems to be dreaming about holding a new referendum on sovereignty. Quebec seems to have chosen, even before the rise of Mario Dumont, the path of national affirmation, what is being called "autonomism."

All the same, I was pleased to realize that it's possible to talk openly with an English Canadian. It often worries me that it is rare, when English Canadians are discussing Canada, for Quebecers to take part in the conversation, as if our only responsibility is not to separate, and as if we have no need to worry about the future of the federation as a whole. It is Bill Clinton's second principle that doesn't get enough respect, the one about the shared responsibility for the success of the community.

Finally, to continue with Bill Clinton's three basic conditions for success, we should also obviously worry about the third one, the sense of belonging. On several occasions, especially in the referenda of 1980 and 1995, Quebecers chose to stay in Canada. But, and it has been said over and over again, this was a rational and reasonable choice, not an emotional decision having to do with any deep attachment to the Canada of today. As we see every year during the national summer celebrations, the primary allegiance of most Quebecers is to Quebec. Primarily, our reasons for staying within Canada are as follows:

• THE ECONOMY: No one has ever been able to persuade us that sovereignty wouldn't come without a certain economic impact. While the sovereignists criticize the fear campaigns run by the federalists, their own position is even more difficult to defend because they are asking Quebecers to assume a real risk. When the present leader of the sovereignist movement, Pauline Marois, referred to a period of turbulence that would follow a successful referendum, she may have made a strategic mistake but she didn't surprise anyone. This idea of economic risk has been an integral part of the debate for forty years.

• INTERNATIONAL AFFAIRS: On the world stage, Canada enjoys a unique position and prestige. Much has been written, in the past few years, about the crumbling of Canada's contribution to world peace, the country's almost automatic alignment with the United States, the wasting away of Mr. Pearson's legacy. All the same, Canada still takes part in all the important international conferences and plays a leading role there, especially among such organizations as the G8, the Asia-Pacific Economic Cooperation, the Commonwealth, La Francophonie, while retaining its high level of credibility among developing nations. Separated from Canada, Quebec would almost certainly be marginalized internationally; at best, it might hope to be treated like a miniature Sweden.

• FLEXIBILITY: Let me repeat that Quebecers certainly feel more affinity for Quebec than for Canada. Paradoxically, one of the main reasons to love Canada is that the Canadian structure, for all its rigidity and its constraints—real or imagined, has allowed Quebec to develop as a society and, as we say now, a nation. Others besides me have and will continue to inventory the "gains"

Quebec has made, but that list is now so long that the nationalists are having trouble figuring out what their next big demands should be. To begin with, think of the "co-operative federalism" of the sixties, especially Lester B. Pearson's policy of openness towards the Quiet Revolution. Then, look at the "open federalism" of today, and how Prime Minister Stephen Harper (note that it has been the prime ministers from English Canada who have demonstrated flexibility in their approach to federalism) led Canada's Parliament to recognize the Québécois nation and to absorb part of the mythical fiscal imbalance. In this context it is tough to mobilize the sovereignist troops.

• THE HESITATION TO LEAVE CANADA: Despite having a stronger national sentiment towards Quebec than Canada, Quebecers feel, for a number of reasons, a certain reticence about abandoning Canada. Essentially, even for the most nationalist of Quebecers who are neither afraid of the consequences of separation nor believe in the progress that could be made within Canada, separation still raises two major problems. First, Canada was founded by our ancestors, and it was the French who gave it its name. Leaving the country would mean abandoning a part of our own history. Second (and this is kind of a taboo subject), there are a number of francophone communities all across Canada for whom Quebec constitutes a kind of "metropolis," and which would find themselves more or less orphaned in the event of a separation.

These days, Quebecers are not preoccupied by these questions the way they were in the sixties or the eighties. In English Canada, on the contrary, existential questioning seems to me to have become a part of daily life, even popular culture, to the point where it's not surprising any more for Quebecers to find themselves discussing the future of the country whenever they're among English Canadians. We wonder, when you get together among yourselves, whether this subject keeps coming up in the same way. There are lots of examples—I come across them constantly while reading the newspaper, watching English-language television or travelling in English Canada:

• Columnists in English Canadian newspapers and magazines are always wondering about what Canada really is, about the Canadian identity, about the feasibility of a multinational country, about the future of the country. I especially enjoy reading Andrew Coyne in *Maclean's* because his articles always seem to depict the most pessimistic side of Canada. He notes that the country doesn't have a very developed national feeling, and he believes that we should be drawing on all our resources to build this Canadian nation and make it a great country. On his Web site, www.andrewcoyne.com, you can read his columns from the past few years, pleading for the development of a new Canadian nationalism.

• In an impressive number of books on Canada published over the last several years, the authors speculate about whether the country *can* have a future. At a certain time, not that long ago, such books were appearing in Quebec, and they dealt either with the future of Quebec or the modernization of federalism. Today, English Canadians are asking themselves these questions. Among those I've read or skimmed, let me mention *Reflections of a Siamese Twin: Canada at the End of the Twentieth Century* by John Ralston Saul; *Great Questions of Canada* edited by Rudyard Griffiths of the Dominion Institute, a Toronto-based think tank devoted to Canadian history; *The Polite Revolution: Perfecting the Canadian Dream* by John Ibbitson, a *Globe and Mail* columnist, who claims that Canada is a huge success; *Fire and Ice: The United States, Canada and the Myth of Converging Values* by pollster Michael Adams of Environics; *The Rights Revolution* by Michael Ignatieff; *What Is a Canadian: Forty-Three Thought-Provoking Responses*, a collection of articles on the Canadian identity by well-known Canadians (very few of them Quebecers); and *The Unfinished Canadian: The People We Are* by Andrew Cohen, who declares that a Canadian identity has yet to emerge. There are dozens more that demonstrate that English Canada is in a state of self-examination, that it's searching for itself.

• All over the Internet, young Canadians are going to town speaking out (well, digitally) about their country, their identity, their future. All you have to do is go to www.bloggingtories.ca, a meeting ground for young Conservative bloggers, to see just how actively people are blogging about politics. Each of the major parties is supported by hundreds of young bloggers, as are all kinds of independent groups. You won't find this fervour in Quebec, even at the heart of the sovereignist movement, which is thought to be strongly anchored among young Quebecers.

• Even in popular culture, in everyday life, it seems to me that English Canadians are still asking themselves about their "Canadianness" and what it really means. Think of the ad for Molson Canadian beer, the one in which the young guy speaks so passionately about what makes him a Canadian ("My name is Joe and I am a Canadian"). Think of the hundreds of Canadian flags flying during all the international sporting events, the Olympics included. You would never have seen outpourings like this, even barely twenty-five years ago. Think of the English Canadian reaction to press baron Conrad Black's trial, where the question that mostly seemed to preoccupy Canadians was this: Is Black—with his cantankerous personality, his competitiveness in business, his luxurious tastes—*really* Canadian? A recent poll indicated that Canadians are the world's biggest pot smokers. As much as this news made them smile, Canadians were prompted to reflect on the essence of the Canadian identity. Thus we saw that *chez vous*, in English Canada, though the country is developing along the multicultural model, there is some interest in redefining the identity and the personality of Canada. This is healthy, no doubt, but it is important that the investigation involve *all* Canadians, including Quebecers.

In his speech in Quebec City, Bill Clinton suggested we look at the world we live in and ask ourselves five simple questions in order to advance our thinking about it. If we apply these questions to Canada, they become the following: What is the basic nature of Canada? Is it a good or a bad thing? How might we change it? What actions should be taken to achieve these changes? Who should undertake these? I find this an excellent way to approach the subject, even if some of the questions are extremely difficult to answer.

Canada's Essential Character

I'm involved in this kind of discussion pretty frequently, and I think it's safe to say that there isn't really a consensus on Canada's essential character. Without sinking into cliché, we can still list three main traits that define Canada and Canadians as they see themselves: first, a certain humility that may have grown out of our harsh climate and our proximity to the world's greatest power, and that often expresses itself in a sort of contempt for success, even a bit of hostility towards those who are successful; second, generosity, great tolerance and a respect for difference, which have allowed the birth of multiculturalism and the adoption of the Charter of Rights and Freedoms; third, a constant search for compromise, for the golden mean, for moderation, which sometimes looks like ambiguity or indecision but really underlies the wide-ranging social programs that have helped us to avoid huge gaps between rich and poor and to survive despite our differences. The best example of this moderation is the inclusion in the Charter of the notwithstanding clause.

Dear Peter, you can do the following exercise for yourself, just as I did to identify the different classical elements of the Canadian identity (I mean those that come up most often in writings or in conversations), then try to see if they apply to Quebec and to Quebecers, or to other Canadian cultural minorities such as First Nations peoples or immigrants.

ASPECTS OF THE CANADIAN IDENTITY	RELEVANCE TO QUEBEC
Tolerance and multiculturalism	Yes, but this is recent.
Kindness, politeness, generosity	We're similar, though the Latin temperament is different from the Anglo-Saxon one.
Envy or jealousy regarding success (especially of Canadians living abroad)	We share this trait, but Quebec has a culture of celebrity that English Canada does not.
The Charter of Rights and Freedoms	Quebec doesn't share your passion for the Charter, but it has its own Charter.
Peacekeeping	Quebecers are less supportive of foreign military intervention.
Health insurance	We don't make this an identity issue in Quebec; we're probably less committed to the public sector.
Hockey	Everyone values hockey, but we realize that certain other sports, for example soccer, are starting to overtake it.

These results are interesting because they allow us to determine what differentiates the Canadian identity from Quebec's.

You could probably keep going with this exercise, using all kinds of characteristics that correspond to the image that Canadians or foreigners have of Canada. You will still see, I think, that Canada as a whole is characterized by a few words, such as "openness," "humbleness" and "moderation," and that some parts of this country, which is so big and diverse, especially francophone Quebec, only fit some of these definitions.

To illustrate this profound difference that exists between Quebecers and other Canadians, I'd like to tell you a little story about something I witnessed that will make you smile. After she stepped down as governor general, Adrienne Clarkson published her memoirs. I'm told that the book was hugely popular in English Canada, that people lined up to meet Madame Clarkson, who is an important Canadian figure. Well, at the Salon du Livre in Montreal in 2006, Madame Clarkson's table was next to Dominique Michel's, the actress-comedienne, who had just released a book of her own. The lineup to meet Dominique Michel—a woman who could probably walk around Calgary for six months without being recognized—was so long that people waited for more than two hours. Madame Clarkson, however, sat at her table all alone and seemed to be dying of boredom.

There are two important lessons to draw from this little story. First, Quebec and Canada have been evolving separately, almost in parallel, for a long time, to the point where the cultural references in the two communities have become completely different. Although our lifestyles are pretty similar, both heavily influenced by the Americans, Quebec and English Canada don't watch the same TV programs or listen to the same musicians or seek out the same sources of information or dance to the same rhythms.

There's also a culture of celebrity in Quebec that allows a Dominique Michel, who's been working as an actress and comedienne for several decades, to hold on to her star status almost automatically. This culture is sustained by a gossip magazine industry, by huge annual galas and television specials, and it resembles, proportionately, that of the United States. That's not very "Canadian." Not very modest. Not very discreet.

All the same, without knowing it all that well, I suspect that elsewhere in Canada there are many other more or less parallel cultures that differ from the dominant English Canadian traits of moderation, modesty and cool, which are modelled on the British culture. It is clear, for example, that First Nations peoples are clinging to their special qualities and have no desire to be assimilated into a national Canadian culture. There are also obviously a lot of new immigrants who, encouraged by our multicultural policy, have little interest in the country's traditional Anglo-Saxon identity or in the idea of duality that is so dear to Quebecers and to all French Canadians.

Also, to drive home the point, the very idea of rejecting a dominant culture—what in Canada we call multiculturalism (as they do in England also, by the way)—has become a significant element of the Canadian identity.

So, to come back to the question of the fundamental character of the country, I would say this: Canada is a country whose essence and institutions are basically British, with British qualities, but which has not tried, or succeeded, in imposing this dominant culture on all its people or regions. French Quebec is just the most striking example of this rejection of the dominant English culture. The result is that even 140 years after Confederation the country remains pretty divided along linguistic, religious and regional lines, and it doesn't seem to be on the verge of becoming more unified. But it survives.

Bill Clinton suggested that, having identified a country's basic character, we then ask if it's a good or a bad thing. It's hard to answer that question without saying "yes and no." Indeed, you know as well as I do that Canada can count on some extraordinary pluses as far as its natural resources, the quality of its citizens, its peaceful relationships with its neighbours, its ability to solve problems in a reasonable way. Canada has succeeded in keeping itself wealthy, free and safe. That's already an accomplishment.

You still have to wonder, though, how it's possible that with all this wealth and this potential the country isn't doing even better. It wouldn't be out of line to imagine that Canada should be at the very head of the world's top group of nations, in matters of prosperity, creativity, arts or sport. But it's not. With all that potential, Canada, among the developed countries, is no more than average at every level. It may be that the lack of cohesion, shared identity and common purpose has slowed the development of the country that Wilfrid Laurier and others envisioned for it in the twentieth century. Today, who would dare say that the twenty-first century will belong to Canada?

Some Things Must Be Changed, But What?

Without trying to reinvent the wheel, it might be helpful to imagine what tomorrow's Canada could become: a Canada that allows citizens who are not part of the dominant Anglo-Saxon model—francophones, say, or recent immigrants or First Nations peoples—to feel they belong. The recognition of and respect for difference is part of what makes up Canada today. It's hard to imagine a unitary Canada with a clearly defined culture and national identity that all citizens share.

However—and here is the Great Canadian Challenge—we can't go on settling for the idea, as we have since the Meech Lake Accord, that it's better not to experiment, that, having achieved this precarious stability, trying to change things is just too risky. The crises that lie ahead—whether they be in the environment, security, energy, demographics or the economy—will be too much for the country to confront in its present condition, divided and corroded by regional rivalries, without cohesion and real leadership.

Obviously we can't expect our political leaders to start a process of renewal. The politicians who negotiated the Meech Lake Accord and the ones who were active in the years just afterward have now moved on to other things, leaving to our present elected officials the spectre of existential debates that look suicidal to them today. Their horizons have become too narrow to say anything other than "the time isn't ripe," when asked for a vision of the future. You can understand why they don't want to take chances.

But we *can* imagine that all Canadian citizens, from one ocean to the other and from south to north, share a feeling of pride and have the will to carry out a common project. It's just a matter of spelling out what dreams, what projects, what challenges those will be. We know that the country comes together during great international sports events, especially when Team Canada is poised to bring home another gold medal. Even if it's only a hockey game, regional and linguistic differences don't seem to count so much then. So, why don't we try to develop national projects that allow us all to work together, and succeed together, just like a hockey team?

So here, roughly, are some ideas to explore together over the next few months with a view to creating some momentum to bring Canada out of its paralysis and turn it into a real world leader, genuinely modern and imaginative, a more united and happier country:

• MODERNIZE OUR INSTITUTIONS: Canadians like to say that Canada is a young country. Well, our national institutions were defined in a constitutional document that dates back to 1867. That's 140 years ago. In fact, the country is relatively old and it wouldn't hurt to rejuvenate some of our institutions a bit.

The first one that comes to mind is the monarchy. It's too easy to say that it's just a symbol. Think about it for a minute: the head of state of Canada is a foreigner, a Brit, whose only qualification is that she is the daughter of the previous king. That's absurd. If we want to carry this craziness a bit further, just suppose that the sovereign in question is getting on a bit and we find ourselves with, as head of state, Prince Charles, a notorious incompetent whom no one respects. That would be a tragedy if it weren't so laughable and so ridiculous. I really like the idea I've heard a few times of asking members of the Order of Canada to choose the next head of state from among Canadian citizens (it would be all right, and very Canadian, to wait until the Queen's death to enact this, so as not to seem too "revolutionary"). While they're at it, the members of the Order of Canada could choose the senators, if we still need a Senate.

Bilingualism is not widespread enough. When Chinese immigrants land in Canada today, they could be forgiven for asking why French is an official language and Mandarin is not. We have to give French an enhanced presence, a leading role in the daily life of the country. We have to start at the top. A prime minister or a provincial premier should speak both languages. All the other ministers as well. And deputy ministers. And possibly Supreme Court judges. It's a non-negotiable condition of entry throughout the country.

The Charter is a beautiful creation, but in many communities it has led to an attitude of entitlement. It's high time that a certain number of duties be attached to the Charter. I like the idea of a Charter of Responsibilities that primarily would explain to Canadians the secular nature of our society, the notion of equality among all citizens (women and men, among others), and that would remind us of the basic concepts of good citizenship.

Immigration and citizenship should doubtless also be modernized in a society like ours, which depends on newcomers to refresh it. As for immigration, I bet I'm not alone in thinking it odd that we pay thousands of bureaucrats to "find" immigrants, while hundreds of thousands of foreigners are eager to come here. In the communications age, isn't there an easier way to figure out who is qualified than by dispatching bureaucrats to the four corners of the world to look for them? And why the devil, when we're trying to recruit new Canadians, are we wasting time and money throwing out families of illegal immigrants who have been here for years? Couldn't we be a bit more pragmatic (another great Canadian attribute, supposedly) on this matter?

As to what constitutes citizenship, as far as I know, no other country in the world grants theirs as easily as Canada does. We give citizenship to people who have lived in Canada only three years, sometimes even less, and we grant it almost automatically, for life. And these people have no obligation other than to renew their passport every five years. We should have a debate about dual citizenship too. I don't know a whole lot about it, but I refuse to accept that it's normal to have two classes of citizens, those who are citizens of Canada only and those who have a double allegiance (or triple or quadruple).

• HISTORY AND HERITAGE: Canadians, as all the studies demonstrate, don't know their history. Even as it is taught, this history is not the same from one region to another. Without wanting to force francophones to sing the praises of the Conquest, which would be counterproductive, it might still be useful to better care for the country's historic sites, to better fund existing museums and build new museums and history centres all over the country, and to give preference to projects aimed at supporting the study and better knowledge of the country's history. Even though the interpretation of facts will always differ, we should, all the same, encourage citizens to know their history.

• IMPROVE OUR DEMOCRACY: We take for granted that democracy is one of the pillars of our country, as the Supreme Court indicated in its ruling regarding the secession of Quebec (the three other basic principles of the country, according to the court, being federalism, the rule of law and respect for minorities). However, citizen commitment to democratic principles is now in free fall, and we find our elected officials less credible than ever before. There's no need to re-invent the wheel, our democracy just has to learn from our neighbours and from several European countries. Here are some striking examples of what we could be working on:

The Senate: It is no longer acceptable for a democratic country to have a Senate made up of members appointed by the prime minister. Not only is it shameful, it shows a flagrant lack of respect for our citizens. Nor can the Senate be fixed bit by bit or on the sly as the Harper government is doing. We have to shake things up, even if that upsets some people.

Elections: Sooner or later, we'll have to introduce some aspects of proportional representation, just as other countries have done. We should think about formalizing how we set election dates, as several provinces have already started to do. Personally, I really like the idea of two-stage elections, allowing members of Parliament to count on absolute majorities and clear mandates after a run-off vote (it works in France, for example). I also like the idea of term limits and recall initiatives, which would allow us to get rid of members who are not doing their job well.

Direct democracy: In several countries, like Switzerland and the United States, major government initiatives are submitted to the public in referenda. These are very rare in Canada, and the government often ignores the results anyway. They are afraid of the paralysis that can result from a referendum, but the upside is that citizens participate, pronouncing directly on important issues.

The role of the elected: In our highly sophisticated systems, real power often lies in the hands of the prime minister, his closest aides and senior bureaucrats. It will always be desirable to see the roles and responsibilities of elected members increase, because, unlike bureaucrats, they answer to the citizens. Imagine members challenging bureaucrats more, carefully reviewing prime ministerial appointments and exercising tighter control over budgetary matters, as they do in the United States.

• MODERN AND VISIONARY PUBLIC POLICIES: If the Canadian government began to innovate and to devise new and modern programs as it once did, governed with long-term vision instead of just looking towards the next elections, took a leading role on the international stage, it is likely that all citizens—including Quebec's—would feel a deeper connection to their government and by extension to their country. The number of areas in which Canada could make good on bad situations is endless:

A real environmental policy: Canada should not settle for playing the Kyoto game. Climate change is not the only environmental issue at stake. We hold an important part of the world's water reserves—what are we doing about that? What are we doing about our boreal forests, our rare birds, our toxic waste dump sites? What about our agricultural land? And what about the quality of the foods grown on our farms? Our bureaucrats and professors and even our politicians are smart enough to think about these things. But who is urging them to?

Growth policy, the creation of wealth: Everyone knows that the dominant economies of tomorrow will be the ones that favour creativity and innovation. So why don't we stop trying to save moribund industries and instead create a genuine Canadian model that, like the Swedish or Irish ones, would rekindle our national pride?

Initiatives on the international front: We successfully distanced ourselves from the United States over the Iraq War. While admirable, this is not enough. Where is Canada in the Arab-Israeli conflict? Where is Canada in the creation of a commercial zone with all the Americas? Where is Canada in talks about free trade with Europe, an initiative that Premier Jean Charest is trying to launch on his own? Where is the Canada of Lester B. Pearson that exercised real leadership in the postwar period?

Dynamic city centres: Cities are the engine of development of modern societies, we know that. Now, in Canada, cities are the "creatures of the provinces" and aren't really able to take on this role. It's high time we granted them their own constitutional status and gave them the means to reach their full potential. And we need a way for citizens to impose their will, a more direct form of democracy, when city managers are incapable of action, as, tragically, is the case in the great old metropolis of Montreal.

A forward-looking energy policy: Canada sees itself as—and is beginning to behave like—an energy superpower. We must not make the same mistake as the Arab countries and put all our eggs in the oil basket. Instead, we need to make the most of our petropower by preparing for the changes of the coming decades and becoming a leader in the development and distribution of new energy sources. Beyond that, we have to focus on new ways to use this energy, in such areas as housing design, transportation, industry and daily life.

• A MORE ENGAGED CIVIL SOCIETY that gets involved in the public debate: More and more I'm becoming convinced we can no longer count on politicians to take the country forward. I'm not criticizing their caution in the face of a frivolous and uninterested electorate, but I think we have to find a way to give them some support, especially in studying the future and coming up with plans, on the one hand; and, on the other hand, somehow helping to bring together and inform citizens who, at the moment, don't always listen very closely when their politicians speak to them. To be more specific, here's what I believe is needed:

Set up local and regional organizations to examine the country's future. The idea would be to bring together citizens, experts and local groups to come up with innovative approaches that the political parties could then implement. Organizations like these could then regroup and set up pan-Canadian exchange networks covering all the key issues.

Keep an eye on the media. In our country, the media play a dangerous role, often disproportionately representing the views of minorities when changes are being studied. We saw it in Quebec after the announcement of certain public projects. We saw it in the debate over whether or not to ratify the Meech Lake Accord, when absolutely anyone who was against it could get heard on the TV news. And we continue to see it in an issue like Kyoto, which brings out the worst clichés and simplistic commentaries that are devoid of any scientific study. Of course, I'm not talking about censoring or controlling the media. But I wouldn't mind seeing a few media watchdogs, like in the United States, that monitor our news providers and challenge them publicly when they don't do their job properly.

A civilian force. In 2004, Prime Minister Paul Martin announced the creation of the Canada Corps, based on the U.S. Peace Corps that President Kennedy established in 1961. Unfortunately, this Canada Corps didn't really work out and was absorbed by one of the Canadian International Development Agency's bureaucratic tentacles. It was a good idea, though, and it surely wouldn't be too hard to develop something else that would help (and perhaps eventually oblige) young Canadian university graduates to take on some kind of constructive project. Think of a short assignment in another province or abroad, in some kind of development project, community service, something like that.

I don't know if I've really dealt with the important questions Bill Clinton raised in Quebec City last year. I only know that they're challenging questions and that we shouldn't allow ourselves to put them aside. We can't just hope that other people will act for us. So I'm inviting you—well, I'm inviting everyone—to work together so that our communities, regions, provinces and nations will all become important players in Canada's future success.

For that to happen, I believe that all of us have to make some important concessions and we have to make them ourselves because no politician is going to dare ask us to.

You anglophones will probably have to accept that the Canada of tomorrow will look less and less like the British Dominion it used to be. The Canada we have to build will be republican and genuinely democratic; it will put all our citizens on the same footing, whatever their native language.

As for us francophones, we'll have to ask ourselves whether our myth of two founding peoples still means anything to most Canadians. Maybe we should just settle for a bilingual country and a strong national government in Quebec. Can we still use this idea of "duality" as the basic principle of the country?

The First Nations will also have to think about integrating themselves into the life of the country rather than keep on trying to go back to a traditional way of life that is no longer feasible.

Finally, immigrants coming from countries other than the traditional ones (that is, neither English- nor French-speaking) will have to explicitly agree to be part of a secular and bilingual country that is based on the rule of law and the rights and equality of individuals.

Of course, such choices must be made individually, but it will be our public institutions that will lead the way in understanding and accepting this reality. To bring about these changes and explain them to the public will require a commitment that we don't see among our leaders right now. Our job is to encourage them in this direction, and if they can't do it, to replace them. We'll talk more about this soon, my good friend.

PATRICE RYAN

LETTER TO AN INDÉPENDANTISTE FRIEND

HELLO, FRIEND. You'll have noticed the title of my letter, won't you? Forgive me, it's just that the word "sovereignist" simply doesn't have the same impact. It's a delusion that turns up in referendum rhetoric sometimes, for the purpose—unacknowledged, of course—of earning a few extra votes. It is well known that "sovereignist" is not as threatening a word as *"indépendantiste"* or, even worse, "separatist." You have to admit, though, that these last two terms are clear and transparent, indeed they say what they mean to say. But sovereignist? I don't know. Have you ever heard of Corsican sovereignists? Catalan sovereignists? Scottish sovereignists? After all, isn't Quebec already sovereign in the many areas of jurisdiction delegated by the Canadian constitution?

Anyway, look, I'm allowing myself to call you an *indépendantiste.* Because that's really what you are, isn't it? And I'm using it because the terms "separatist" or "secessionist" sound a bit harsh and aggressive. Also, and please believe me when I say this, they have the opposite tone to the one I want in this little missive. I want to be both frank and calm. Why? Because too often we fall almost systematically into a pattern of personal attacks and labels and baseless accusations. These are the arguments used to try and build popularity by discrediting political opponents, and, by definition, they avoid the real debate. You see, some people think this dialogue with the rest of Canada is worn out. It's possible. Even probable. If you ask me, I think it's particularly stagnant between the federalists and the *indépendantistes.* You don't believe me? Okay, when was the last serious intellectual debate between these two groups?

What has brought about this total absence of rational debate? Those same personal attacks, labels and gratuitous accusations. They are both the easiest and strangely the most effective tactics

in partisan politics. You know how much damage the sponsorship scandal did to my side? The media, supported by your camp,
managed to plant in the collective imagination the following
idea: the federal regime is corrupt. As if that particular scandal
was specific to one political system more than another. A little
as if a unitary system could never suffer from this kind of cor-
ruption. A little as if France, to name just one example, had never
been cheated by opportunists or profiteers. A little as if you could
be certain that an independent Quebec would never fall victim to
such a practice. Well, it's a little as if this scandal of ours had just
been the result of some structural faults in the federal state and
nothing more.

It doesn't really matter, obviously, but you have to admit that
this whole affair dealt a nasty blow to the federalist idea. You
think I'm exaggerating? Well, you'll recall that the Bloc was heading towards a serious defeat before the scandal was exposed. Isn't
that the best proof of the idea you've succeeded in creating: that
the federalist option is corrupt by its very nature? Otherwise,
how do you explain the link between the burgeoning support for
the Bloc and the scandal? Why didn't these voters choose to support any other federal party? Because to score political points it's
always more effective to skirt around the issues, purposely avoiding the real and often complicated facets of any question. All this
is only to say that I'm going to try, personally, to avoid falling into
that trap. Will I succeed? You'll tell me that this is likely to be a
difficult and dangerous exercise: our respective arguments have
been steeped for too long in the current demagoguery, on both
sides. But I'm going to try anyway, I promise. Because despite
everything one says and especially hears, politics is still too
important to leave in purely partisan, stale and fossilized hands.

Having said this, let's get back to the point: why this letter?
Because, my friend, I'd like to tell you why I'm a federalist, or, if
you prefer, why I'm not an *indépendantiste*. Because even though

I respect the federalist model I am not, and likely never will be, a Canadian nationalist. This is mostly because I distrust nationalism, of any kind. Because I think it too often clouds political judgement, provokes irrational thinking and sets up useless barriers between people. Because I'm always expressing reservations about its meaning, its value and its real symbolic power. Because I can see myself in Don Cherry about as well as a Newfoundlander can see him or herself in Pierre Falardeau. Because I feel no particular attraction for the monarchy, finding it archaic and frankly ridiculous, probably even as much as the mounted police. Because while I find the Rocky Mountains very pretty to look at, that's about all. Because I doubt that we're talking here about the best country in the world, and, in any case, I'm not going to be the naïve standard-bearer of unshakable loyalty. And so, why am I a federalist? Basically for two reasons.

First, because I think federalism offers the best solution to the new world we live in. Whether we like it or not, we are living in a village that is more and more global. It's a great mix of humanity. So, how do we reconcile cultural specificity with common interests, especially under the rule of law? How do we allow individual minorities, especially linguistic ones, to flourish while still assuring their common interests? How do we meet the many challenges that transcend borders; for example, the environment? Canada, despite its idiosyncrasies and its sometimes irritatingly obsolete symbols, remains a country that provides solutions to all these problems. From the pure social experiment that it was in the beginning, it has become, it seems to me, a model of diverse communities living together. An example of cultural gathering, acceptance, sharing and the exercise of rights and freedoms. And this coexistence, though it can sometimes be frustrating, is, all the same, demonstrably necessary. I'm convinced that it is the new great challenge for humanity. And Canada, despite its detractors, has been meeting it pretty well. At least until now.

Therefore, the second reason for my allegiance is based on the fact that the nation-state model and the nationalist reflex are, at best, anachronisms, and, at worst, obstacles to the healthy development of the human race. A dead end, to some extent. I'll try to prove it to you in the following pages.

Having said this, let me spell out the idea underlying my thinking here: we owe it to ourselves to change the way we conceive of our political animals, to revisit our assumptions. We owe it to ourselves as francophone Quebecers to reconceptualize our relationship with the rest of Canada. We have to free ourselves from the pitfalls of our past and, especially, from the climate of resentment and suspicion and bitterness that has been driving us for quite a while now. We need to wipe the slate clean. We owe it to ourselves to give up the victimization and the egocentricity. We owe it to ourselves to get rid of the myths and other ghosts that are corrupting the way we identify ourselves, and, similarly, stop pigeonholing everyone around us. Indeed, it is high time, my friend, that we look to the future with enthusiasm and confidence and that we exorcise the old demons, both real and (too often) imagined...

If I knew something that would serve my country but would harm mankind, I would never reveal it; for I am a citizen of humanity first and by necessity, and a citizen of France second, and only by accident.

CHARLES DE MONTESQUIEU

Do you know this quotation from Montesquieu? It was written a long time ago, but I strongly believe that it's still relevant. At least it summarizes pretty well, I think, how we ought to conceive of our politics and make our historical analyses. For example, whenever I have to evaluate an issue of public policy or national unity, I try to make myself look at it objectively, like an outside observer. This allows me to put in perspective the ins and outs of political life. To downplay the drama of it as well.

To illustrate my point, I have to wonder if, in the absence of any personal or collective interest, I would consider my province's complaints in the same light, at least in terms of their fairness. Indeed, if it's true that my freedom ends where other people's begins, I have to assume that this same principle underlies the quality of treatment that I have a right to expect. The example of all the classic "wailing and gnashing of teeth" about tax-sharing (which almost invariably has been good for Quebec from the start) is striking here. You'll tell me it's normal that any regional or provincial politician favour their own constituents. Of course you're right, and I have to add that it's also true in any federation. All the same, this kind of reasoning has some limits when it comes to fairness, indeed sometimes even to ethics.

In this regard, I often feel that in Quebec we've developed a pretty Manichean view of our political environment: everything that comes out of Quebec is good, whereas everything that originates in Ottawa is bad. The good (our government) against the evil (the unmanageable intruder). So why is this? Why can't the central government also be the government of Quebecers? Haven't we practically monopolized running it over the past few decades? St. Laurent, Trudeau, Mulroney and Chrétien—weren't they all Quebecers like you and me? What are you saying, that they were all put into power by the rest of Canada in order to defend an anti-Quebec vision of the federation? So how do you explain that these guys often won huge majorities in Quebec, especially among francophones? Have you forgotten the seventy-four out of seventy-five seats Trudeau won in 1980, although he's supposed to have been the worst enemy ever of the Franco-Quebec vision? Are we really that masochistic?

To conclude, let me just say that, contrary to popular belief, a public policy is not necessarily less legitimate or beneficial for our province just because it comes from Ottawa instead of Quebec; that there are sometimes differences between the interests of Quebecers and the Quebec provincial political class; and that a fortiori there are often differences between the interests of the *indépendantiste* élite and those of other Quebecers. I'd go so far as to say that sometimes, depending on the stakes, it is preferable that the central government be responsible for those sectors that go beyond provincial or regional interests. Accepting such supposedly "centralist" politics, I am convinced, in no way prevents the proper management of our public affairs, or, if you like, the preservation of our distinctive character.

I regard as heretical and detestable this adage that when it comes to government a popular majority has the right to do whatever it wants.

ALEXIS DE TOCQUEVILLE

Let's come to back to this question of identity. Even though I love being a francophone Quebecer, I find it hard to identify with strictly nationalist causes. It seems to me that, by definition, they put the "us" ahead of everything else. And that is even more dangerous, as Tocqueville would say, when the "us" in question is the majority in our government. When all is said and done, the "us" argument seems to me at the very least a bit obsolete and sometimes, if you'll allow me to say so, a little old-fashioned. It's extremely improbable that history, which I believe to have a direction, is really taking that path.

Indeed, who is this "us" that we're talking about in Quebec? Obviously I could remind you of Jacques Parizeau's "us" from his October 1995 speech. But since you then condemned what he said, at least in public, you would accuse me of bad faith. So instead I'll mention Louise Beaudoin's "us," as she is said to be an open-minded *indépendantiste*. And this "us," you'll see, is more in line with your way of thinking. And, furthermore, it has had a strong effect on my own. In an interview she gave some years ago, Madame Beaudoin, asked by a journalist about the relevance of securing independence for Quebec, said, essentially, "Why, it is so that we will be in the majority in our own country!" You'll agree with me that we've often heard this argument, even among the most progressive *indépendantistes*.

So let's continue with a brief semantic analysis: which majority was Madame Beaudoin talking about? There's no doubt that it could only be the francophone majority who live in Quebec. So what, I hear you saying. Well, everything I'm arguing for is implicit in this little group of words. The *indépendantiste* movement is designed essentially *by* and *for* francophones. Please understand that I'm not trying to give you the impression that your whole movement wants to leave out Anglo-Quebecers or members of the ethnic communities. Nor do I think that an independent Quebec would ever try to exclude or maliciously discriminate against any Quebecers who were not pure laine. What I do believe, however, is that your movement, despite what you say, has nothing really collective about it. It is a movement, I say again, conceived *by* and *for* francophones. Of course, you'd like it if the "others" bought into your plans, but this is more for reasons of legitimacy or simple referendum arithmetic than anything else. All the same, this objective could be extremely difficult to achieve if the history of the past forty years is anything to go by. And why, in your opinion? Doesn't this exactly prove my point? Don't give me that argument I keep hearing about how it's really the "Quebec territory" that will get its independence, or, in other words, that your nationalism is purely "territorial." A territory doesn't *do* anything. It's not alive, it doesn't vote and it sure doesn't give a damn about independence...

I'm going to give you another very simple reason that proves your project is intended only for francophones: because if it were not, then the idea would be, in some way, to create a second Canada! It's six of one, a half dozen of the other. I mean a multicultural country where different communities coexist, respecting the rights of linguistic, ethnic and religious minorities. A social experiment in which negotiating the complex interactions between groups requires a regime that's based on compromise. An entity that's difficult to define generically, whose somewhat confused structure would satisfy some and irritate others. A country without homogeneity, without a shared common culture and pretty well deprived of sociological references. A kind of humanistic mess, eh? Now, personally, I'd be delighted. Over the years I've learned to let go of my sometimes overly defensive reflexes and, instead, to enjoy this cultural mosaic that's as rich as it is complex. All this having been said, admit that it's a tad ironic that you'd put all this time and effort into breaking up Canada in order to reproduce a small-scale version that's deprived of the economic and political clout of the original!

The political myth is a belief system with very strong evocative power.
STÉPHANE PAQUIN

Finally, more or less in the same vein, let me ask you one last question: if we were independent, how would this necessarily increase the use of French? Would you go as far as boosting the content and application of Bill 101, thus probably contravening the decisions of the Supreme Court? I'll remind you that, contrary to popular belief, those decisions were influenced as much by the Quebec Charter as by the Canadian. Would you dare to quote Duplessis in this instance and say that the Supreme Court, like the Tower of Pisa, always leans the same way? That, after all, the Supreme Court judges are all appointed by the federal government? Aren't these arguments, which are basically very simplistic and demagogic, really from an earlier era, especially since the *Renvoi*[1] on secession, whose conclusions, let me remind you, you adopted with great pageantry?

So then, in addition to dismissing the theory of a Trudeauist plot meant to weaken the French fact by means of a national charter, all this leads us to another question: would you be prepared to go as far as weakening the Quebec Charter in order to strengthen Bill 101? No? That's reassuring. But then, specifically, what could we do to protect and advance the cause of our language? And as a corollary, how does the federation now prevent us, in light of the provisions of our own Charter, from being as French as we want to be? Doesn't Bill 101 already require that French be Quebec's only official language? Lucien Bouchard, when he was the leader of your party, didn't he boast of the fact that 94 per cent of Quebecers speak French? That seems fairly acceptable to me, especially for a people who, if we listen to you, are threatened with extinction... In other words, is it possible that French is in pretty good shape just now in Quebec? And if so, isn't that a bit of a stumbling block to your argument? Unless, of course, we just want to keep on raising the spectre of assimilation so we can be sure the choice is always available.

Having said all this, and to come back to the discussion, you have every right to promote an essentially francophone scheme. Even though I think you're swimming against the tide of history, I respect your ambitions and your convictions. So, instead, let me share a couple of purely personal proposals with you.

First, it would be a good idea to demonstrate a bit more transparency, as much with regards to the motives of your proposal as in the referendum process. Stop confusing issues. What exactly are you after, in fact? An independent Quebec run by a majority of francophones who, from now on, are the sole decision-makers? Fine, but just say so, simply and clearly. I know that you do so occasionally. But not always, far from it. Too often we hear some clever language that is meant to conceal the real intent of the project, such as the example I gave earlier about alleged territorial nationalism. Such a dose of false political rectitude sugarcoats the reality, sows confusion and does a disservice, you'll agree, to our democratic life. The same goes, a fortiori, for the referendum process. I won't come back to that question again here. Many others have already considered it over and over again. I'll simply remind you that, as André Maurois used to say, "Clarity of text is a sign of an honest mind."

Next, have some respect for francophones who don't share any part of your desire to create a new country. If you only knew how often I've been called a traitor, an opportunist, even better an extraterrestrial, you wouldn't believe it. And why, exactly? Am I any less a Quebecer than you are just because I think my people would be better off as part of a larger politico-economic entity? Am I less of a Quebecer because I feel as much a Canadian? Am I somehow less of a francophone just because I'm willing to share my central government with other citizens who may never understand a word of French? I could also ask how a unilingualist from Moose Jaw would have more negative impact on national unity than a unilingualist from Mont Laurier, but that's another story. Am I less committed to Quebec's survival just because I approve of the Supreme Court's decision to reject some irksome sections of Bill 101, which were from the start purely discriminatory (let me remind you again of Montesquieu's words)? Am I somehow less of a defender of Quebec's interests just because I try to put myself in the shoes of other Canadians when I'm looking at our claims on Ottawa; for example, when we're dealing with issues of tax-sharing? In fact, if I don't quite know what additional power to claim, why would I do so? Isn't that the real question here?

The *indépendantistes* (for electoral reasons) and now the "auton-omists" often talk about needing to obtain more powers from Ottawa. However, when it comes time to say which powers, the task suddenly becomes very difficult. Could you do it? The banks? The army? Criminal law? Please admit, at the very least, that we're a long way from a national consensus on this. What are you telling me? The Allaire Report? In other words, take Canada out of Quebec if we can't take Quebec out of Canada? Am I being sarcastic? No. It's more like proof that any analysis undertaken with nationalism in mind too often ends up mired in dogmatism. That's why I say, again, that, better sooner than later, we have to rethink both our way of looking at Canada and our way of identi-fying ourselves as Quebec francophones. We have to give up the misleading arguments and the drama, just as we have to let go of this almost visceral bitterness about the past, which poisons our debates and gets in the way of our moving ahead as a society.

We must bear in mind that there is nothing more difficult and danger-ous, or more doubtful of success, than to introduce a new order of things in any state.

NICCOLO MACHIAVELLI

You want more proof? Okay, let's talk about other Canadians' recognition of our status. I know that as an *indépendantiste* you often use this question as the basis of your own argument. In fact, why do we have such an imperious need to be recognized as different? Don't we already know it? Isn't it obvious? If so, then why do we keep needing to be told? Are we still, in 2008, that "insecure" about being a nation? Having said that, and as you know, the Harper government as well as practically all the mem-bers of the House of Commons recently recognized us formally as a nation. Are we better off, then? Not really, confess it. And why not? For two reasons, in my opinion. First, because despite our constant demands for gestures of good faith and openness from the rest of Canada, our bitterness around the constitutional debate keeps leading us to call these same actions opportunistic or calculated. Isn't this paradoxical? Second, because we consider futile any non-constitutional recognition that comes without plenty of additional powers.

So, now, I have two more questions for you. How would entrenching this recognition in a constitutional document, which most of our fellow citizens would probably never read anyway, make us any happier? The permanent nature of the thing? Right. But do you really think any future government would have the audacity to renounce the existing resolution and declare that, quite the opposite, Quebec does not constitute a nation? That would be political suicide, my friend. So, what are the additional powers we need? I'd be happy to receive more powers, but which ones? In what areas, under the present federal arrangement, are we lacking sufficient powers to advance our collective needs? It's not clear, is it? And you know why? Because all of the powers we need for our cultural and linguistic growth are already within the provincial jurisdiction, at least until we prove otherwise. So, what now? Are we trying to change the constitution for vague and purely symbolic reasons, the symbolic aspect of which has already basically been recognized by that last resolution? Allow me to remind you of the quote from Machiavelli. In other words, it doesn't seem very wise to me to embark on such a dangerous path if we haven't even agreed among "us" exactly what it is we want from "them."

If a minority will secede rather than acquiesce, they make a precedent which, in turn, will divide and ruin them; for a minority of their own will secede from them, whenever a majority refuses to be controlled by such minority.

ABRAHAM LINCOLN

On another level, am I less of a patriot just because I accept, in my francophone reality, that I'm a minority in terms of Canada as a whole? You'd agree, moreover, that if we're all hoping to become a majority, we're soon going to have a huge problem. In concrete terms, the belief that every nation should have its own state isn't going to lead to a very nice future for humanity, is it? I should add that Quebec's francophone minority, as long as it is being dealt with fairly in the Canadian context (Official Languages Act; tax-sharing; multiple jurisdictions in education, economic rights, civil law, etc.), would have a hard time—barring some extremely serious reasons—claiming that it needs to become a majority. In fact, if we, francophone Quebecers, reject our minority status, how can we legitimately impose the same status on the other minorities living in our territory? In other words, at what point do we become so important as a people that we can claim the right to be independent while still refusing the same right to others? If no nation accepts that it's a minority, you might as well say that no majority remains, and as a result we soon find ourselves right back where we started. And if I tell you that there are more than 3000 peoples or nations (I never have understood the difference between the two) on Earth, you'll see where I'm going. And if I add that there are more than 615 First Nations in Canada alone, are you still with me? I mean, it seems clear that accepting such a syllogism (every nation deserves a state) can only plunge the human race into unprecedented chaos. That's why, and with good reason, international law allows secession only in cases of oppression, institutionalized discrimination or colonialism.

Having said that, I am very much aware of the *indépendantiste* aspirations, and I respect them. It is, as the Supreme Court recognized in the *Renvoi sur la sécession,* a legitimate objective. I'm only saying that the philosophical bases of *indépendantisme,* given their sociological and juridical impact, can't be taken as lightly as we sometimes seem to. Such nonchalance, paired with a certain amount of navel-gazing, is as unwise as it is threatening to our social life.

Right. So where are we? What about francophones outside of Quebec? You have to admit that this is one of the main weaknesses of your position. Take the Acadians, for example. How many are they? Several hundred thousand? Not bad, all the same, in a province of 750,000 citizens, is it? They contribute, you have to agree, to the influence of French culture in North America, indeed in the world. You know, as I do, that they've had to struggle for their cultural survival at least as much as we, Quebec francophones, have. But you never—or hardly ever—mention the Acadians. Why? Let me suggest a three-part hypothesis.

First of all, your silence is provoked by the fact that the Acadians, just like all the other francophone communities outside of Quebec, illustrate very precisely the contradiction of one of your main claims: that the French fact can't survive and flourish in the Anglo-Saxon ocean of the Canadian federation. Consider, however, that the Acadians number nearly 300,000 citizens, which is a lot more than at the beginning of the twentieth century. I might add that during the same period the Franco-Quebec population went from one million to six million. You have to confess that when it comes to assimilation we've seen worse. All the same, you'll reply that our influence within Canada has since been weakened, and you're right. And yet, how can we talk of the threat to the survival of French when the number of citizens who call themselves francophone continues to grow? And you have to remember that the progress, at least in terms of numbers, of the French fact both in Quebec and in Acadia took place within Canada. Is that not undeniable proof of the effectiveness of those provincial powers designed to protect and promote one of the two official languages? Could we not also conclude that the federal government has contributed, at least in part, to this success? This seems especially true when you look at the Official Languages Act, at the right of francophone minorities to be educated in their own language and at the (late) Court Challenges Program. You'll tell me that other francophone communities haven't had the same luck as the Acadians, and you're right. But do you really believe that a unitary rather than a federal system would have made their survival easier?

Second, I believe that your silence is explained equally by the fact that following the independence you're hoping for, francophones outside of Quebec, especially the Acadians, would risk finding themselves hampered by the disappearance of their Quebec siblings. Would they flourish in the same way without the considerable political weight that we have now within Canada? And if the number of francophones outside Quebec declined after we left, how would that contribute to the influence of French culture in North America? Would we not be losing some proud and forceful allies in the struggle for the survival of our language? In other words, isn't it likely that one of the major side-effects of independence would be, paradoxically, to threaten its first objective?

As for my third point, again it will provoke both questions and some discomfort. Sociologically speaking, the Acadians constitute a nation or a people just as much as we do. However, do you hear them demanding more powers just because they're a nation? Do you hear them threatening to leave the federation if we don't satisfy one or another of their demands? Did you hear them demanding recognition as a nation following the recent resolution of the Harper government? Wouldn't they have been justified in doing so? For reasons I don't understand, the Acadians seem to be at once fiercely proud of their origins and completely happy to be part of the Canadian whole. Good for them, you'll say. And I would answer, "But why, in your opinion?" Historically speaking, didn't they suffer serious prejudice and injustice on the part of the Imperial Government? Culturally and statistically, aren't they much more of a minority than we'll probably ever be? As a result wouldn't they be—at least as much as we are—perfectly justified in making the most of their complaints, in threatening to leave the country or at least in knocking at the portals of the temple known as the Canadian constitution as soon as possible? So why are they not doing this?

Here's my theory: because their intelligentsia, unlike our own, have not spent decades nursing the myth of additional powers, the culture of bitterness or prejudice towards this "other" that calls itself the federal government, or the Anglos of Toronto or the religious right of Alberta. And I could go on, sadly enough. You think I am exaggerating? Okay, then what do you think of the rejection of the Meech Lake Accord by these other Canadians? What about the Conquest? The War Measures Act? The repatriation of the constitution? Finally, how do you explain that we twice refused to leave Canada, after all these crippling blows. Is it because we're scared? Masochistic? Well, I would suggest that it's because, despite its idiosyncrasies and other imperfections, Canada still holds a privileged position in the hearts (and especially the minds) of a majority of Quebecers. Just imagine what this country would be like if our elites stopped, even partially, systematically and simplistically denigrating Canada.

Had enough of this talk about the Acadians? Our situation is different, you say? Sure, but in what respect? Oh, I see. You're saying that we, Quebecers, are different from other Canadians. Quite right, I grant you that. But Newfoundlanders, aren't they equally different from Albertans? And the First Nations peoples (pick whichever of the 615 nations strikes your fancy) from our Lebanese? And the Romansh-speaking Swiss from the Swiss Germans, and the Flemish from the Walloons? Of course, it's obvious that we're different from other Canadians, especially on the language front. But all the same, that doesn't stop them from being equally different from each other, somehow without setting off this endless and incurable constitutional angst. Are you still with me?

Fundamentally, I doubt that we're as different as people would have us believe we are. Isn't it undeniable that Canada was built much more on shared values than on all kinds of differences? Wasn't the Canadian Charter, which enshrines a good number of these values, based on the Quebec Charter, which already enshrined those values for Quebecers? Haven't we created a country where, for all its faults, the living is pretty good both in social and economic terms? Apart from quarrels among politicians at different levels of government, aren't Canadians proud of belonging to this country, especially when travelling abroad? Haven't we set up, together, social programs designed to minimize the inequalities among the citizens of our different regions? And haven't we, francophone Quebecers, profited from the generosity and brilliance of the other provinces as much as their citizens have benefited from our drive and our diplomatic and commercial connections with the francophone world? Wasn't this whole country, at every level, built under the strong influence of Quebec francophones? I'm convinced of it, just as I believe that our shared history, studied objectively, would bear out my claim.

Obviously, it's good strategy for you, *indépendantistes*, to stress real, potential and imagined differences to justify your position. But it's a bit irritating all the same, this strategy of yours. Doesn't every country, whatever its political system, have its own collection of frustrations and wrangling and compromise? To play on these in an often inflammatory way won't do anything, you know, to improve the health of our democratic way of life. It's a pointless strategy, devoid of any merit whatsoever: fuelling hatred and bitterness is too easy and certainly immature, at least philosophically.

You should work at being reasonable, not at being right; sincerity, not infallibility.
JOSEPH JOUBERT

I hope I've led you to see the worth of my thinking and my conclusions. I especially hope you'll understand the extent to which I feel myself a Quebecer, certainly as much as you do. The extent to which I love our language, our culture, our special qualities. The measure in which I love Quebec, committed federalist though I may be. The extent to which I sincerely hope we'll be able to continue spreading our genius, our arts, our business sense.

Having said this, there's no doubt that we differ on the question of how to get there. For my part, I am persuaded that it's a whole lot better for us, and for the rest of the human race, to put our trust in living together rather than becoming insular. To share some central institutions, including a government, with people who are not necessarily identical culturally or linguistically. To emphasize our common values rather than our differences, real or imagined. To abandon myth in favour of a pragmatic and rational analysis of history. To drop this Manichean take on provincial-federal relations. To slow down this verbal and literary rhetoric that's aimed only at scoring electoral points. To keep up a dialogue with the "other," bearing in mind that they may not be all that different from "us." To begin by getting to know and appreciate the Canada that exists. To stop trying to hijack the discussion on constitutional matters. To rigorously examine what's actually going on in order to avoid compulsively making demands that are sometimes outmoded, vengeful or simply symbolic. To advance, when appropriate, proposals that are concrete, modern and reflect both our needs and those of our federal partners. To somehow realize the thinking of Montesquieu. It is just not practical to seriously think of reform without first modifying our attitudes and our political situation. Without changes to our behaviour, any attempts at constitutional reform will, as history bears witness, be doomed to failure.

In short, I believe it's essential that we abandon our all-too-often egocentric outlook and learn to think in a new way. That we re-examine our political and cultural paradigms. That we start with a clean slate. Not cleansed of our history, but of our bitterness and our defensive reflexes.

Yours, FRÉDÉRIC BÉRARD

PATRICE RYAN *is president of Ryan Affaires Publiques, a public relations consulting firm he founded in 2006. He is a member of the Political Commission of the Liberal Party of Quebec.*

FRÉDÉRIC BÉRARD *teaches law at the University of Montreal and is a consultant on corporate affairs at Hill & Knowlton, an internationally recognized company.*

Note

1. *Renvoi*, or "reference," is a term applied to a Supreme Court decision, in this case (1998) supporting the federal government's position that Quebec cannot unilaterally declare independence.

FRANÇOIS PRATTE

SEIZING CANADA WITH BOTH HANDS

I STOOD in the Paul-Sauvé Arena on November 15, 1976, when René Lévesque and the Parti Québécois swept to power promising a referendum on sovereignty for Quebec. And I wept on May 20, 1980, when Quebec voters returned a No vote on the question of Quebec's independence from Canada. I have always defended Quebec's identity, writing letters on the subject to such newspapers as *La Presse*, *Le Jour* and *Le Devoir* even when I was a teenager.

Am I a sovereignist? No. Am I a federalist? Once again, no! For most people, the choice is between one or the other, no more, no less. When it comes to me, I am not out to defend Canada as it is, and I am even less interested in the independent Quebec the sovereignists seem to define. Their vision is pure fantasy. An embarrassing anachronism. A sophism. Am I an autonomist, then? If I say yes, it is yes to the idea of autonomy for all provinces and territories... yes to a Canada that could become stronger still.

The era of New France, the period of the British North American colonies and the centuries of habitation by the people known as the First Nations are not really part of Canada's history. They constitute a prehistory. Looking at the events from our past is helpful in knowing where we came from, but using them to rationalize the decisions handed down in our courts today seems to me about as absurd as trying defendants in these same courts according to seventeenth-century law. In short, it is not possible to be in 1608 and 2008 at the same time. And it is unfair to apply two weigh scales or two yardsticks at the same time.

In writing these words, I knew very well that I would be revealing an apparent ignorance of our history and that I would be committing certain intellectual sins, or worse, blunders. For example, introducing the expression "First Nations" with four words ("the people known as") that seem to discredit the expression, I gave the impression that I was denying the existence of certain inhabitants or groups of inhabitants of Canada called indigenous peoples, as well, perhaps, as questioning that they belong to their own nations. That is not the case: in my sentence, they are, in fact, the descendants of the first humans to dwell on this continent, several thousand years ago. However, the First Nations did not invent the peopling of Earth: all over the world, humans have learned how to move in groups and settle, as needed, on territories they have conquered.

In sum, we are all immigrants or the descendants of immigrants. The First Nations included.

Here is another offence: I wrote "not really part of Canada's history." It is this premise, in my opinion, that forces us to ask some of the questions that are fundamental issues of this book: How old is Canada: one hundred and forty? or twenty-five? Has an independent and autonomous Canada even been born yet? What is a Canadian? What is a sovereign state in the twenty-first century?

Quebecers, Francophone Quebecers and French Canadians

I was born in Shawinigan-Sud in February 1958. At the time of my birth—less than ten years after Newfoundland came into Confederation, ninety-one years (an entire human lifespan) after the signing of the first British North America Act (the Constitution Act, 1867) and about a quarter century before the repatriation of the constitution in 1982—I was, like folk singer and poet Félix Leclerc, a French Canadian. There is no point bringing up the sixties and the progressive transformation of the French Canadians of Quebec into just plain Quebecers. That is not what I am talking about. On this subject, though, it is useful to point out to any Quebecer born after 1970 that the translation of the expression "French Canadian" used to be *Canadien français,* before being systematically replaced by "Québécois" in the vocabulary of a lot of people who seem not to take into account that Canadians of French descent exist in provinces and territories other than Quebec, that all Quebecers are not necessarily French Canadians (no, the expression "francophone Quebecer" is not redundant) and that French Canadians in the rest of Canada (ROC) are not always expatriates of Quebec. But I will come back to that. It is too important a subject to neglect in an exercise intended to define a country that is trying to prove its legitimate existence.

FEBRUARY 1976. A little village on the Côte-d'Ivoire. For nearly six months, I have been part of a group of eight Canadians from different provinces and territories participating in a cultural exchange and economic development program sponsored by the Canadian International Development Agency (CIDA). It is called Canada World Youth. It is a young organization founded by Jacques Hébert, the great defender of Canada and close friend of then–Prime Minister Pierre Elliott Trudeau. Each group is made up of young people from every region of the country, with representation in proportion to the size of each province's population.

It is a bit artificial, but we understand the principle: twenty-four hours a day we make up a microcosm of "the great Canadian family." And each of these groups is composed of an equivalent number of members from the host country. There it is. Four months in Canada (in two provinces, Quebec and Ontario) and four months in a "developing country." It is a human experiment intended to show, among other things, that Canadians are a big united family despite their differences.

A united family? Well, no. Experience shows mostly that we are antagonists. We are absolutely not "united in diversity," an expression that will become the motto of the European Union several decades later.

Côte-d'Ivoire is francophone. However, most of the Canadians in our group are anglophones, reflecting their demographic influence in the country. However, since all the Ivorians speak French, three quarters of our "family" converse in that language. So the anglophones in the group are living in unusual circumstances: they are a minority!

In the middle of the bush, where there is neither running water nor electricity, I am surrounded by children from dawn to dark. I also become good friends with many of the other villagers, who always welcome me with open arms and offer me something to eat. Endlessly curious, I watch, I listen, I taste surprising dishes, including a rat killed with a machete while coming out of a termite nest. I like these people, but sometimes I want to be with other "Europeans" (as the Ivorians call us). Is that not normal? My prayer is granted one day when a Belgian, a French-speaking White Father as it happens, visits the village. As soon as I see him I am delighted, thinking: "Ah! Another person like me, with whom I can share my impressions of Africa!" The subtext, of course, is someone with the same background as me, someone of my own culture! I instantly go over to him and shake his hand...

but after five minutes of conversation I am stunned to discover that I feel more distant from him, from his values and his thinking, than I do from the Ivorians I have been hanging around with for months.

This five-minute meeting leaves a lasting impression. Because it is from that day on that I become aware of the fact that the notion of race and culture is entirely relative. I say to Cathy, a girl in our group, "You know what? If I was on the planet Mars surrounded by little green men for a few months, and I bumped into a Chinese man, I know I would throw my arms around his neck and shout 'Brother!' Yet, on Earth, this Chinaman would be a foreigner."

Canada: An Officially Bilingual Country

At the end of that Canada World Youth experience, in May 1976, the francophone Quebecers in our group had all become bilingual (the French Canadians from the other provinces and territories were bilingual to begin with), but just one anglophone, from Toronto, had learned enough French to get by in conversation. Two other anglophones, Albertans, were beginning to manage a little bit. Question: How is it that most of the English Canadians in the group managed not to learn to speak in their country's second official language, despite having access to French immersion programs for years? Answer: They refused to try. And all of them, except that smart guy from Toronto and the two exceptions from the Prairies, justified their intellectual laziness, if one can call it that, by suggesting that it was useless to learn a French they would never again speak in the rest of their lives. At least, they were convinced of that. Because *their* Canada was not bilingual. Where they lived—a Vancouver suburb, a remote Ontario village, a Saskatchewan town or elsewhere—French was absent from their daily life except on cereal boxes or signs adorning federal government buildings. In the minds of these Canadians living outside of Quebec, English was the language of the future. Probably even the only one that would survive in Canada, if not on the whole planet.

I have to remind you that this was 1976; the world would evolve a little bit after that.

If I am clearly remembering the conversations we had during the review we did a few weeks after arriving home, all the francophone Quebecers felt their experience showed that Canada was made up of two more or less impenetrable linguistic groups. The two solitudes could get along and even have a nice time together, but they belonged to two distinct worlds. Two distinct *countries*. Quebec was the only Canadian province in which it was possible for francophones to study, live, grow, read, write, work and sing in their own language anywhere within its borders.

We probably all voted for the Parti Québécois on November 15, 1976.

ALEXANDRE TRUDEAU, who was only two years old when I was in the Côte-d'Ivoire, is now (2008) chairman of Canada World Youth/Jeunesse Canada Monde. The second son of Pierre Elliott Trudeau, he was, in 2007, one of only three French Canadians on its board of directors, the other two being founder Jacques Hébert[1] and former participant Pascale Fournier, who is now a law professor in Ottawa. The ten others were anglophones, which included English Canadians and some allophones, among whom were probably some francophiles. I repeat: three francophones out of thirteen, that is 23 per cent! Should we be surprised? No, since Jacques Hébert seems to have been obsessed by the representational issue within Canada World Youth. And, according to Statistics Canada, 23 per cent is the number of Canadians across the country who actually speak French at home.

So what is irritating francophones? What gives them the impression of occupying such a marginal place in the Canadian establishment? The answer is language: even if the descendants of the British are scarcely more numerous than those of French heritage, their language is, by far, the most widely spoken from one end of Canada to the other. And as the years go by, this proportion grows, since the large urban centres, which are all anglophone except for our bilingual Montreal, are magnets for exponential growth. The population of the Greater Toronto Area, for example, according to Statistics Canada, is about 5.5 million, a number equal to three quarters of the entire population of Quebec!

Here is a very real fact: francophone immigrants usually speak English in their daily lives in Vancouver, Calgary and Toronto. And another fact: the majority of francophones living in British Columbia, Newfoundland and Alberta were not born there. They are mostly from other provinces and territories, and among them is a relatively significant percentage of francophones who were born abroad. In British Columbia, for example, 13 per cent of the residents whose maternal language is French were born outside Canada, and 77 per cent were born in another part of the country. And these statistics are from 1996.

Although the rich provinces and territories (which are becoming richer and richer) benefit from interprovincial and international migration, the demographic influence of Quebec is progressively shrinking, as is the francophone population within Canada.

The spokespeople for a certain vision of Canada, when they defend Canadian "multiculturalism" (a definition that changes from one person to the next), continue to declare that the descendants of the British and the French are the two founding peoples of Canada. Therefore "equal." It is time to stop using us like baggage: the federal government has gone to huge lengths to achieve results that are probably opposite to the ones they were hoping for.

The road to hell is paved with good intentions. ·

IN 1963 the federal government set up the Royal Commission on Bilingualism and Biculturalism, the famous Laurendeau-Dunton Commission. Among other objectives it was meant to help us better understand the relationship between the country's anglophones and francophones. For six years, its members travelled to every corner of Canada. They met with provincial and territorial politicians, citizens, business people, academics, artists. The results: a six-volume report and, more importantly, the adoption · in 1969 of the Official Languages Act, which consecrated bilingualism in Canada.

What kind of bilingualism? Clearly this was not at the individual level, which would oblige every citizen to know both languages. That was not the idea. Besides, the members of the commission understood that English was, and would doubtless remain, the only language spoken in many Canadian regions, especially in the West. Which brings us back to the original question: what bilingualism? In May 1969, Secretary of State Gérard Pelletier explained the bill to a Radio-Canada journalist: "This is a bilingualism that says that the government will speak both languages, that Canadian citizens, all across Canada, can speak to government officials in the language of their choice, that is, for francophones in French, and anglophones in English. So it is a matter of allowing, by means of a legal document— and requiring—that the federal government provide services in the official language chosen by the citizen who wants to deal with it!"[2]

Nearly forty years have passed. But still, in 2008, there are those who believe that Mr. Trudeau's Official Languages Act was meant to "bilingualize" Canada. Or at least, in recognizing francophones and anglophones as the country's founding peoples, to give them the right to express themselves and to work in their own language all across Canada. Is this a flawed interpretation? It is the one that most Canadians have remembered, in any case. The message was equivocal.

Since 1982 the protection of the two official languages has been enshrined in the Canadian constitution. Section 16(1) specifically stipulates it: "English and French are the official languages of Canada and have the equality of status and equal rights and privileges as to their use in all institutions of the Parliament and government of Canada."[3]

So, theoretically, a Tremblay from Chicoutimi who moves to Newfoundland can brandish his or her status as one of the founding peoples and demand, without any embarrassment, in towns large or small, in the post office or any federal building, that people reply in French. That is the spirit of the law (even if it is not applicable in most of the country's municipalities outside Quebec), even if this Tremblay is the only French speaker in the village where he or she has decided to live.

In short, English and French are public languages wherever they are spoken, and state languages where they are not!

Language is the one element that binds citizens together, reinforces their sense of belonging to a whole, allows them to take part in their society's development. If, in some small place—a town, say—two significant language groups are living side by side, it is clear that those who have mastered both languages are going to fare better. Because in their mouths they have the key to unlock all doors. The unilinguals, however, are isolated. They partially deprive themselves of some of the richness of the mixed society in which they live. In such a situation, the use of at least one common language that everyone understands is an absolute necessity. And so, one language always comes out on top.

Canada is so vast that it covers half a continent. What other major city in this country brings together two such impressive linguistic communities as those made up by the francophones and anglophones of Montreal? None. All across the country, outside of Quebec, the prevailing language is English. In Montreal, a city dominated by French and officially French but, in fact, bilingual, most of the citizens are bilingual: they can express themselves to differing degrees in both languages. And better still, the allophones are often trilingual, which puts them in an enviable position in this era of globalization.

This is all to say that this picture of the Canadian population as a whole has nothing to do with the one from 1969. In the 2001 census, Canadians named more than a hundred different languages in answer to the question about their mother tongue.

So does the official languages policy still have any raison d'être? Yes. In any case, whether or not it is declared to be official, a language asserts itself. Immigrants learn the language of the majority. It is a matter of survival. Of integration. Of employment. Of economics. And outside of Quebec, with the exception of a few cities in New Brunswick and Ontario, the dominant language is English. This is true to such an extent that even if francophones (who are less and less populous) still speak their own language at home, they forget it the moment they step outside to go shopping, to go to work or to visit their local recreation centre.

Every year, the Commissioner of Official Languages issues a report in which he or she censures federal institutions and organizations (especially the armed forces) that flout the bicultural reality of Canada. The annual delivery of this report, which is always done in a way that will guarantee it good media coverage, feeds a myth: that francophones can always receive service in French just by lifting their little finger. Indeed, I think that herein lies the problem: we have planted the idea in francophones' heads that they have the right to be attended to in French all across the country. Expectations have been raised. Rights have been declared. Francophones have been accorded a status... that, in reality, they lost ages ago. Indeed, wherever English reigns, French is no more than another second language rather than *the* second language, reduced to the same status as the various mother tongues spoken by Canada's immigrants. Except, of course, in the minds of those who aspire to a better-paid job in the federal government or in national firms that require bilingualism for certain positions.

Because with the Official Languages Act, bilingualism became an industry.

Despite the fact that the use of French is mandated, being a francophone in a largely English-speaking environment can sometimes be demoralizing. In order to withstand the shock of the virtually unilingual anglophone world that is the ROC, there is a fail-safe trick: accept the fact that Canada is, in reality, made up of individual unilingual provinces and territories. Then it is possible to stop feeling cheated by an Official Languages Act that, in any case, looks more like a trademark than a mark of trust. When they get off a plane in Philadelphia or in New York, do francophone Quebecers feel slighted if a staffperson speaks to them in English? Of course not, they expect it. In my opinion, they ought to have the same expectations almost everywhere in Canada. And, of course, an anglophone visiting a small town in the middle of Quebec should not be offended if an employee at the local post office cannot answer in English (although we all know, from experience, that the effort to become bilingual is more common among francophones). If we were not so insistent on bilingualism in regions where one language clearly predominates, I do understand that the annual report of the Commissioner of Official Languages would, as a result, be a bit thinner, but relations between anglophones and francophones would probably be friendlier because they would be more honest.

Canada is officially bilingual. The European Union is officially multilingual. On packages in each of the member-states, the labels, instructions and ingredient lists are always written in several languages. But when Germans travel in France, they cannot insist on being served in German! The opposite is also true, of course: French citizens in Germany cannot insist on service in their own language.

One of these days we are going to have to face the facts: insisting on bilingualism for all federal institutions everywhere in the country is a utopian dream. It is as chimerical an idea as the Quebec sovereignists' dream of independence.

Frankly, as a national dream, as a national glue, could we not find better?

Canada: A Multicultural Country in Search of Its "True" Culture

What do Canadians from all provinces and territories have in common? What do they share that nobody else can claim to have? What kind of feeling of belonging have they developed towards Canada?

When I can speak of Canadians in the first person plural, when I can honestly and spontaneously say "we" instead of using a detached "they," then I will be convinced that *we* actually have a Canada that holds together. A Canada that is solid and united despite our differences, if not thanks to them: because then we will admit our differences here and there, and we will respect each other without condescension. We will be a real country, just like France, the United States, Germany or Italy, inhabited by people who "want to live together," to use a popular expression. But this will not happen automatically. We will need more than good intentions.

A country cannot be sold like merchandise. A country is a film that is produced because everyone involved is persuaded that, on the one hand, it could not be made without them, and, on the other hand, that they will be assured a mention in the credits. We will need a real magician of a screenwriter, a great director, a visionary producer and an enthusiastic crew. There is no question of giving francophones (especially Quebecers) only minor acting parts or assistant jobs behind the camera, or starring roles just for the sake of appearances. Using positive discrimination is a shallow and insincere approach; it is just a matter of hypocrisy. The same goes for the anglophones. And for First Nations peoples. And for "new" Canadians. In short, everyone must be on the same footing, without any special privileges, agreeing to put aside the secular beliefs of the conqueror or the victim of the conqueror. The grievances of another era only lead again and again to a dead end.

In other words, instead of demanding some kind of pseudo-independence for Quebec, let us reclaim Canada as a whole and do what we can to make it into the fine country it claims to be. We have much to gain from doing so.

Canada is the result of what was done in the past. But it is not obliged to keep digging blindly, sinking deeper into the hole in which it found itself stuck during the twentieth century. Likewise, Quebec must also be able to choose paths other than the dead end that our governments have led us down since the No vote on sovereignty in 1980. There is no chance that I for one will put up with the awkward uncertainty of a Canada with vague objectives or the dead-end policies of a Quebec that defines itself according to its passing moods and that sustains itself with illusions of sovereignty.

To build a Canada that really works, we will have to begin by honestly declaring our intents, even if we are not always eager to hear them, and by asking candid questions, without shame or modesty. Above all, we must take nothing for granted. And we must exclude all resistance to new approaches. Fear of change is, by definition, the least constructive attitude of all.

The truth is that Canada is developing much more chaotically than we would have thought—it really is a *work in progress*—and its cultural foundations, which are in fact what we are talking about when we speak of languages and peoples and nations, are far from being solid and well defined. In fact, the regions of Canada are gaining strength (economic, cultural) and distinguishing themselves more and more from each other, mainly because of the different origins of their populations. The old duality—Quebec and the ROC—is blurring. And that is good news for the country. But the connecting thread, the cultural link among its peoples, is tenuous and neglected.

Have we any right, in Quebec, to reproach the rest of Canada for being dynamic and the different regions for prospering? If, like a bird under stress that plucks its own feathers, we turn upon ourselves, can we honestly blame the other provinces? Of course not, because it is we who are pulling out our own feathers. Indeed, when we play the victim within Canada we act just like parrots, jealously guarding our territory and slowly inflicting injury upon ourselves. And all the while we chatter to mask the damage.

In Quebec, we must either take hold of our own destiny and Canada's, or else we will just go on spinning our wheels and complaining.

Canada: A Sovereign Country?

What is the definition of a sovereign country in 2008? Does sovereignty really exist? What part of a given country belongs to the planet as a whole and what part to its inhabitants?

From a certain perspective, I find it presumptuous for Canada to declare itself a sovereign country. Because every July 1, instead of celebrating our independence, we celebrate belonging to an empire! In fact, this British dependence runs so deep in Canada's genes that when it had the opportunity to sever this connection completely in 1982, it did not do so. There was a golden opportunity to revisit the constitution in its entirety, but instead it was repatriated, while maintaining the monarchy. The constitutional monarchy! For twenty-five years, we have been talking not about the new constitution of a country that has won its independence but about additions to an existing document. We complicated the British North America Act, calling it from then on the Constitution Act, 1867, because we were incapable of making our own decision to cut the link that tied us to an empire for more than two hundred years, and we added a supplementary element, another juridical layer: the Canadian Charter of Rights and Freedoms. Never mind the numerous contradictions and endless debates already before the courts!

One fact is certain: the lawyers and the constitutionalists will not be taking their retirement anytime soon.

Some would say that Canada is not the only Commonwealth country to have held on to a connection, even symbolic, with England. That is true. Australia and other countries have, too. But in my humble view as a citizen of Canada, it is an aberration. A country is either as independent as every other country or it is not independent at all. If the repatriation of April 17, 1982, had truly been Canada's declaration of independence from the British Empire, we would have moved our national holiday to April 17.

Until the beginning of the sixties, Quebec was under the influence of the clergy, who stuck their noses in everywhere: schools, hospitals, television networks, radio stations, cultural institutions, publishing houses, newspapers, unions! That level of control, a real mass conditioning of Quebecers, prevented us from envisioning a different kind of Quebec. However, there followed a very rapid transition, almost immediately, that laid the foundation of a modern, more open Quebec.

Sooner or later, if Canada truly wants to function as an independent country, it will have to jettison any kind of juridical connection with England. Many Canadians, and probably most Quebecers, support that decision. One day, Canada will have to transfer the British crown to a museum, in the same way that Quebec was able to separate the church from the state. After all, we have not eliminated the church from our public life. It is still there in a minor way, as a part of our tradition and our history. However, we no longer live under a theocratic regime.

Also, since we are discussing God, is it not time to officially withdraw any mention of Him in the Canadian constitution? The preamble to the Canadian Charter of Rights and Freedoms reads: "Whereas Canada is founded upon principles that recognize the supremacy of God and the rule of law..."[4] This matter has already been debated in the past, though I had almost forgotten it. In 1999, New Democratic MP Svend Robinson brought forth the wrath of editorialists, members of Parliament and even his own party leader, Alexa McDonough, when he presented to the House of Commons a petition signed by a thousand people demanding that the word "God" be removed from the Canadian constitution.

Well, as the expression goes, there is many a slip 'twixt the cup and the lip. I am suddenly having a hard time imagining how one could persuade the House of Commons and the premiers of all the Canadian provinces and territories to cut the umbilical cord that connects Canada to England. Would it not be seen as sacrilege? The task would not just be a simple formality. It would be like subjecting Canada to withdrawal from a long-standing addiction to the monarchy!

It is easy for Quebecers to make fun of some English Canadians who show a deep attachment to their mother country, England. But before we criticize our neighbours... Not long ago, I heard a radio interview with Antoine Robitaille, a journalist from *Le Devoir*, in which he said he was shocked because a famous bookstore in Quebec, Librairie Pantoute, dared to put its French literature in the foreign literature section... His reaction was absurd, of course: we are not French and French literature is, indeed, foreign literature. That is a truism. In the midst of this great movement towards independence (whether of Quebec or of Canada), Mr. Robitaille's remark seems to me just as contradictory as English Canada's refusal to cut its tie with England.

Like a good detective who tries to find every possible motive for a crime, we must look at the issues from many angles. Who benefits from the present situation? Who has something to lose if we unify Canada in order to help it on its way to its destiny?

The Canadian Identity

It is said that tourism has become the world's most important industry. When foreigners, in their own countries, flip through the pages of magazines and newspapers dedicated to "Canada" as a destination, what do they find? What are they looking for? Is our technique for attracting tourists—whether we be a Canadian, a Quebecer or a Montrealer—to show them the real picture or to artificially create attractions?

Those who built certain monuments, in other times and in other countries, believed that these symbols would be seen and that they would endure. They did not build those monuments with an eye to public opinion polls or market surveys. They created them to mark historic events, exploits, values, religions, gods, heroes... and many other reasons. They built them to commemorate their people and their civilization. Our own monuments and our own countries ought to reflect what it is that we are, what we have become or what we are on the way to becoming. Not according to other people but according to ourselves. Given, of course, that we are willing to define ourselves. This takes courage, but above all less demagoguery and more leadership.

Canada, according to many, would not survive without Quebec. I share that view. But I also share the view of those who think that Quebec would not survive without Canada. We make up an indissoluble whole, even though our constituent parts are unequal in influence, in area and in human composition.

This said, one forgets the key role that Quebec played in the creation of the Canadian confederation. It is the rebellions of 1837, in Lower and Upper Canada, which led to the Act of Union of 1840, which gave birth to the short-lived Province of Canada, which created malcontents everywhere and brought about the Quebec Conference in 1864, which in turn led to the creation of the Dominion of Canada in 1867. And who would become one of the "Fathers of Confederation"? George-Étienne Cartier, a lawyer who belonged to the Patriot movement, which pledged allegiance to Britain. The same man who presented the Parliament of the Province of Canada with a bill to create the Grand Trunk Railway Company, that great project that was very likely the impetus for the Canadian dream.

And so, to the four original provinces—Nova Scotia, New Brunswick, Quebec and Ontario—were gradually joined the six others over the period until 1949. The country is an amalgam of territories that found it beneficial to get together in order to modernize. Isolation was not an option.

The Canadian provinces and territories are all lands of immigrants. They were populated by migrations of groups from one province to another and by the arrival of immigrants from around the world. In 1881, according to the Laurendeau-Dunton Commission, newcomers with heritage other than

British or French made up 11 per cent of the Canadian population. By 1961, this percentage had more than doubled, to 26 per cent. Today, the First Nations and the descendants of the British and the French amount to barely half the total Canadian population. So the mixed nature of the citizenry is part of the national identity: since 1867, Canada has accepted more than fourteen million immigrants.

And in which provinces and territories do these immigrants choose to settle? Given that around 80 per cent of them speak only English as their first or second language—but not French, most of them prefer to locate elsewhere than Quebec. Where? The answer is in the provinces with the strongest economies: the richer they are, the more people they attract. And the more people they attract, the richer they become! The reverse is also true: the poorer the province or territory, the less attractive it is. The less it attracts immigrants, the older the average age of its population becomes. The older the population, the poorer it becomes. And the poorer…

Quebec is the province in which the population is aging the most quickly. It is also the one with the greatest number of poor people: more than 42 per cent of Quebec's citizens do not pay income tax.

Ah! Quebec! How often have we heard that our province is the envy of a certain ROC? So, the province is poor. It makes trouble, feeds a conflicting relationship with the rest of Canada. Canadians love Quebec, hate it or envy it. But no matter how one looks at the province and analyzes it, whether it be the numbers, the language, the culture or the international stature, Quebec has one trait that the rest of Canada seems to aspire to: a highly defined identity. Yes, I mean the distinct society. The Quebec Nation.

I think Quebec began to develop once it shook off the yoke of the clergy and the tyranny of Maurice Duplessis. What followed was not all roses, that is for sure. I am the first to deplore the follies and the poor decisions of our politicians and public servants. I regularly condemn, in private conversation—and in public when the occasion presents itself—government negligence and demagoguery. And I could go on. But all that is healthy. The debate demonstrates that our society is alive and evolving.

The other provinces and territories have never developed identities as spectacular and flamboyant as Quebec's. But it would be wrong and unfair, as well as dishonest, unrealistic and chauvinistic, to suggest that the ROC is homogeneous, without its own history, personality or culture. The question is, how do those provinces and territories perceive themselves? Have they come to, or in fact passed, the same phase of collective navel-gazing that has made Quebec what it is today? Do they see themselves as contributors to a wealthy country without a history but in which the living is easy? Or do they see themselves as players fully engaged in a country built in their own image, in whose destiny they share?

Every country seems to create and feed its own internal demons. In the United States, Americans still fuel their history of slavery by maintaining the division between Blacks and Whites. In Quebec, we carefully preserve the boundary between francophones and anglophones. In the rest of Canada, they sustain the guilt complex of the conqueror. Centuries later, this mentality still generates ambivalent relations towards the First Nations (about 3 per cent of the country's total population, including the Inuit) and all the generations of immigrants that followed, the latter being considered a single group of foreigners just visiting the First Nations, even if the ancestors of these immigrants arrived here more than four hundred years ago and even if more than one third of those polled in the 2001 census said that they were Canadians by origin (rather than English, French or Ukrainian, for example).

Canada's official bilingualism is, at its root, an industry. Surrounding this industry is another one, which developed around the complex we have vis-à-vis the First Nations. Recently, I obtained an abridged version of *Canada's Food Guide*, designed especially for our First Nations. This is not a joke. I am not talking about a guide that was translated into aboriginal languages, but a pamphlet meant for normal, healthy people living in Canada. Entitled *Eating Well with Canada's Food Guide: First Nations, Inuit and Métis*, this little illustrated four-page pamphlet, published in 2007, perfectly demonstrates the unconscious condescension that Canadians show to people whose lands our ancestors conquered many centuries ago. I will be told, of course, this guide results from our understanding that the diet of our First Nations peoples is different, that they live by hunting and fishing, that in the Far North, for example, fresh fruits and vegetables are not always available, and so on and so forth. No, but... what is all this? Do we have to produce a food guide for every community in the country, in the name of multiculturalism?

Here is yet a third industry that is flourishing thanks to our collective neuroses: all the goods and services that flow from our obsession with national unity, including projects that entail a serious waste of public money. We have only to think of the Gomery Commission, which investigated the sponsorship scandal. This phobia is likely fed and motivated by the terrific threat potentially posed by our American "friend," our elephantine neighbour who continues to call into question our sovereignty in parts of the Far North and who never hesitates to challenge our commercial agreements when they do not suit them. But in trying, through artificial and extreme methods, to persuade citizens that the country is "united," what is the real message that the government of Canada is sending? That the country is fragile.

These Canadian complexes—and there are more of them— have cost us dearly. And not just financially. The bureaucracy that they have engendered has kept us from seeing the country except through a lens of paranoia.

To build, modernize and solidify Canada, we will need a strong state, a strong country. In the minds of most people, that could mean "centralizing the state," even though that is not necessarily the case. Quite the opposite, even! In my view, a strong Canadian government would be dynamic and modern and do more than just manage relations between the provinces. It would promote the decentralization of power while strengthening those powers that justified its existence and its role as the centre of a confederation of states that have chosen to share a territory, some customs and certain realities.

Decentralization *is* confederation. Autonomism is neither a novelty nor a Quebec invention. From the beginning, Confederation was based upon a measure of respect for the autonomy of the provinces. That is what gave it its strength. Canada did not come into existence as a single entity. It was constructed according to the principle of agglomeration: the territories and colonies were not conquered, they were persuaded to join the Dominion of Canada. In other words, our country is not a pit bull. It is a Labrador.

Throughout its century and a half of existence, Canada has lived through several metamorphoses, each set off by great projects or great movements. The railroad is a fine example: it is certainly its construction that gave birth to the country. Then there were the world wars, the first and the second. Finally, we must not forget the twentieth century and its modernity: the government has assumed a greater and greater role in the life of each of its citizens. And, of course, there were the great upheavals of the sixties and the seventies, which, once again, Quebec helped to set in motion.

If I put myself in the shoes of Canadians outside of Quebec, I realize they must be weary of watching us decide the future of the country! They must fed up with watching Ottawa react constantly to demands made by Quebec!

So am I. I would like us to move on. And I am not alone.

A Possible Future for Canada

A country is not built overnight. We take steps today knowing full well that it is hard to predict their consequences.

Ideally, we will lay the groundwork to ensure, as far as we can, a better future for our descendants, even if we have no idea what they will face, in the end. We simply do not know the ramifications of today's decisions. In contrast, we do know their foundations because that is the part we can control.

Among our many pretensions as human beings is the belief that we can predict all outcomes. That we can control them too. But we live in a permanent state of cognitive dissonance: our beliefs are continually contradicted by the facts. Yet, we are "know-it-alls," that is, a lot more ignorant than we think. Let me go even farther. Human beings of our era know less than our ancestors about the essential facts because we lack a fundamental understanding: we do not even realize what we do not know.

Should the decisions that we make today not be based on our deepest values rather than on simple calculations and projections?

Our directions are not destinations since we do not know what upheavals lie in wait for our successors. We can make guesses about the future, but we cannot control it. We take a path, guided by what brings us consensus: our values. Whether it is a matter of concrete projects, laws or treaties, this is our approach.

The great strength of a country, its secret weapon, is its population. Culture and shared identity are far more important than we would think in a country's development. That is why, contrary to what I have always thought until recently, Heritage Canada ought to be even stronger than it is. But, of course, within a framework that is entirely different from the three complexes that I have mentioned, that is, the divide between francophones and anglophones in Quebec, our feelings of guilt towards the First Nations and our obsession with national unity, not to mention multiculturalism! After all, a Canadian "monoculture" does not exist any longer. It is equally necessary that that the other provinces and territories be as autonomous as Quebec is. Yes, especially on the cultural development front. I would like to see Canada adopt the motto of the European Union: "united in diversity" (*In varietate concordia*). A country's strength is not only economic or military. And Canada needs that strength to face future challenges. Letting each province and territory become stronger makes Canada stronger as a whole.

When we look at Canada from a global perspective, we can make some generalizations that are also cause for alarm.

Canada occupies an absolutely gigantic area of the planet. Its earth is rich, its climate enviable, it has the greatest reserves of fresh water on Earth... all the while supporting only thirty-three million people. In this era of globalization and growing concerns about the environment and overpopulation, it is obvious that this imbalance will be called into question repeatedly in the coming decades. Already this has begun. If I am not mistaken the Arctic waters are considered to be Canadian by only one country: Canada.

In other words, in this world of globalization and free markets, where borders are becoming more and more fragile, where large national companies are often sold to foreigners and managed by them, where mines and natural resources are exploited by foreigners too, where people travel not only to visit but also to work and even become immigrants, a huge country like Canada, with its abundant resources but comparatively small population, could certainly become an object of desire. But I will not play the devil's advocate.

Who makes up Canada today? Older people who have a knowledge of the past, and younger people who will shape the country's future. Well, who are these young people? More than half of them are not Canadians descended from French or British heritage. They like to travel, they are less tied to tradition than their parents were and they gather their information and their values from the Internet, where many of them occupy a virtual space in a community that recognizes no national borders.

The world having changed during the fifties, sixties and seventies because of the baby boom, let us not underestimate the influence of the younger population. This new generation will grow up fast, and it is they who, in large measure, will decide everyone's future. Not only will this coming generation be numerous, they will also be more energetic and—probably too— richer and more powerful than their parents.

A century from now, virtually no one on the planet today will still be alive. We will all have been replaced by others who will have to live with the decisions that we are making. There will be evolution. And transformation. What direction do we want Canada to take? What would we like for the future inhabitants of the buildings we are putting up today? What will there be of us in the museums and the history books?

My biggest wish is this: that, as Canada matures, it becomes a welcoming and thriving land, built in a spirit of solidarity for the planet as a whole.

FRANÇOIS PRATTE *is a writer. In 2003, he was a candidate for the Action démocratique du Québec.*

Notes

1. Note: Jacques Hébert died a few weeks after the publication of the original French version of this book.

2. Source: http://archives.radio-canada.ca/politique/langue_culture/ clips/592-3071/ (accessed May 27, 2008).

3. Canada. *Constitution Act, 1982*, s. 16. See http://laws.justice.gc.ca/en/const/ annex_e.html#I (accessed May 27, 2008).

4. Canada. *Constitution Act, 1982*, preamble. See http://laws.justice.gc.ca/en/ const/annex_e.html#I (accessed May 27, 2008).

7

MARTIN CAUCHON

DURING THE LULL IN THE STORM, LET US LOOK FOR SOME BALANCE[1]

THE YEAR 1993 marked my start in federal politics. Under the Liberal banner, I was elected as the member of Parliament for Outremont. Proud of the confidence shown me by my constituents, I went to Ottawa with all the enthusiasm and energy of a young idealist out to change the world. I was eager to take my seat in the House of Commons and delve into the many matters facing government, each of which I found truly fascinating. Think back for a moment to the issues of the day. First there was the question of the public purse and how to deal with burgeoning deficits in the aftermath of a punishing recession, then there was the reform of the Canadian social safety net and the reorganization of the civil service. We were also called upon to set a new direction in economic development, to address the challenges of globalization, and I could go on.

The work to be done was all the more demanding because it had to be carried out in a House of Commons where the Opposition was deeply divided by regional parties, such as the Reform

Party and the Bloc Québécois. After only a few weeks in the House of Commons, I became aware of the particular dynamic created by the presence of these regional parties, a dynamic that works against the very spirit of federalism. This is especially true with the Bloc Québécois, which is in Ottawa awaiting the creation of an independent Quebec. Of course, Quebecers had spoken by voting for the Bloc and their democratic choice must be respected, especially when that choice conveys such a clear political message. And so, within the context of a federal government, we had not only to continue our work but also to try to come to terms with a group that intends to rock the boat from within. And before long, the Bloc, which more often than not claims to speak for all Quebecers, began to completely confuse the interests of Quebec with the issue of separation. Day after day, I witnessed these tactics. Essentially, this party distorts the rules of federalism by analyzing almost every political issue from a purely Quebec-focussed point of view, without ever considering what might be at stake for Canada.

After a while, the Bloc strategy begins to look redundant and its formula, a little tired. It aims to show that the federation is not working and, in fact, curbs Quebec's evolution. The Bloc also claims that Quebec does not possess all the tools it needs for development, that it does not receive a fair share of the tax revenue and that the Canadian federation is at a standstill. Therefore, it claims, the only valid choice for Quebecers is separation, which will bring them that terrestrial nirvana called an independent Quebec.

In the House of Commons, I always fought vigorously against this vision. I believe the Canadian federal system to be sufficiently generous, flexible and respectful of all the provinces and territories and their aspirations, while at the same time being solid enough to allow us to continue building Canada as a whole. Indeed, the country has changed a lot since 1867.

Now that the Bloc Québécois has been in existence for several years and that we have waged several great political battles, there is a certain calm descending on the political environment, which is also reflected in the results of recent public opinion polls. It is worth noting as well that the presence of a Liberal government in Quebec, along with the gains of the Action démocratique in the last provincial election, seems to be sending the same message. Obviously, I do not believe that the sovereignist movement has disappeared. However, I do think we have a chance now to sit down together and reflect on our past and who we would like to become, so that we can decide collectively how we might best approach the future. First, a brief look at the past, just to refresh our memory.

The Canadian Federation: A Unique Foundation

A federation is an organized political structure in which powers are divided between the central government and all the other component parts, which, in the Canadian case, are the provinces.[2] Each level of government is sovereign within the jurisdictional spheres assigned it by the constitution. Each one, respecting the federal spirit, is charged with preserving fundamental values such as democracy, the protection of personal freedoms, solidarity and respect for the rule of law.

The federal system, as we know it today, dates from the creation of the United States of America in 1787. Although our neighbour was the first to form a modern federal state, and subsequently inspired others to do so, it did not establish a "right" way of doing this. In fact, there are as many variations on the original model as there are federations. Historically, countries that have chosen the federal system have found ways to adapt and refine it to suit their needs.

For its part, Canada was the first federation based on the British parliamentary system.[3] Although many influences favoured

the establishment of a federation in Canada, the two most important were the American Civil War and economic considerations.
This is the context in which the British North America Act was
passed in 1867, setting up Canada as a federation. While sections
91 and 92 of the Constitution Act, 1982 outlined the powers
belonging to Parliament alongside those of the provincial leg-
islatures, a closer reading reveals the desire of the Fathers of
Confederation to create a strong central government. The distinguished political scientist and governmental consultant David R.
Cameron wrote on this subject: "Canada was founded in 1867 as
a centralized federation, with the key powers of the day vested
in Ottawa and a strong paternalistic oversight role assigned to
Ottawa vis-à-vis the provinces."[4] The federal government was
charged with the power of disallowance and of reservation, as
well as spending power and residual powers.

Notwithstanding the realities of this fairly dominant federal
government, the new federation reflected the society it had just
reorganized, and respected, at least in part, certain historic agreements, among them the Quebec Act of 1774, which recognized
the French fact, the Catholic religion and the civil law of Quebec.

This is how the foundations of Canada were laid down: a federal system with a strong central government whose structure
already demonstrated clearly what gives federalism—especially
Canadian federalism—its particular strength, which is its capacity for accommodation. So, how is it faring today? Did the
Founding Fathers achieve their goal of a powerful central government? Has the Canadian federation, as it has evolved, proved
to be effective at meeting our many challenges? Or has Canada
actually hindered the provinces' development?

The Evolution

A system of government does not evolve in isolation. It has to
engage with a population that has its own characteristics and

changes constantly. Consequently, a good system of government has to allow for and adapt to this reality over the years. If it does not, it will soon break down.

To fully understand a federation, it is necessary to look at its founding document, its supreme code of laws, the constitution. In Canada, as in many countries, the constitution is not based on documents alone. It is also made up of customs and traditions. As the Supreme Court of Canada, in the famous *Renvoi* of 1982 dealing with the resolution to modify the constitution (the repatriation), put it so eloquently, the constitution is composed of some written elements but also draws on common law (court decisions) and constitutional covenants.[5] So, to understand the evolutionary character of our constitution, it is important to look at all these components. Careful examination shows, that since 1867, there has been a considerable trend towards decentralization and a rebalancing of the power relationship between the federal government and the provinces.

There were several constitutional amendments between 1867 and 1982. However, except for a few, most of them have had no more than a limited impact on federal-provincial relations. Among those worth mentioning, there is the creation of new provinces and the Statute of Westminster of 1931, whereby Canada became a sovereign country without completely severing the colonial connection. It was only with the repatriation of the constitution in 1982 that Canada formally cut its ties to the United Kingdom. It is also worth highlighting the constitutional amendment of 1940, which initiated the welfare program known today as employment insurance.

The constitutional agreements and judicial interpretations handed down from the Judicial Committee of the Privy Council in London until 1949 and from the Supreme Court of Canada thereafter show another side of the story. Throughout the years, the courts have tended to favour the provinces, especially with regards to the sharing of legislative responsibilities, and have thereby contributed to rebalancing Canadian federalism. Take, for example, certain powers that have widely been considered paternalistic. First, the federal government's power of disallowance, which is found in sections 56 and 91 of the Constitution Act, 1867, gives the federal government the authority to disallow any law passed by a province. It goes without saying that this power, which was used often initially, led to much gnashing of teeth by the provinces. Fortunately, court decisions have now rendered this control all but obsolete. In fact, in its famous judgement on the secession of Quebec, the Supreme Court of Canada declared:

> It is undisputed that Canada is a federal state. Yet many commentators have observed that, according to the precise terms of the *Constitution Act, 1867*, the federal system was only partial. See, e.g., K.C. Wheare, *Federal Government* (4th ed. 1963), at pp. 18–20. This was so because, on paper, the federal government retained sweeping powers which threatened to undermine the autonomy of the provinces. Here again, however, a review of the written provisions of the Constitution does not provide the entire picture. Our political and constitutional practice has adhered to an underlying principle of federalism, and has interpreted the written provisions of the Constitution in this light. For example, although the federal power of disallowance was included in the *Constitution Act, 1867*, the underlying principle of federalism triumphed early. Many constitutional scholars contend that the federal power of disallowance has been abandoned (e.g., P.W. Hogg, *Constitutional Law of Canada* (4th ed. 1997), at p. 120).[6]

The same fate that befell the power of disallowance also affected the power of reservation that had been given to the provincial lieutenant governors. In this case, lieutenant governors could refuse to grant assent to a law passed by the provincial legislature, thus compelling the provinces to deal directly with the federal government in order to obtain approval. The virtual disappearance of these two powers has effectively strengthened the role of the provinces in all of their jurisdictions.

In addition to court judgements, the fifties saw the start of an assertiveness on the part of certain provinces, a move that contributed considerably to the development of the Canadian federation. Quebec led the way, when it instituted its own personal income tax in 1954. Today, Quebec, Ontario and Alberta have also assumed, to varying degrees, a measure of autonomy in the matter of taxes. For Quebec, especially, this power has taken on a symbolic significance. I was Minister of National Revenue in Ottawa in 1999, when the Department of National Revenue became the Canada Customs and Revenue Agency, now the Canada Revenue Agency. In addition to granting greater independence to the institution that collects taxes, one of the purposes of this reform was to enable the new agency to offer its services and expertise directly to the provinces and territories, capitalizing on substantial economies of scale. The decision caused an outcry in Quebec; in this context, I believe the Quebec government feared that it would lead to a political battle over tax collection, therefore putting at risk its mandate.

Despite the fact that the new agency could have saved money and avoided duplication, this idea that Quebec return the responsibility for tax collection to the central government was so symbolically powerful that it did not even occur to the federal officials, never mind the politicians, to suggest it.

During the sixties, this new provincial assertiveness opened the door to the possibility of withdrawing from federal programs but receiving full compensation as transfer payments, a change accomplished through purely administrative moves. Jean Lesage was the first premier to take advantage of this change, in 1966, when he opted out of the federal program and set up Quebec's own provincial pension plan. The seventies brought about the signing of formal administrative agreements. As an example, consider immigration. In 1978 Quebec signed an agreement, which it renewed in 1991, giving the province a lot more power over who and how many new Canadians it would accept. Since then, Ontario has followed suit, signing its own agreement in November 2005.

There are many examples of other special arrangements between the federal power and the various provinces. My goal here, however, is not to provide an exhaustive list but to show that from the moment of Confederation, Canada began to change. It has evolved for the better and continues to do so even after the repatriation of the constitution in 1982, which came about despite troubled circumstances.

From 1982 until now, Canada has enjoyed a level of political dynamism that has, in its search for solutions, made possible some major reforms. At the constitutional amendment level, take, for example, the "deconfessionalization" of schools in Quebec and Newfoundland and Labrador, a change that relieves each province of its educational obligations to Catholics and Protestants going back to Confederation.[7] On a more administrative level, note the agreement on labour signed by the federal government and Quebec and the agreement on health care worked out with the provinces and territories in 2004. The latter recognizes the principle of asymmetry in the context of the Canadian constitution.[8] As well, there is the social union framework agreement, which, while not signed by Quebec, acknowledges the federal government's willingness to restrain its spending power, and there is Bill c-110, which governs regional vetoes by the provinces. Finally, the resolution on the "distinct society" clause presented to the House of Commons by Jean Chrétien's Liberal government on December 11, 1995, ultimately led to Quebec being recognized as a nation in the fall of 2006, when Prime Minister Stephen Harper's Conservative government put that resolution through the House. This evolution of Quebec-as-nation also cut the ground out from under the feet of the sovereignists, who were hoping to develop a new symbol of rejection. These reforms clearly point to a federalism that is alive and well.

Of course, there are other problems just over the horizon, and, to be honest, there probably always will be. Based on our past experiences, however, I know that we will be able to meet these new challenges, and I believe that a federation is the best system to do this. The power dynamic that exists within a federation allows divergent positions to be managed without ever losing sight of the common purpose.

So Where Does That Leave Us?

The track record that I have just described shows a country that, while far from perfect, is on the whole in fairly good shape. All the same, I perceive signs of life from the sovereignist movement heading for the barricades. I can hear them saying that even if the Constitution Act, 1982 legally applies to Quebec, it is still no less the case that Quebec never signed it. And yet this same constitution gave us the Charter of Rights and Freedoms, whose section 16 declares French and English to be the official languages. Others will argue that the constitutional talks that led to the failed Meech Lake and Charlottetown Accords demonstrate Canada's inability to redefine itself and adapt to change. Finally, others will maintain that Quebec should sign the constitution so that all Canadian provinces and territories can move forward together. This last idea is important and deserves a few words.

The Constitution: To Sign or Not to Sign?

To address this question, I want to tell you about a meeting I had with an anglophone political analyst just after I left active political life. He wanted to review the whole Canadian political scene and specifically to talk about the mood of Quebecers. This meeting led to some very interesting exchanges, especially when we broached the always thorny question of the repatriation of the constitution in 1982 and the absence of Quebec as a signatory.

As we know, the absence of this signature presents a fundamental moral and political problem for Canada. Nonetheless, on a purely pragmatic level, the constitution, which is the supreme law of the land, does have the force of law in Quebec. As we have already seen, the Canadian federation has not stopped evolving, despite this dilemma. In my opinion, the greatest effect of Quebec's not having signed the constitution has been to fuel the political debate, often to the great pleasure of the sovereignists, who have made the issue into a symbol.

In my view, it is imperative for Canadian unity that Quebec fully abide by the constitution of 1982. This means saying yes to signing the constitution. But when? That is the fundamental question whose answer lies in our character, in who we are as Canadians, by which I mean people of different mindsets but profoundly tolerant and respectful.

To come back to my meeting with this political analyst, our lively discussion led me to understand some significant differences in our two approaches to the question. On one side, there is my Latin temperament, my Cartesian view of the world and my training in civil law that predisposes me to codify things. On the other side, there is the point of view of an Anglo-Saxon, who likes to see things evolve through practice, custom, precedent and without too much fuss—essentially in the image of common law. As an example, remember that the United Kingdom does not have a written constitution, yet it can hardly be said to be lacking a constitution.

Soon enough, we found ourselves at an impasse. Essentially, we both wanted the same thing, that is, to see Quebec fully integrated into the great Canadian family. However, our approaches, our mindsets, our ways of seeing things were so diametrically opposed that we ended up looking to resolve our differences through compromise. After all, to be Canadian means accepting differences and searching for solutions. And so, reflecting the dynamic that exists in our federation, we worked out a Canadian-style solution, declaring Quebec's return to be a necessity, while agreeing that we'd be starting down the wrong path if we tried to impose any kind of deadline. This is a desirable outcome because any attempt that did not have a happy ending would plunge us once more into a constitutional and political crisis. To say that Quebec and Canada do not want to live through another checkmate on the constitutional chessboard is to put it lightly. We have to act prudently. We have to buy into the dynamics of the whole federal system, work towards its evolution and wait for just the right moment. I am convinced that in doing so we are not waiting for Godot; rather, that some day soon, Quebec will be able to sign the constitution willingly.

The New Power Relationship

Our federal system has been and always will be subject to tensions that lead to doubts and second thoughts. These tensions are not only healthy in a federal system; they are, in my view, desirable. The creation of the Council of the Federation in 2003 literally strengthened the foundation of our Canadian federal system. One of the council's fundamental objectives is to respect the constitution and to recognize the diversity within the federation. Beyond this very praiseworthy objective, the council will help bring about a new power-sharing relationship with the federal government. If, within the council, the provinces and territories can come together in spite of their disagreements, this could effectively create a new dynamic, which would allow the federation to evolve naturally. Furthermore, this might show Quebecers that they are not going to be alone when it comes time to make changes.

Although the council's effectiveness has yet to be tested, there have been a certain number of improvements, especially with respect to fiscal imbalance, which is after all a political problem far more than it is a structural one. It is also important to acknowledge the work that has been done in the areas of health and interprovincial trade. However, despite this progress in a few areas, there is still a lot to be done to establish a new power structure that would make it possible to deal with these matters as national issues. To better understand my point, it is worth taking a look at health care and interprovincial trade in more detail.

Health Care Is Sick!

Medicare as we know it today has its roots in the 1950s. It symbolizes the spirit of mutual assistance and generosity that characterizes Canadian society. Over time, the Canada Health Act, which guarantees universal access to health care, has become one of this country's fundamental values. In fact, throughout the years, many politicians have defended this law, especially its five underlying principles, namely: comprehensiveness, accessibility, transferability, transparency and universality.

Today, with the aging of the population, the development of new technologies, the shortage of health professionals and the problems with patient access to treatment, we are forced to concede that the Canadian public health care system is facing daunting challenges. In all of the provinces, the list of ineligible services is growing and people are looking for creative ways to circumvent the system. Even though the federal government has pumped more and more money into this sector, the situation has not improved. In 2005, in the *Chaoulli* case, in which physician Jacques Chaoulli challenged the law preventing patients from seeking private medical service, the Supreme Court of Canada took a critical look at the health care system. In fact, over the signatures of Chief Justice Beverley McLachlin and Judge John Major, the court affirmed:

> We conclude that on the evidence adduced in this case, the appellants have established that in the face of delays in treatment that cause psychological and physical suffering, the prohibition on private insurance jeopardizes the right to life, liberty and security of the person of Canadians in an arbitrary manner, and is therefore not in accordance with the principles of fundamental justice.[9]

And also:

> Finally, the benefits of the prohibition do not outweigh the deleterious effects. Prohibiting citizens from obtaining private health care insurance may, as discussed, leave people no choice but to accept excessive delays in the public health system. The physical and psychological suffering and risk of death that may result outweigh whatever benefit (and none has been demonstrated to us here) there may be to the system as a whole.[10]

Looking at a judgement as harsh as this one, I find it hard to understand why the federal government, which sets the conditions, does not, in concert with the provinces and the territories, which manage the health sector, initiate a huge public consultation on the possibility of reform, involving the entire Canadian population and all the interest groups. As a society, we must investigate how the existing system can be improved without losing sight of those imperatives—mutual assistance and personal dignity—that Canadians hold so dear. Politically, the stakes are high, but this is an important issue and discussion and debate are part of the very nature of democracy. To reject the basic idea of challenging, comparing, analyzing the options is scarcely comprehensible in a democratic society like ours.

Already, a parallel system of private health care is being developed in many provinces without any say from the country as a whole. Having missed out on such a fundamental discussion, we are discovering a parallel system whose terms we do not control and which is already having an effect on the public system.

Some time ago, I had the honour of being invited to an evening reception put on by representatives of the health care system. During dinner, the woman seated next to me introduced herself, saying that she managed human resources in the surgical unit of a hospital. She explained that hospital work was becoming more and more difficult because this parallel system was causing serious problems. Increasingly, staff were leaving the hospital to go and work in private health clinics, and this exodus was causing not only a shortage of personnel but a considerable loss of expertise within the public hospitals. There are many other examples like this. If as a society we decide that we do want to do something about this situation, if the Council of the Federation is truly determined, this is exactly the type of issue that we could address and resolve. We need to fix our Medicare system or we may lose it in the future.

Interprovincial Trade

The year 2007 marked the fiftieth anniversary of the Treaties of Rome, and more importantly of the treaty that brought the European Economic Community into existence. To mark the occasion, the twenty-seven member-states of the European Union signed in Berlin on March 25, 2007, the text of the Berlin Declaration, which celebrated the achievements of a union that has hugely contributed to the economic, political and social stability of Europe.

There is no doubt that the cornerstone of this treaty—it is called a treaty because it brings together sovereign states—is what are called the Four Freedoms of the European Community, namely the free movement of goods, services, capital and, finally, people. Over and above the great principle of community solidarity, these four freedoms helped to build the new unified Europe and fostered a stronger feeling of belonging. In short, they created what we can now call a European identity.

What seems so evident to us fifty years on was not so clear at the start. Nevertheless, a glance at the past reveals the progress of a Europe that has, in many respects, become much more integrated than all of the Canadian provinces and territories. Indeed, even though Canada is a country, among our provinces and territories we will not find that group of Four Freedoms, which defines the European community.

Even though Europe's institutions as well as its geopolitical realities are very different from Canada's, I believe that Canada ought to pursue those Four Freedoms, adapted to our own reality. Among other things, this would bring about: an increase in competition leading to benefits for consumers; a rise, for businesses, in the number of trained workers and better access to this labour pool; a contribution to the economic growth and stability of our country through accumulated interprovincial trade relations. In that respect, the agreement on internal trade signed in 1994 is a step in the right direction. Article 100 of that document states clearly:

> It is the objective of the Parties to reduce and eliminate, to the extent possible, barriers to the free movement of persons, goods, services and investments within Canada and to establish an open, efficient and stable domestic market. All

Parties recognize and agree that enhancing trade and mobility within Canada would contribute to the attainment of this goal.[11]

What this article does, essentially, is to reflect the Four Freedoms of the European Union. And yet, notwithstanding this signed agreement, the creation of a federal-provincial-territorial committee of ministers of internal trade, and the fact that the council has made internal trade its battle cry, not much progress has been made. This is particularly true of the important sectors of labour and the harmonization of rules and standards dealing with business within each province and territory. In a meeting on September 7, 2006, the Ministerial Council on Internal Trade worked out a plan of action specifically dealing with the issue of labour mobility, the results of which are expected in April 2009. One can only hope that the plan will be a step forward. However, if the past is any indication, it is likely that the road ahead will be rough, primarily because there is so little real political will. These matters directly affect our prosperity as a country and also touch on our cohesion and our national unity.

During a conference of first ministers from western Canada, which was held in Nunavut in July 2007, the premier of British Columbia, Gordon Campbell, whose province signed an agreement with Alberta in April 2006, did not hesitate to ask the fundamental question: when are we going to decide that we are a country? When are we going to decide that the free movement of goods and people and services is something that is part of what a national identity should be?[12]

To do this, to realize concrete results, the agreement on internal trade should become more binding, perhaps by being formally ratified by all the provinces and territories. I am not going to detail all the changes that have been suggested to make this agreement more effective. Suffice it to say that this is a serious challenge for our federation, and it will have repercussions across the political stage.

Health care and internal trade are two areas the council ought to insist upon as key objectives. The council could also turn its attention to a few other matters. Natural resources, for example. At a time when natural resources have become synonymous with wealth, should we not be rethinking our policies? Should we not be thinking about our future generations? And when the First Nations peoples have to call a national day of protest to be heard, should we not be giving priority to their needs? Finally, should we not be paying more attention to the "western alienation" that is the result of, among other things, under-representation in the House of Commons and the Senate?

Of course, the council can never replace the federal government, and that is not its purpose. In fact, the federal government will always hold a unique position that gives it an overall view of the entire Canadian society. This overview allows it, in concert with the provinces and territories, to set both our direction and our goals. Undoubtedly, the council could act as a catalyst in the sphere of federal-provincial-territorial relations. It could seek out the shared bond in an environment where common sense does not always prevail over often divergent political and partisan interests.

The Right Moment

The future still holds many challenges. Today, I believe I can say that we will meet these challenges, collectively, within Canada. Quebec, with the help of the other provinces and territories, has contributed significantly to the development of a country that reflects our values, that is, profoundly democratic, respectful and tolerant. It is a land that knows the value of its own diversity. The farther we go into this era of globalization, the more we realize the uniqueness and the beauty of the Canadian model. We can make a difference to the world, because collectively, within Canada, we have already worked out the answers to a great number of issues.

In both my political and private life, I have had the chance to meet with people from coast to coast and to appreciate Canada's diversity. I have also travelled abroad to talk about federalism and to see what other countries are doing politically. Everywhere I go, people marvel about the miracle that is Canada, about how we bridge the linguistic and cultural divides to live together in harmony. I have come to realize that we live in an exceptional country whose values have inspired and motivated many generations. Consider the Second World War veterans, whom I met in Quebec City at a ceremony in their honour. I had just given a speech on the importance of their sacrifices to protect the freedoms that we enjoy today. Barely had I finished my speech when an old man came up to me, with tears in his eyes and visibly moved, to thank me. Humbly I answered this man that it was I who should be thanking him. It is because of his sacrifices, and those of others like him, that we are now able to cherish our values freely and within a democracy that has no equal. The courage of this veteran and so many others in defending our values should inspire us to go even farther.

As I said earlier, I think I see a lull in the storm. So let us take advantage of this calm to listen carefully to our own country. Let us rebalance the federation, building on the work of many provinces and territories that have already sought to redress this issue. And speaking of the challenges of Canadian federalism, Professor Gérald Beaudoin—who was also a senator—said:

> Only one Canadian province has a majority of French speakers. And as far as we can tell, no other seems destined for the same, even though in 1870, the francophone leaders in Manitoba might have aspired to it. In New Brunswick, officially bilingual since 1982, 34% of the population is French speaking.

If we want to keep Quebec in the Canadian federation, an objective that I believe is by far the best both for Quebec and for Canada, then Canadian federalism has to be refined. That is its destiny!

A sort of exaggerated "provincialism" is weakening the central Parliament and is becoming troublesome. Besides, several provinces don't want it. And if they did, they know they would not have the financial resources. Indeed, they are too dependent for their survival upon federal transfer payments and equalization.

Quebec would not get along well with an overly centralized state. Everything depends upon the acceptable degree of centralization and on a degree of centralization appropriate to the needs of the time.[13]

In a federation, the search for balance is an endless task. We, Quebecers, must join in wholeheartedly and set aside the idea of independence. Today, I think the time is ripe to do this, to initiate a wide-ranging public consultation with all Canadians. This dialogue, which could be run by a sort of consulting commission, would allow us to update our concept of the country and to better understand the concerns of the whole population. Its recommendations, without setting a deadline, would undoubtedly guide our governments in their future decisions. Of course, this kind of decision is not without its risks. However, I believe that riskier still is doing nothing at all.

MARTIN CAUCHON *is a barrister, solicitor and partner in the national law firm of Gowling Lafleur Henderson* LLP. *He also sits on several boards of directors. Elected in the federal constituency of Outremont in 1993, he was, among other roles, Minister of Justice and Attorney General for Canada, as well as Minister Responsible for Quebec. He decided not to run for re-election in 2003.*

Notes

1. This essay is translated from the original French version published in *Reconquérir le Canada—Un nouveau projet pour la nation québécoise* in 2007. It may contain minor differences that do not have any impact on the substance of the argument.

2. There are three territories (the Yukon, the Northwest Territories and Nunavut) whose juridical status is quite different from that of the provinces. The territories acquire their powers through laws passed by the federal Parliament. The present essay deals primarily with federal-provincial relationships.

3. David R. Cameron in *Handbook of Federal Countries* (Anne L. Griffiths, ed. with the collaboration of Karl Nerenberg), Montreal/Kingston: McGill-Queen's University Press, 2005, p. 108.

4. *Ibid.*, p. 109.

5. Reference: Resolution to Amend the Constitution, [1981] 1 SCR 753.

6. Reference: The secession of Quebec, [1998] 2 SCR 217, par. 55.

7. Gérald-A. Beaudoin, *La Constitution du Canada: institutions, partage des pouvoirs, Charte canadienne des droits et libertés*, 3rd ed., Montreal: Wilson & Lafleur, 2004, pp. 313, 314.

8. Gérald-A. Beaudoin, "Nouveau, le fédéralisme asymétrique? La Constitution canadienne prévoit plusieurs asymétries," *Le Devoir*, September 28, 2004.

9. *Chaoulli v. Quebec (Attorney General)*, [2005] 1 SCR 791, 2005 SCC 35, par. 153.

10. *Ibid.*, par. 157.

11. Agreement on internal trade, September 1994, art. 100. Available online at www.ait-aci.ca/en/ait/AIT%20Original%20with%20signatures.pdf (accessed May 27, 2008).

12. Words appearing in an article by Katherine Harding, "B.C. Premier shines spotlight on free trade," *The Globe and Mail*, July 7, 2007, p. A7.

13. Gérald-A. Beaudoin, *La Constitution du Canada*, pp. 30–31. (translation)

8

ANDRÉ PRATTE

WIPING THE SLATE CLEAN

Reviewing Our Past to Build a Better Future

FOR AT LEAST half a century we, Quebecers, have been defining our future and our relationship with the rest of Canada based on the same basic facts. Federalists like sovereignists agree, fundamentally, that the status quo is not acceptable and that the constitution absolutely must be changed if Quebec is to develop within Canada. Sovereignists believe that the impossibility of such changes has already been demonstrated and that, as a result, the only way for Quebec to achieve its goals is to become an independent country. Federalists are a bit more patient, that is all. Few of them are willing to argue publicly that being part of Canada offers Quebec undeniable advantages. The few who do so loudly and clearly are mostly in federal politics; they are seen by their fellow citizens as oddballs at best, and as "sellouts" at worst.

Despite the shock of seeing the Action démocratique du Québec (ADQ) become the Official Opposition in the 2007 provincial election, all indications suggest that Quebec politics will continue to work along the same old lines. Indeed, in this regard, strictly speaking the ADQ adds nothing new. Provincial Liberals, Péquistes and Adéquistes will still claim in chorus that Quebec needs more powers in order to evolve, that most federal policies are bad for Quebec and that our national government should fight Ottawa. Among the views of the three major provincial parties in the matter of federal-provincial relations, there may be differences of degree but not of substance. They have to do with who is really the most "autonomist" and who best looks out for the "higher interests" of Quebec, by definition opposite views to those of the rest of Canada.

This way of looking at matters is no longer appropriate in today's Quebec, in today's Canada or in today's world. It is this vision, not federalism or the anglophones, that is keeping modern Quebec from making progress, through the stale debates it breeds, and the irresponsibility and the victim complexes it feeds. Neither some theoretical renewed federalism nor independence will help Quebecers to tackle the considerable challenges they face. What it will take, first, is a change in the way they view themselves within Canada and in the world. It will mean, as the political scientists would say, a new paradigm.

It is a matter of starting with a clean slate. Not of forgetting our past, but of learning to see it in a new way. Of daring to question our myths. Of looking at our problems in a new light rather than studying them again and again through the distorted lens of "our Master, the past."[1] Of remembering, yes, but of using memory as a way forward. Today's Quebecers are no longer the fragile, dominated, exploited people of old. Why are they clinging to this burden of past complexes and reflexes?

Since today's dominant ideology—shared by all the major provincial parties—comes out of the history Quebecers have been taught and the potent political consensus that it created, it will not be easy to change. However, the magnitude of the task makes it even more urgent and important.

I Remember[2]…Whatever Suits Me

A few months before his death, I had one last meeting with the former editorialist and politician Claude Ryan, for whom I always had the greatest admiration. Mr. Ryan gave me a book that I had not heard of: *Le mythe de la modernisation du Québec—Des années 1930 à la Révolution tranquille.* This volume, published in 1991, went almost unnoticed at the time. And yet it is fascinating.

The author, historian Claude Couture of the University of Alberta, deconstructs the old myth according to which Quebec, right up until 1960, was a backward place, under the complete domination of a reactionary church and of anglophones who were as rich as they were racist. A land of peasants, clerics and clerks, French-speaking Quebec was allergic to industrialization and capitalism, which it left, through a mix of choice and necessity, to the anglophones.

Like all myths, this one is partly based on reality. But French Quebec was also energized by a powerful current of liberalism, about which too little is said in our history classes. Steadfastly modern, convinced of the necessity of separating church and state, active in business, these people may not have been in the majority, but they were not a marginal group either. Their opinions showed up especially in large-circulation newspapers such as *La Presse* and *Le Soleil*. For a long time, this strain of history went unreported by mainstream sources, whose reports were based on the analyses of *Le Devoir*, the Catholic hierarchy's favourite daily newspaper. However, in 1929, *Le Devoir* was printing 14,000 copies a day against the 154,000 of *La Presse*.

According to the accepted version of our history, Quebec sank into a social, cultural and economic black hole after the defeat of Louis-Joseph Papineau and the Patriots (1837–1838), and remained in it until Jean Lesage came to power 122 years later. This version has been spread widely among our people by most of our intellectuals, politicians and artists. Well, Mr. Couture demonstrates that the story is not that simple. Two or three decades after the Rebellion, "French Canadians seemed to be overcoming the problems that accompanied urban change, and to be responding quite well to the challenges of their time"[3] to the point where, at the dawn of the twentieth century, French-speaking Quebec had at least nine banks. That is not bad for people who were supposedly uneducated in business matters! According to some sources, in 1931, 57 per cent of the owners of manufacturing businesses in Quebec were francophones.

From the beginning of the twentieth century, Montreal was a dynamic industrial city, while the agrarian population of Quebec was in steady and rapid decline. The francophone bourgeoisie and its press were far from sympathetic to colonization, which in any case was neither as widespread as had long been supposed nor exclusive to Quebec. Colonization was generally viewed as a stopgap solution, just one way among many to recover from the depression of 1929.

All this by way of saying that the francophone Quebec of the past was not, as claimed by the "canonical version" of our history,[4] an exclusively exploited, oppressed, colonized and backward society. The more closely we study Quebec's history, the more we realize that a lot of Quebec francophones, especially the LaFontaines and Cartiers who are so little talked about these days, understood very well how to stand up and promote the advancement of their society, and, indeed, did cause it to move forward. "Quebec was already quite modern, in the sense that the values of today's business community were in place before 1960,"[5] according to Claude Couture. "Quebec Inc." was born a good century before it was baptized and celebrated!

If we take into account the obstacles the francophones of that time had to deal with, the birth of a prosperous and influential business class amounts to a huge success. A success that is never mentioned now, because Quebec's official history has been written by the Quiet Revolutionaries, for whom the modern era began with their politics and for whom the salvation of francophone Quebecers is entirely due to the work of the post-1960 provincial government. "Offering an entrepreneurial vision of pre-1960 Quebec, showing evidence of the existence of a measure of modernity, of a progressive economy, of a liberal and individualistic culture, of rational behaviour and rising prosperity, all that became unacceptable. To accept such a revisionist cosmology would only lead to doubts about the certainties and dogmas that had been built upon the altar of the Quiet Revolution."[6]

It is to the liberals of the nineteenth and twentieth centuries that Quebec owes its democratic institutions and its economic survival. And it is these liberals also who, contrary to what a lot of "nationalists" believe, challenged the clergy's domination of our intellectual life and rejected any sympathy for the European dictators of the mid-twentieth century.

This is not to deny that Canadian francophones were the object of discrimination and contempt from Canadians of British descent. Evidence of this fact can be neither ignored nor forgotten. But history is never as straightforward as the ideologues would like it to be.

Claude Couture is not the first to have unearthed this myth-making, of course. Other historians have challenged the "official history." For example, more than thirty years ago, historian Paul-André Linteau emphasized that if the Quebec higher bourgeoisie was essentially composed of anglophones, francophones made up a very large part of the middle bourgeoisie.

And it is this middle bourgeoisie that Mr. Couture is talking about. Unlike the upper classes, it had few connections with the

Empire or the rest of the continent. Within Quebec itself, however, it wielded substantial economic and political influence. The middle bourgeoisie owned banks and built railroads. "Between these two levels," Dr. Linteau writes, "the difference is not one of kind but of degree. It is the case of a single bourgeoisie, possessing capital and dominating economic activity, within which you find contradictions, clashes of interest and different levels of power."[7]

So, some francophones succeeded in overcoming prejudice—and that was decades before the Quiet Revolution and Bill 101—both in the political sphere and (admittedly, more rarely) in the economic one. They prevailed because of their competence, their ability, their skill at negotiating with the "Conqueror." They were often called "traitors," in the same way people today scorn those of us who have made good beyond our borders, whether their names be Pierre Trudeau or Guy Laliberté.[8] Every Quebec francophone who makes it to the top of his or her field shows that our nation's progress depends not only on structural changes and the openness of others, but largely on us. There are no valid excuses. We have been *maîtres chez nous* for a long time now. And masters of our own destiny.

Now, about Mr. Trudeau. In the initial group we assembled in preparation for this book was an intellectual whose insight and acute understanding of the Quebec soul I have always admired. However, when he learned that Pierre-Gerlier Forest, the president of the Trudeau Foundation, had joined us, he withdrew. Never mind that Mr. Forest is in no way a "hard-and-fast" federalist like many federal Liberals, nor that the Trudeau Foundation does not get involved in politics, he did not want to be associated in any way with the name Trudeau, even from a distance.

So there is another win for "official history," a yoke that we would benefit from throwing off. Mr. Trudeau made two serious mistakes during his political career. First, repatriating the constitution without the agreement of Quebec's National Assembly. Second, denouncing the Meech Lake Accord, which comforted the decision of Premiers Frank McKenna and Clyde Wells and which led to the collapse that we remember. Like many Quebecers, I, too, resent Mr. Trudeau for that. But these mistakes do not sum up his career. They do not justify his being seen in Quebec as the Devil incarnate. The Quebec intellectuals and politicians who peddle this negative image of the former prime minister conveniently forget that Mr. Trudeau was very popular in Quebec throughout his career. In fact, while he was prime minister, he was far more popular than René Lévesque.

And Mr. Trudeau also did some great things. He urged us to excel at the national level rather than just being content to sequester ourselves in Quebec. The Canadian Charter of Rights and Freedoms, which our intellectuals denounce because it supposedly led to the "butchering of Bill 101," is much appreciated by most Quebecers, as many surveys have demonstrated. Mr. Trudeau succeeded in making the Canadian government officially bilingual, thus meeting one of the fundamental demands of the Quebec nationalists of the time. He provided francophones outside of Quebec with the tools they needed for cultural survival. Now, is every francophone who keeps the language alive not an asset for the preservation of French in North America? Unfortunately, Quebecers follow their artists in this respect, showing a lot more interest in what happens to the Cajuns of Louisiana—a declining population that receives no help at all from its central government—while they yawn with boredom at the slightest mention of Franco-Ontarians or Franco-Manitobans.

On the twenty-fifth anniversary of the repatriation of the constitution, I was looking again at pictures of the ceremony held in Ottawa on April 17, 1982, in the presence of the Queen.

Who was there, in the front row? Pierre Trudeau, Jean Chrétien, André Ouellet... three more francophone Quebecers who, in the steps of Louis-Hippolyte LaFontaine, George-Étienne Cartier, Wilfrid Laurier, Ernest Lapointe, Louis St. Laurent and others, built Canada. Quebec nationalists detest them. Because they would not take a purely defensive stance. Because they chose to demonstrate their abilities and their own genius across the whole country instead of limiting it to Quebec. Should we not, instead, be proud of them (which in no way prevents us from disagreeing with some of their politics)?

But, instead, we have chosen to depict them as sellouts, mandated by the "English" to "put Quebec in its place." There is some confusion here. It is true that many of these politicians opposed certain plans of the Quebec provincial government. All the same, this government is not Quebec's only representative. Quebecers vote at the federal level too, and those votes count as much as the ones they cast in provincial ballot boxes. Would Bloc Québécois MPs dare to claim that they are any less representative of their constituents than their provincial counterparts? To put it another way, when a federal politician from Quebec defends a position that is different from the one held by the Quebec government, it is not a betrayal of Quebecers: it is simply a different view of their needs. And it sometimes happens that federal politicians are right.

It is very easy for minorities to blame all their problems on the majority and on a few *rois nègres*.[9] However, our history is not that of a crushed nation. It is the history of a people who came out on the losing side after the Conquest, certainly, but who also knew how to get themselves out of a tight spot; who often had to deal with the intolerance of the English majority, but who also profited from their skills and, sometimes, from their generosity; whose problems, sometimes, were the result of their own decisions and not imposed by the conqueror; who, having prospered in the worst of circumstances, can certainly do so today; who have not to fight for some liberty, because they are already "free and able to achieve [their] destiny and [their] development,"[10] as Robert Bourassa, the Quebec premier at the time, said the day after the collapse of the Meech Lake Accord.

How we remember our history is not just a matter of theoretical interest. If we look on it as an endless series of setbacks and frustrations, then every rough period that follows will be seen as another chapter in an ongoing tragedy. Instead, if we see our history as an alternating sequence of victories and losses, great moments and mistakes—like the history of any other people— then we will be able to stand back a bit, downplay the drama of recent events and react in a more rational and considered way.

It would also be wise to look at the history of other Canadians, as well as at our own shared past seen from their point of view. Such an attitude of openness was the beginning of the resolution of the "troubles" in Northern Ireland, according to the British minister responsible for this file, Peter Hain: "Knowing a lot of history is not enough: to make progress, each side has to understand the other's history."[11] Quebecers would certainly benefit from a greater curiosity about other Canadians.

The simplistic perception we have of our history took root in the analysis of our first great trauma, the Conquest. Even the choice of this word to describe what happened between 1759 and 1763 is significant. It conveys the image of a conqueror crushing French Canada underfoot, permanently destroying its will and paving the way for centuries of exploitation. Now, this is pure fantasy! When General James Wolfe defeated General Louis-Joseph de Montcalm on the Plains of Abraham, it was not French Canada he vanquished, it was France. The English had not gone to war to wipe out the French Canadians but to enlarge their empire at the expense of the French Empire, not just in North America but in Europe, India and the Caribbean. The Seven Years' War was a global war, in which Canada was just one of many battlefields.

What was to become Quebec was not at the time an independent country. It was a colony controlled by a capital that, even though it had bequeathed it a language and a religion, was domineering nonetheless. And how domineering! Those last years of the French regime were extremely painful for the residents of New France, subject as they were to the abuses of Intendant François Bigot and his band of profiteers. "When we did not feel utter destitution, the monopolists were working to create it, undermining the morale of the army and the people; and then, once they had managed to achieve it, they took full advantage of the situation. In the winter of 1757–1758, which was a prelude to even worse conditions, the people of Quebec suffered great hardships. They were dying of hunger."[12]

Canada was neither colonized nor conquered in 1760: already colonized, already exploited, already abused, the French Canadian people just passed from one master to another. Obviously it was not a trivial change, the new capital having a very different culture from the old. The French Canadians would subsequently be subject to tremendous hardship and suffering, some of it a result of the contempt the English merchants and politicians had for them, some of it a by-product of the great global economic currents that they did not want or were not able to adapt to, and still some of it a consequence of the weaknesses and shortsightedness of their ruling class. It is easy simply to focus all of our attention on the Conquest, the Durham Report and the quelling of the Rebellions; that just makes us victims of the "other." Which we often were, admittedly. But we were also victims of circumstance. And of our own mistakes.

It would be less romantic, and would not have galvanized our nationalism to the same extent, to talk about the Abandonment of 1759 (which would deserve a capital letter just as much as the Conquest does). For, first and foremost, that is what it is all about. Although France may have dreamed of the New World, the country never committed all of its energy, its faith or its military. "The British were more attached to their American colonies,"[13] Fernand Dumont concluded after studying eighteenth-century Canada. When General Wolfe's ships came in sight of Cap Diamant, Louis xv had already dropped Canada, refusing to send General Montcalm the reinforcements that would have saved Quebec.[14]

In any case, the fate of New France had already been decided. Immigration was too small, the economy too underdeveloped (based only on the fur trade), the administration too incompetent, the climate too inhospitable. In 1760, French Canada numbered 70,000 people; the British colonies to the south had twenty times that. No one can say what would have happened if General Wolfe had lost the Battle of the Plains; however, nothing about New France at the time would have suggested a radiant future. What impact would the French Revolution have had here? And the Terror? What would Napoleon have done with those "few acres of snow"?

To a certain extent, French Canadians benefited from the fact that the nineteenth century belonged to England, especially in economic terms. Canada's economy prospered by becoming part of the Empire's. And French Canadians gained from the creation of a parliamentary regime. Despite various obstacles set up by their English governors, French Canadians found in their legislative institutions a forum for validating their complaints, rallying public opinion and, finally, forcing the ruling nation to make some concessions.

These facts doubtless explain why many French Canadian leaders at the start of the nineteenth century saw the Conquest as more of a blessing than a disaster. No one other than Louis-Joseph Papineau termed the French regime an "arbitrary and aggressive government" and declared that under the English "the rule of law had given way to violence."[15]

So the real history of French Canada is not one of a lovely seventeenth-century French nation savagely crushed by English beasts. Quite the opposite, the Conquest brought some undeniable advantages. This fact does not allow us to minimize or silently pass over the abuses the English committed against the French Canadians. But it does mean that we have to acknowledge these positive elements.

For this reason, the outcry generated by the rumour that Queen Elizabeth II would visit Quebec to celebrate the four hundredth anniversary of the city's founding was an extraordinary bit of idiocy. "I think she has absolutely no reason to be there. It [the monarchy] is an outmoded symbol and it would be a definite misrepresentation of history. We are celebrating the anniversary of the city Samuel de Champlain founded four hundred years ago. The Queen should stay home,"[16] said Gilles Duceppe. But it is the leader of the Bloc Québécois who is misrepresenting history here. During 259 of those 400 years (65 per cent), Quebec has been part of the British sphere of influence. The city has long included an important anglophone community that has contributed extensively to making the capital what it is today. Without the link to England, would the Port of Quebec have become what it is now? We can say, in any case, that La Grande Allée[17] would never have been laid out nor the Château Frontenac built.

A century ago, francophone Quebecers had a more accurate take on their own history. And so, during the tercentenary celebrations in Quebec, the Prince of Wales was cordially welcomed. Those ceremonies of 1908 owed their grandiose character to the governor general of the time, the Englishman Lord Grey, to whom we also owe the planning of Battlefields Park (just as the restoration of the ramparts and ancient gates was sponsored by his predecessor Lord Dufferin). And while Great Britain was represented by its heir to the throne, and the United States by its vice-president, France was content to send a senior civil servant.

At the opening of the celebration, the mayor of Quebec, Jean-Georges Garneau, emphasized the French Canadians' gratitude to France "always beloved, to whom we are indebted for our life and our great traditions," and to England, whose rule "has made us free to grow while keeping our religion, our language and our institutions."[18] A hundred years later, the sovereignists would like to act as if, between the defeat of 1759 and the Quiet Revolution, absolutely nothing had happened. Or rather, that everything that did happen was bad for the francophones and, especially, for the city of Quebec.

And of course, the same people who denounced the Queen's possible visit will welcome French President Nikolas Sarkozy with a great outpouring of emotion, ignoring the fact that, contrary to what their fantasies tell them, the city of Quebec owes more to the English throne than to the Republic. But no one dares say that. We much prefer our own distorted version of history. What does it matter that it has more to do with a film by Pierre Falardeau[19] than with any proven facts?

The Conscription Crisis of 1942 is another example of the narrow perception of history that we have acquired, a history in which we are always victims. Rarely do we hear anything, on this subject, other than the indignation Quebecers feel for the federal authorities who forced our ancestors, against their general and deep-rooted opposition, into a war led by the British Empire. If we looked at this issue from another perspective, our resentment might be lessened. Imagine, for example, that Quebec had still been under the influence of France. Would the pressure to come to the aid of the mother country during the two world wars not have been even stronger? For those wars, we should remember, involved France as much as England!

Most of all, we should make note of one other detail: William Lyon Mackenzie King was right! Throughout almost all of the Second World War, he did everything he could to keep his promise to French Canadians not to impose conscription, while at the same time trying to calm the English Canadians, who were growing impatient. However, the prime minister had to consider the evidence: the war was going to continue, Canada was not sending enough soldiers to meet the demands coming from the European front, and the country had the military and moral obligations to contribute as much as it possibly could.

Considering the extraordinary nature of the struggle against Adolf Hitler, we can only conclude that in opposing conscription the Quebecers of that era had it wrong. They were wrong to see the war only as a quarrel between empires, wrong to ignore the fate of the European Jews, wrong to support Philippe Pétain against Charles de Gaulle. Was it just ignorance? For the general population, it was. But there is no forgiving the elites. By 1942, the fate of the Jews was being extensively reported in the newspapers, especially in Jean-Charles Harvey's *Le Jour*.

Today, who could conceivably agree with what the anti-conscriptionist François-Albert Angers said at the time? The French Canadians, he wrote, "have absolutely no interest in getting involved in the quarrels of some Great Powers whose arrogance and whose desire to take or maintain advanced positions amount to a permanent source of conflict."[20] Or the words of the federal MP Wilfrid Lacroix, who maintained that "This war is not Canada's war, but only that of the British Empire"?[21] At that time Mr. Harvey, one of the few Quebecers who approved of Mr. de Gaulle and of conscription, was called all kinds of names. They even dubbed him "John-Tcharles" to underscore just how much he was a lackey of the English Canadians.

And even though a referendum in 1942 relieved Prime Minister Mackenzie King of his commitment, he still delayed overseas conscription as long as he possibly could. In fact, he was able to hold it off until just six months before the conflict in Europe came to an end. A scant few thousand conscripts were sent to the Old World, sixty-nine of whom were killed. By far the majority of French-Canadian casualties in the Second World War were... volunteers.

In the book he wrote about this controversy in 1962, André Laurendeau set out to denounce the attitude of the Canadian government. The few passages dealing with the situation in Europe are pathetic, so badly does this great journalist just avoid the fundamental issue: did French Canadians not have the same obligation as every civilized person in the world to go and fight Hitler? "It is true that Pétain was admired in French Canada," wrote Mr. Laurendeau, "and perhaps that is because he did what we were forbidden to do: he got his country out of the war."[22] Got his country out of the war! How could such a brilliant intellectual write a line like that twenty years after the conflict? The Pétain government did not "get his country out of the war" but turned it over to Hitler, as well as collaborating with the Nazis to the point of handing over thousands of Jews who ended their days in the camps.

Mr. Laurendeau again: "In those days I often just closed my eyes, thinking of the misery of the men on the battlefields and in the bombarded towns of Europe. I felt... totally powerless to help them."[23] Supporting conscription instead of opposing it might have been an excellent way to help them, might it not? It seems that Mr. Laurendeau never thought of that option, either in 1942 or twenty years later.

The story of the 1942 Conscription Crisis is not simply an account of the English majority imposing its will on the French minority; it is also a case of a historical error on our part. Just as the many Canadian constitutional crises are not only the result of English Canada's refusal to acknowledge Quebec's difference— although this has indeed happened several times. Some of the crises have arisen from lost opportunities, such as when Quebecers have rejected agreements out of hand without realizing these would have brought considerable advantages in the long run, especially the right to veto any constitutional change (Victoria, 1971) and—we will come back to this—a guaranteed 25 per cent of the seats in the House of Commons (Charlottetown, 1992).

Over the next few years, we will not hear anything more about fiscal imbalance. The problem, almost everyone agrees today, is effectively settled. Was this Quebec triumph ever celebrated in the streets? Did the National Assembly pass a unanimous resolution congratulating the federal government for having acted in the best interests of Quebec, the other provinces and territories and the federation? Of course not. In fact, when Parliament passed a resolution acknowledging that the Québécois constitute a nation, it was quickly consigned to the memory hole that is reserved for any gains made by Quebec. One after the other, they are locked away so that nothing may risk beautifying what we would like to be our Canadian Way of the Cross.

If we took a different approach to our history, we would be able to criticize Quebec's own strategies and tactics when appropriate. And we would be in a better position to make compromises that would not always be seen as a surrender of principle. Let us admit it: if we had ratified the agreement from the Victoria Conference or the Charlottetown Accord, imperfect though they were, we would be a lot farther ahead than we are today "thanks" to our bitter-end strategy.

It Is No Longer 1867

Since long before the Conquest, as I have said already, we have been in a weak demographic position in North America. This weakness is not just the result of the territory having been populated by American Loyalists and British subjects. It is not the outcome of Lord Durham's strategy. Even when we were a French colony, the number of anglophones immigrating to North America far exceeded the number of francophones.

The perception that we, francophone Quebecers, have always had of the confederative pact is that it was an agreement between two equal nations. This vision still predominates among the federalists as well as the sovereignists. The former see the nature of this agreement to be one demanding special status for Quebec, one of the two founding nations. The latter consider that an illusory quest; they believe that the only way to re-establish an egalitarian relationship between the two nations is to turn Quebec into an independent country, just like Canada. Now, even admitting that Confederation was originally a pact between two nations (and many would challenge this), today this thesis is just as obsolete in reality as it is seductive in our imaginations. Not much concerned with what goes on in the rest of Canada, Quebecers have not noticed the extent to which it has changed, and how much this evolution has rendered completely unreal, and even absurd, the quest for this kind of equality.

At the time that Canada was founded, in 1867, the new Dominion numbered 3.7 million inhabitants, three quarters of them in Quebec (32 per cent) and in Ontario (44 per cent). When they joined the new country just a few years later, British Columbia had a tiny population of 36,000 and Alberta only 73,000. Since then, Quebec's population has multiplied seven times, Ontario's eight. In the meantime, the population of the West has literally exploded: British Columbia is 120 times more populous than it was 140 years ago; Alberta, 47 times. In 1901, Quebec was seven times more populous than these two provinces combined. In 2007, their population has slightly overtaken ours... and is growing faster.

Canada is also a much more complex country than it was. For example, the northern territories are asking for, and being granted, more and more autonomy. Although the territories are still sparsely populated, their economic growth is swift, accelerated by exploration and, before long, by the exploitation of their prodigious natural resources. The opening of a "Northwest Passage," an eventual rival to the Panama Canal, could equally stimulate the development of these territories. One day they will become as prosperous as Alberta is now. In the meantime, Newfoundland has become, for equalization purposes, a "have" province. So Canada is more and more multipolar: Ontario no longer dominates the country's economy so completely, nor can Quebec expect to monopolize its politics.

For several years, Quebec sovereignists hoped the independent Quebec–Canada relationship would be modelled on the one developed by members of the European Union (EU), where each member-state is theoretically equal to the others. Well, since the time of the original nine member-states that made up the EU that René Lévesque so envied, things have changed a lot in the Old World. Now, within the twenty-seven–country European Union, no country could claim to be absolutely sovereign (and, in fact, they are all less and less so) and none of them is equal to another. As the EU grew, the voting system was changed to reflect the demographic influence of each member. That change was confirmed in the "simplified treaty" that the Union heads of government agreed upon in 2007. Poland, wanting equality with Germany for historical reasons (despite having only half the population), was simply put in its place. Equality among members—unequal in terms of population, power and wealth—is as much a fantasy in Europe as it is at the United Nations or in a federation.

And so the more we see the growth and determination of these new regional power centres, Canada, in its complexity and its immensity, looks more and more like a continental union. In this context, it would be futile to hope, and absurd to demand of the rest of Canada, that Quebec be given the status of "equal" to the rest of the country (a premise put forward in the electoral platform of the Action démocratique du Québec). It would be equally impossible were Quebec an independent country, just as Poland's struggle within the EU was unreasonable and doomed to failure.

Quebecers have had several opportunities to entrench the special status they wanted into the constitution. From 1960 to 1995, the Quebec question was central to Canadian politics; that was our "window of opportunity." It led to the agreement from the Victoria Conference (1971), which gave Quebec the right to veto all constitutional amendments (an agreement renounced by Robert Bourassa under pressure from the nationalists); the Meech Lake Accord, which was rejected by two provinces; and the Charlottetown Accord, which was turned down by a majority of Canadians, including Quebecers. This last agreement, which was extremely complex, was an attempt to come to grips with what Canada had become while still satisfying Quebec's demands. In particular, it guaranteed our province a minimum of 25 per cent of the seats in the House of Commons, whatever the future demographics of the other regions in the country. That was a gain of major importance. We dismissed it out of hand, Mario Dumont in the lead.

Fifteen years later, the federal government proposed a bill to correct the under-representation of British Columbia and Alberta in the House of Commons. Quebec provincial politicians, notably the sovereignists and Mr. Dumont, were quick to denounce this bill which, reflecting demographic data, would have had the effect of slightly reducing Quebec's position in the federal Parliament. The same group that led the fight against the Charlottetown Accord is now demanding that Ottawa guarantee Quebec a 25 per cent position in the Commons! And they will justify this about-face by saying that the 25 per cent was in and of itself always a good idea, but that the Charlottetown Accord contained other compromises that were unacceptable to Quebec. It is this attitude that, for forty years, has prevented Quebec from making constitutional headway: the refusal to compromise. Our demands always appear to be legitimate; the others', never. After all, are we not a "nation"? A "founding people"?

This refusal to compromise originated no doubt in our insecurity. But today, it is more a matter of a superiority complex: Quebec is a nation, sir; Alberta is just a bunch of cowboys and polluters. This kind of unreasonable attitude, whether within Canada or, eventually, in the "community of nations," will not get us anywhere.

The response of Quebec politicians and commentators to the Harper government's initiative is revealing in another respect. I recall, for example, my friend Joseph Facal, a former member of Parti Québécois governments, saying, "This programmed minoritization of Quebec is built into every word of the Constitution that was imposed on Quebec in 1982 without our agreement, and is still not signed!"[24] A *programmed minoritization??* What is unfair about Quebec, like the other provinces and territories, being represented in Parliament according to the size of its population? In what other political system would it be otherwise?

If Quebec's population is not growing as fast as that of the western provinces, that is not Ottawa's fault. Nothing is stopping us from having more children. Nothing is stopping us from accepting more immigrants: the immigration agreement signed with the federal government—which would be part of the constitution if we had accepted the Charlottetown Accord—even allows us five percentage points more immigrants than our population should permit. If over the last five years we had taken advantage of this larger share, we would have had 270,000 immigrants instead of 210,000. A good way to reduce the impact of a demographic decline. Why did we not do it? In this field, as in many others, our fate was in our own hands.[25]

When I wrote an editorial to this effect, Mr. Facal replied in his *Journal de Montréal* column, maintaining that Quebec is weakening "because the Quebec federalists now are so unconditionally federalist that English Canada has known for a long time that it can get them to accept anything at all."[26] Since I agree that Quebec should be represented in the federal Parliament in proportion to its population, an indisputable democratic principle (at least as indisputable as the 50 per cent plus one so dear to the sovereignists!), I must be an "unconditional federalist" ready to swallow "anything at all!" And Mr. Facal was, of course, opposed to the Charlottetown Accord...

Clearly, as a "founding people" we are entitled to demand certain privileges, certain protections. But in making our demands, and in our negotiating strategies, we ought to take into account what Canada has become: an immense and complicated ensemble within which some powerful regions and strong cultures are living side by side. We cannot find our place in this confederation by demanding what we had in 1867 or in 1608 any more than

The Netherlands can demand that it be considered a superpower because Holland was one four centuries ago. We have to do what the others do: make our case through our economic strength, our energy, our creativity, our labour force, our skill at building alliances with our partners. That is certainly what we would have to do as an independent country, without the asset of the political influence we now hold vis-à-vis the central government.

Today's Quebec is a modern nation with no reason to envy any other nation in the world. We should be mature enough to see Canada as it is, not as it was or as it might have been. Realism is not a synonym for resignation. Quite the opposite. Once we are free of the mirages that have too often shaped our attitudes, we will find ways to increase our influence, as every country has to do when it is geographically or demographically disadvantaged.

Becoming Truly Autonomous

Passing through Vancouver in the spring of 2007, California's governor, Arnold Schwarzenegger, spoke about his state's influence in the area of climate change. "Even though California is a big place, it's the seventh largest economy in the world, I think it is important to recognize that even though we are a little spot on the globe, the power of influence we have is the equivalent of a nation, or even a continent."[27] California's influence in the world is undeniable. Whether the state adopts a new policy or launches a new style, the world pays attention. Why? Because California has a seat at the United Nations? No. Because California is dynamic, avant-garde, populous and rich. With its thirty-six million people, this state—as the governor stressed—is the world's seventh-largest economy, just ahead of... Canada. There are 190 countries less economically powerful than the Golden State.

As for Quebec, it has the world's fortieth-largest economy, placing it ahead of such countries as Denmark, Ireland and

Portugal... In terms of gross domestic product per capita, Quebec ranks even higher, number twenty-two. So what is keeping us from becoming the California of the North? What is stopping us from becoming, in our own way, an enviable model in fields such as education, health, the environment, energy? Oh, I forgot. We are waiting until we have "full powers." "All our taxes." "Autonomy." Did California wait for that? What powers are we lacking to develop the best education system in Canada? The best-managed health system? A healthier environment? We will not find genuine autonomy, true independence in the concessions that Mario Dumont and the sovereignists are trying to obtain from Ottawa. Genuine autonomy is the will to take charge, to fully assume one's responsibilities.

When the Action démocratique talks about getting more powers from Ottawa, do they tell us which ones? Or for what purpose? No. "Quebec's optimal development evolves with the strengthening of its autonomy," says the party platform. More powers are necessary, says the French version, because that is "natural." Should we not rather be taking maximum advantage of the considerable sovereignty and autonomy that we already enjoy? The Quebec government has seen many gains over the past few decades. Have all of these translated into better services for Quebecers? We have repatriated the constitutional responsibility for worker training; are our workers better trained than they were before?

Blaming Ottawa for all our difficulties allows us to avoid our obligations. Waiting for independence as if it were the magic solution to all our problems allows us to do nothing while we are waiting. Yet, in how many other independent countries would you rather live than in the province of Quebec?

California may very well be as powerful as a continent, as Mr. Schwarzenegger has reminded us, but "one state alone cannot do it... So it's very important for us, as a state, to go and to reach out and to form partnerships, to form as many partnerships as possible."[28] And what is true of the environment is true of all other fields. Country or province, we have to partner with others. Yet in Quebec, we do not often reach out to those who should be our preferred allies, the other Canadian provinces and territories. Once again, we seem to be waiting for that great evening when we declare our independence and when we can finally talk "equal to equal" with Washington, Paris and Beijing. What an illusion! How much influence do you think Quebec's ambassador in Washington would really have?

Why not, instead, from hereon in, build solid and diversified links with Ontario, British Columbia and Alberta, three of the most dynamic political entities in North America? If we did this at every level—political, economic, scientific and cultural— we would be much farther ahead in our ability to profit from being part of Canada. We would also have more influence with the federal government, not because of some circumstantial alliances (which, by their very nature, are fragile) arising from one or two federal-provincial conferences, but thanks to solid links forged over time. If the partnership strategy is good for California, would it not be good for Quebec?

Taking Our Place

Over the last few years, political commentators have often deplored the weak francophone representation in the Prime Minister's Office (Mr. Martin's and Mr. Harper's, especially) and in the Cabinet. They also condemn the growing lack of concern for official bilingualism in federal institutions. The 2006–2007 report of the Commissioner of Official Languages, Graham Fraser, stresses, "The official languages dimension always seems to be easily forgotten, especially when it comes to language of service and communications, and even more so when it comes to language of work." And he goes on, "It is unfortunate, however, that 41 years after Lester B. Pearson's language policy was adopted, 37 years after the Act came into effect and 25 years after the Canadian Charter of Rights and Freedoms was signed, it still takes a strong leader or bad press to make changes happen. The value of official languages must become entrenched in our collective conscious-ness and in the organizational culture of federal institutions."[29]

These observations are correct, and sadly so. Today, we are a long way from that élan that Mr. Trudeau's "French Power" slogan gave to bilingualism. However, we must also concede that Que-becers' lack of interest in federal institutions has something to do with this. Prime Minister Paul Martin, for example, made several attempts to attract Quebec francophones to top-level positions in his office. Yet, his efforts were in vain.

In Ottawa, there are constant complaints about how difficult it is to recruit Quebec francophones to work in or manage fed-eral organizations. It is a vicious circle: Quebecers do not want to work in the federal machine, mostly because they are afraid of the frustrations that will inevitably result from their minority status. Their absence only exacerbates this phenomenon: in the absence of Quebec francophones, why would anglophones even think to consider the needs of Quebec or of the French language?

It is often said that the Harper government does not have a very strong Quebec team. No doubt, this is probably true, but can you blame the prime minister for this? Quebec cannot both go ahead and elect Bloquistes—a perfectly legitimate choice, of course—and, at the same time, want to be represented in the federal Cabinet. If Quebecers want to vote for a protest party because they feel that is where the "real power" lies, they are free to do so. But they should not then begin to whine about Quebec having so little influence in the federal political machinery!

In a particularly passionate speech he made to Quebec supporters in June 2007, Liberal leader Stéphane Dion reminded them of the importance of Quebec participation in federal politics. (Partisanship led him to speak only about the Liberal Party, but the reasoning applies across the board.)

> Everything great and influential that has ever happened in the history of Canada has been made possible because Quebecers invested their energy and talents in the Liberal Party of Canada. This was the case under Wilfrid Laurier, just as it was under Mackenzie King. Some great ministers came from Quebec at the time of Mackenzie King, people like Ernest Lapointe and Louis Saint-Laurent; and it was also an amazing period of construction for Canada. And of course Pierre Elliott Trudeau...
>
> Look at each of these periods and you will always find Quebeckers who have taken on enormous responsibilities, whether as ministers, members of Parliament, chairs of committees or senior officials.
>
> Canada would not be where it is without all of these Quebecers who believed in the Liberal Party of Canada.[30]

The more Quebec francophones there are in Ottawa, the better the interests of Quebecers will be defended, including the French language. Moreover, it was a Quebecer—Mr. Dion himself—who gave bilingualism a second wind by launching the Action Plan for Official Languages. This substantial initiative, which committed $750 million over five years, has, according to the Commissioner of Official Languages, "given the new momentum that was so desperately needed to the official languages policy and has helped offset the budget cuts that affected official languages communities in the years prior to the Plan." And it was another Quebecer, the Conservative minister Michael Fortier, that Commissioner Fraser praised, saying, "Thanks to the leadership of the Minister of Public Works and Government Services Canada in recent months, this institution has finally begun to follow through on the numerous recommendations made as a result of several investigations and an audit."[31]

It is time for Quebecers to return to our federal institutions, whether they be political or administrative. I admit that this will not be easy. Francophone Quebecers will always be in the minority at the federal level. Which means that their views will not always receive proper attention. Which means that, more often than not, and even with an Official Languages Act, they will have to work in English. They will have to deal with prejudice, and they will have to explain, convince, pound their fists on the table, and demonstrate both an irreproachable competence and an unparalleled originality. Quebecers, however, are not the only ones to bear this cross: it is the lot of every minority. And none of that would change if we became an independent country, contrary to the illusions the sovereignists hold. Within the shared Quebec-Canada institutions that would almost certainly be put in place, Quebecers would inevitably have less influence, as is the case with the smaller member-states in the European Union.

It is time to concede that we are a minority, not due to some sinister plot going back to the Durham Report, but because, since the eighteenth century, circumstances have continued to favour English-language immigration to North America. Admitting this fact does not mean that we are kowtowing to anyone. However, instead of refusing to enter the ring until that blessed day when our partners grant us some kind of factitious equality, we should come into it fully aware of both our strengths and our weaknesses.

How can smaller powers triumph over larger ones? By forging alliances. And that is why Quebec's first concern should be not its diplomatic relations with France but its diplomatic relations with every other province and territory in the country. Of course, it is less exhilarating to meet with politicians, business-people, union representatives and journalists in Winnipeg than with their counterparts in Paris. However, when it comes to advancing Quebec's interests, the former is just as useful. To deal with regular issues like fiscal imbalance. And also to undertake longer-term projects, such as future constitutional changes. Let us not wait for the First Ministers to reconvene around that historic bargaining table. From now on, we should aim to be present throughout English Canada, in every sector, so that when the time is right, Canadians' opinion of Quebecers will be a lot more positive than it was at the time of the Meech Lake Accord.

The economic hub of the country is shifting westward, towards provinces that are more suspicious of Ottawa and less knowledgeable about Quebec than Ontario generally is. There is much work to be done building relations with the western provinces, work that is more important than lobbying for a quarter or half of a seat at the United Nations Educational, Scientific and Cultural Organization (UNESCO). And yet, which Quebec politician makes regular visits to Alberta? To British Columbia?

Quebecers have decided to stay in Canada. We must now be consistent and take our place proudly and decisively in this country we have chosen. Take it, rather than just sulk until it is given to us. In this way, we will be faithful to our history. Not the history of a conquered people that our mythmakers have invented. But the history of a proud, strong, original, open and creative nation. This is our true history, forged over more than four centuries, by generations of French Canadians.

ANDRÉ PRATTE, who compiled this collection, is the author of five books, the most recent being Aux Pays des Merveilles: Essai sur les mythes politiques québécois (VLB Editeur, 2007). He also co-authored, with Joseph Facal, Qui a raison? (Boréal, 2008). A journalist for the past thirty years, he is currently Editorial Pages Editor at La Presse. In 2007, he won a National Newspaper Award in the Editorials category.

Notes

1. *Notre maître, le passé* was the title of a book by Lionel Groulx, an influential nationalist historian in the 1930s and 1940s.

2. "I Remember" (*Je me souviens*) is the Quebec motto and can be seen on all Quebec licence plates.

3. Claude Couture, *Le mythe de la modernisation du Québec—Des années 1930 à la Révolution tranquille*, Montreal: Editions du Méridien, 1991, p. 20. (translation)

4. Gilles Paquet and Jean-Pierre Wallot, *Un Québec moderne—1760–1840*, Montreal: Editions HMH, 2007, p. 672.

5. Claude Couture, *supra*, p. 123. (translation)

6. Gilles Paquet and Jean-Pierre Wallot, *supra*, p. 677. (translation)

7. Paul-André Linteau, "Quelques réflexions autour de la bourgeoisie québécoise, 1850–1914," *Revue d'histoire de l'Amérique française*, vol. 30, no. 1 (June 1976). (translation)

8. The founder of the hugely internationally successful company *Le Cirque du Soleil*.

9. Literally, "nigger kings," this is a metaphor coined by *Le Devoir* editor André Laurendeau to describe those corrupt Quebec politicians who were able to hold onto their power only because, like some African kings of colonial times, they were helping the colonial invaders maintain their dominance.

10. Robert Bourassa, Quebec National Assembly, *Journal des débats*, June 22, 1990, p. 4134.

11. Peter Hain, "Peacemaking in Northern Ireland: A Model for Conflict Resolution?", speech given at Chatham House, June 12, 2007. See www.peterhain.org/default.asp?pageid=62&mpageid=61&groupid=2 (accessed May 27, 2008).

12. Fernand Ouellet, *Histoire économique et sociale du Québec, 1760–1850*, Montreal: Fides, 1966, p. 48. (translation)

13. Fernand Dumont, *Genèse de la société québécoise*, Montreal: Boréal Compact, 1996, p. 61. (translation)

14. Joy Carroll, *Wolfe et Montcalm—La véritable histoire des deux chefs ennemis*, Montreal: Les Editions de l'Homme, 2006, pp. 160–161.

15. *Ibid.*, p. 150. (translation)

16. Joël-Denis Bellavance, "Que la reine reste chez elle, conseille Duceppe," *La Presse*, April 17, 2007. (translation)

17. The street where the nineteenth-century upper-class built its Victorian homes, today lined with restaurants.

18. See also the fascinating work by H.V. Nelles about the tercentenary celebrations in Quebec, *L'histoire spectacle—Le cas du tricentenaire de Québec*, Montreal: Boréal, 2003.

19. The controversial and very nationalistic Quebec filmmaker. *Octobre* and *15 février 1839* are his best-known political films.

20. Yves Lavertu, *Jean-Charles Harvey, le combattant*, Montreal: Boréal, 2000, p. 333.

21. *Ibid.*, p. 311.

22. André Laurendeau, *La crise de la conscription*, Montreal: Editions du Jour, 1962, p. 115. (translation)

23. *Ibid.*, p. 150. (translation)

24. Joseph Facal, "S'effacer sans s'indigner," *Journal de Montréal*, May 28, 2007. (translation)

25. It is worth noting here that the leader of the Action démocratique du Québec, Mario Dumont, all the while claiming that Quebec's presence in the House of Commons should in no way be diminished, opposed an increase in the immigration thresholds in Quebec. This increase is, however, essential to maintaining Quebec's demographic position relative to the rest of Canada.

26. Joseph Facal, *Journal de Montréal*, May 23, 2007. (translation)

27. See http://gov.ca.gov/speech/6552/ (accessed May 27, 2008).

28. *Ibid.*

29. Graham Fraser, Office of the Commissioner of Official Languages, *Annual Report 2006–2007*, pp. xii, 9.

30. Stéphane Dion, "Making the Liberal Party the Favourite Party of Quebeckers, Once Again," speech delivered on June 16, 2007, in Drummondville, Quebec. See www.liberal.ca/story_12939_e.aspx (accessed May 27, 2008).

31. Graham Fraser, *supra*, pp. 18, 9.

9

PIERRE-GERLIER FOREST

HEALTH POLICY

Enough of the Empty Chair

IN POLITICS, despite what René Descartes says, it is not so much common sense as bad faith that seems to be the most widely shared human characteristic. I still read every day how the Canadian government is usurping provincial responsibilities by meddling in health care matters, as if nothing had changed in the constitutional arrangements since 1867 or as if our idea of health care was still stuck in the nineteenth century: that is to say, hospitals, doctors, epidemics. During the leadership debates in December 2005, to pick just one irritating but very typical example, Bloc Québécois leader Gilles Duceppe humorously dismissed the "ten thousand bureaucrats" in the federal offices of Health Canada in Ottawa, giving the impression that they had nothing useful or important to do. In effect, his statement implied, why would anyone care about the safety of medications or of food, or worry about the toxicity of pesticides or the increase in diabetes in First Nations communities? Even the federal government's

timid appeals in favour of minimum wait times for certain
medical procedures and essential surgeries were met with cries
of indignation. Indeed, the least mention of "national" norms—
read "Canadian"—automatically triggers a flood of objections, all
more or less inspired by the same rigid view of federalism and of
health care.

Let us be clear: the provinces' primary role in matters of
health care is the only viable arrangement, the only suitable
response to managing the various issues that touch our lives so
personally. This is true of risk-sharing. It is also true of adminis-
tering networks and organizations. And it is true of conceiving
of and carrying out programs.

A health care system cannot function without a very precise
balance between the needs of a well-defined population and the
actual services available, a role that the provinces are far more
capable of fulfilling than any central government, doomed as it is
by diversity and the size of the country to constantly seek out the
lowest common denominator.

But we are mistaken if we think that health care is exclusively
a provincial concern. Even in 1867, the constitution reserved
for the federal government some responsibilities for the protection of public health, as well as certain obligations that flowed
from Ottawa's responsibilities towards First Nations and several
other political and financial areas. And that is not all. "Health" is
obviously not confined just to hospitals or to the regulation of
medical practice, areas that both the constitution and tradition
have effectively assigned to the provinces. The health of Quebecers is based on a long series of factors and decisions, involving
such seemingly different considerations as heredity, education,
social environment, economic prosperity and even religious
affiliation. In fact, quite a few of the basic factors that determine
our state of health fall totally or partially within the federal

jurisdiction, including economic policy, immigration policy, trade policy, intellectual property and patents, environmental protection measures and research funding, among others.[1]

To greatly simplify the issue, it could even be said that in Canada the *supply* of health services is mostly a provincial matter: from hospitals to public health, without forgetting drug coverage and visits to the family doctor. And that the *demand* for service— the circumstances that lead to visits to a physician's clinic or a hospital emergency department—is largely influenced, if not determined, by policies set in Ottawa. These policies, of course, may be affected by federal decisions made outside what would usually be thought of as the health care field, including those that contribute to maintaining a healthy and vigorous economy or that seek to counter the degradation of the environment, but also those that allow the commercialization of a new drug or that permit research into new therapies and that have a direct impact on the costs assumed by the health care system. This may also include even less tangible, but equally restrictive, matters, such as norms and values. Rightly or wrongly, many Canadians believe they have a virtually inalienable right to health care— the best possible—whenever the need arises. They also believe that this right is protected by the federal government, mostly thanks to the Canada Health Act 1984, a somewhat mythical law whose effects now far exceed the intent of the original text.[2] This approach to dividing up the jurisdictions is virtually unheard of. In other federations with a comparable constitutional and juridical heritage, such as the United States or Australia, there has been a progressive move away from this model towards a more pragmatic division of responsibilities.

Unlike the political role of lieutenant governors or the requirement that Quebec senators own property in the province, these questions are neither theoretical nor constitutional curiosities.

Health care issues are fundamental public policy issues, not just for individuals but for society as a whole. We invest an important part of our collective wealth in health care and receive in return equally important benefits: a level of well-being, a collective sense of security, a measure of prosperity. Now, a health care system is difficult to manage and especially to reform, even in unitary countries. Ask the French, the British, the Danes. And in Canada, this work of transformation is even more demanding because no level of government has the tools or even the authority to deal with both the supply and the demand at the same time. And, if either Ottawa or the provinces hold strictly to its traditional role—that is, each in its own camp—then, failure is assured.

In spite of a massive injection of funds in such priority areas as primary care, electronic records, prescription drugs, human resources, wait times since the mid-1990s, we are still a long way from achieving promised changes, especially compared with the advances made in the rest of the world during the same period. Canada now ranks last in most international comparative surveys.[3] Every year in Washington, experts and high-level authorities from the great industrialized nations gather as guests of an American foundation to compare their progress in updating their respective health care systems. When I first started to attend these meetings, a little less than a decade ago, Canada was held as a model, because the principles guiding our intended health care reform seemed both clear and accessible. But I came back from the meeting of December 2006 in a sombre mood, and to be frank, a bit humiliated, because the questions being put to the Canadian delegation were all about our problems and about the apparent deterioration of the working conditions in our health care system.[4]

Indeed, across the entire country, the reform program has been bogged down by a series of false starts and half-measures that have resulted from a lack of collaboration and co-ordination. Quebec has not fared much better or worse than the other provinces, despite its empty chair policy—choosing not to participate in the joint efforts of the federal government and the other provinces on health care—and despite the scope it has been given in various national health care agreements, especially since 2000. Alberta, which took a similar position on the same issues during these years, is in a comparable position. It is a basic fact that going it alone in health care is an impossible and absurd task, since too many of the controls lie beyond the reach of provincial health ministers. Besides, even if they were given the combined powers of the provinces and Ottawa, they would still lack those belonging to their colleagues in finance or education or the environment, which must also be exercised within the tangle of federal and provincial jurisdictions.

And it is not enough just to come to the table. After all, it is not just the absence of Quebec or, to a lesser degree, of Alberta that has blocked reforms to the health care system in the other provinces. Yet, none of them has posted spectacular results. Participants or not, all governments in the country are in a way the victims of that traditional constitutional framework, which forbids the provinces and Ottawa to look beyond this archaic division of jurisdictions and enter into talks about how, realistically, to modernize the health care system. Indeed, to go even farther, a few judicious compromises of the kind that sometimes work in politics will not be good enough here. The examples most often cited, such as immunization programs or strategic investments in health research, have produced notable results—albeit with a few spillover benefits. We are going to have to face up to some basic questions, those that touch on the dynamics of federalism itself. So, I propose to begin by exploring this path, coming back later to the health care system and how to reform it.

Centralization and Symmetry

In a presentation on federalism he gave to members of the Royal Society of Canada in 2005, Professor Douglas Brown proposed a distinction between "symmetry" and "centralization" in describing and analyzing federal states.[5] Professor Brown is not the first constitutionalist to use these two terms, far from it. But instead of using the word "symmetry" only as an academic synonym for "centralization," he was applying it to suggest another specific dimension of the juridical and political realities of federal politics. In the Canadian context, it is a useful distinction that makes for a less ideological discussion of the relations between the federal government and the provinces.

Let us start with the idea of symmetry and its opposite, asymmetry. Both terms are a shorthand that allows us to take stock of the ability of a federation's member-states to develop policies suited to the local conditions, whether they be geographic, cultural or socio-structural. The more capacity there is to deviate from general principles, the more asymmetrical a federation will become. For example, the economic policies of Bavaria, the electoral mores of the canton of Glaris (where constituents can vote at the age of sixteen and with a show of hands!) and the penitentiary system in Texas reflect values and choices that are not necessarily shared by other inhabitants of Germany, Switzerland or the United States. So none of these federations is perfectly symmetrical. Even in Canada, despite a strong ideological resistance to asymmetry, there is no shortage of practical examples. In fact, Quebec instantly comes to mind, whether it be a matter of language, civil law, immigration or social policy. However, throughout the history of the country, other Canadian provinces have demanded and obtained special rights and privileges, on issues ranging from First Nations policy to education, not to mention transportation policy and the makeup of the Senate.

The idea of centralization allows us to take into account the work being done to define and maintain national identity, as much in juridical and political as in economic and social matters. To be a German, Swiss or American citizen confers, in each case, a series of fairly uniform rights and obligations, independent of the Land, the canton or the state in which one lives. And the more such expectations are codified in law or juridical texts, the more a federation is said to be centralized. From this perspective, for example, it should be readily apparent that the Canada of the Charter of Rights and Freedoms (1982) is a more centralized country than was the Canada of the British North America Act (1867). But it could be even more so. Germany and Australia, for example, are two federations where social and economic rights have been built into civil rights, which reinforces the centralist aspects of those federations—without, as we have seen with Germany, presenting any obstacle to asymmetry in certain fields or regions.

For me, one of the interesting results of this distinction Professor Brown has suggested (although he does not use this idea himself) is that it allows us to define four different versions of federalism, according to whether a federation is more or less centralized and more or less symmetrical.

• I think, for example, that the autonomist dream of the Action démocratique du Québec (ADQ) is a federation that is at once *asymmetrical* and *decentralized*. On the one hand, an autonomous Quebec could develop and manage all its policies with no other concern than, when necessary, coordinating with the other provinces in the federation. The creation in 2003 of the Health Council of Canada was an example of this kind of asymmetry: one clause of the agreement signed by the First Ministers allowed Quebec to abstain from participating in the work of the council, assuming that it already had a comparable institution or, at least, that it was in the process of creating one. From the autonomist point of view, on the other hand, Quebec could also reject Canadian norms and values should they appear to be in conflict with the province's larger objectives. The repeated attacks by ADQ supporters levelled against the provisions of the Canada Health Act guaranteeing every citizen access to health care services seem to me to be based on this logic. At least this is the way in which I understood the conclusion of an article by political scientist and former ADQ president Guy Laforest that appeared the day after the Quebec election in March 2007, where he came out against "the doctrinaire and symmetrical statism underlying the federal health act," which imperils the "rebalancing of the public/private health care powers that would unblock the way to our dreams."[6]

• There is in English Canada, especially in the West, a populist and reformist trend that seems to me to be fascinated by the prospect of a *decentralized* but *symmetrical* federation. The repeated calls for a "Triple E" Senate, in which the provinces would have an equal number of elected representatives endowed with effective powers, are the expression of a widely held mindset that repudiates any distinctions among members of the federation. It was evident at the time of the Meech Lake Accord and it is visible today in the debates over renewable resources and tax-sharing: convincing most Canadians that one province is different from the others is a very difficult task. A proponent of this view would say that the obvious differences between provinces and territories—their size, culture or geographic location—do not, and must not, bring with them any special juridical accommodations, even with respect to rights and duties and even with such seemingly different entities as Prince Edward Island and Ontario. This belief is also sometimes accompanied by a hostility (based on principle) to any measures imposed by the central government and by a fierce desire to defend the values and rights that reflect local tradition. Members of some political movements in Alberta or Saskatchewan have similarly denounced the most intrusive effects of the Charter of Rights and Freedoms, in a tone that Quebec nationalists would surely recognize. We must be careful, however. These alliances are just as fragile as they are ephemeral: resistance to Ottawa's centralism is accompanied by an almost instinctive resistance to any form of asymmetry from Quebec.

• We usually identify Pierre Elliott Trudeau and the Liberal Party of Canada with *centralized* federalism. We could add that this same approach is often associated with a fairly *symmetrical* view of the role and powers of the provinces. Although Pierre Trudeau's thinking seems much more nuanced to me, in fact, especially in the matter of symmetry, I have to concede that his pronouncements on the Meech Lake Accord contributed to this image.[7] As for the Liberal Party, the "Party of the Charter" as Paul Martin used to say, it seems to me to have, in these last few years, begun a kind of adjustment. Is this new direction lasting and sincere? Time will tell.

The Charter, in any case, is still a key element in the context of this discussion. It codifies and protects some individual rights that transcend local circumstances, as foreseen in Douglas Brown's definition of centralization. But it goes even farther: it gives new meaning to citizenship, and, as a result, even to the idea of a Canadian nation. There is no more need for shared history, and little reason for a flag or other national symbols: from 1982 on, apart from those obligations connected with the effective functioning of a "free and democratic society," Canadian citizenship became an individual matter. It became a kind of juridical blanket that covers and protects each person's varying and self-proclaimed cultural, religious or political preferences, whatever the mix.

Let me add that this approach could have accommodated the relatively wide-ranging powers for the provinces. Even held in check a bit by the Charter, the provinces would have been able to counterbalance the power of the central government, a little like the states in the American political system.[8] But this way of thinking has never been popular in Canada. The political elites have almost always seen the provinces as reactionary (Bill Bennett) or even oppressive (Maurice Duplessis), the government in Ottawa as the incarnation of enlightenment and progress. This is clearly a false premise: in Canada, as in all federations, the capacity for political innovation moves cyclically from one level of government to another. Indeed, rather than keeping the provinces' powers in check and limiting their manoeuvrability—the amendment formula of 1982!—we could have conceived of a model within which their role as "laboratories of democracy," as our American neighbours say, could be fully developed.

• The fourth model of federalism also reconciles, in Douglas Brown's words, *centralized* and *asymmetrical* views: the affirmation of individual rights and shared values, on the one side, and, on the other, the recognition that local dynamics, far from being threatening, can be fruitful. This is a challenging model. Reconciling individual motives and private interests with the norms of a particular community is not possible without negotiation and mutual accommodations. At the same time, it is not easy to make room for issues or responsibilities that are best shared. As was apparent, for example, in 2006, recognizing Quebec's specificity ran headlong into a Canadian reality that allows ethnic diversity only when it is woven into the fabric of a single nation. In fact, the balance between centralization and asymmetry is always unstable, even fleeting, because of competing interests, rival ambitions and differing opinions.

In a political culture as repelled by conflict as ours is—and there is no denying this is the case—finding this balance always involves a difficult choice. When Canadian political scientists

talk about intergovernmental relations, they regularly emphasize the collaboration, the co-operation, the harmony; rarely do
they dwell on the confrontations, the manipulations, the power
struggles that are inherent in federalism.[9] It is obviously a purely
theoretical illusion: as a federal system evolves, it inevitably
passes through tense periods during which the distribution of
powers and the rules of the game are renegotiated. The laborious
progress of the European Union, far from being all passionate
speeches and warm handshakes, should provide a measure of
comfort for those who worry about the slightest hiccup in relations between Ottawa and any of the provinces.[10]

One more word on this subject. One of the key aspects of the
administrative, political and social revolution that transformed
Quebec in the 1960s lies in the series of mutual concessions that
led to the creation of the Quebec Pension Plan, hospital insurance
and student loans. In all these cases, the obvious asymmetry was
adjusted to remain consistent with the fundamental tenets of federalism negotiated by the provinces and the central government:
shared values, a fair fiscal framework, guarantees in regard to
the transfer of benefits and clarity vis-à-vis the obligations of the
beneficiaries. It seems to me that this is a conclusive example that
deserves to be repeatedly recalled, a case where the operational
and political benefits of asymmetry can clearly be increased by
the judicious application of common principles towards the programs and the rights of the beneficiaries.

The Action démocratique was not wrong to force the question
of autonomy into the arena of public debate. I am not convinced
that Canada is a terribly centralized or symmetrical country:
even immigration policy or foreign policy are not purely matters
for the central government, which, by the way, plays a secondary
role in most areas of social policy. Nor do I feel that there is any
appetite in Quebec for a greater level of asymmetry in such areas

as criminal justice. Would we agree, for example, that the provinces could re-establish capital punishment, as thirty-eight out of the fifty American states have done since 1976? But the principle that shifts the burden of proof to those who want to increase the amount of centralization or symmetry within the federation is a good one, and it is similar in essence to the one that requires the sovereignists to demonstrate what would be gained by breaking the federal tie.

Federalism and Health Care

The health care field is a good example of how Canadian federalism works (or should work). In its present form, the health care system is based on a logic that is both strongly centralist and very asymmetrical. Centralization? Federal interventions have created expectations and, even indirectly, imposed certain rights on the provinces. Citizens know, for example, that access to care does not depend—or should not depend—on their financial situation. Fairly uniform standards about the quality of care apply across the country. (The federal government really has no influence in this particular area, but the programs it has promoted and supported have contributed to the development of identical institutions, which health care professionals in different provinces have set up in roughly the same way. Having visited all the provinces, I can confirm that nothing resembles a Canadian hospital so much as another Canadian hospital of the same size...) The underlying principle of redistribution that is inherent in a public health insurance system—shifting resources from the rich to give to the poor, and from the healthy to the ill—has benefited from the superior fiscal strength of the central government, especially during the early stages of the system.

But contrary to proposals and encouragement from many sides, including some of the experts, the system has never become a "national" system as in Great Britain or in France. Although the American health care system is renowned for its fragmentation, the public insurance scheme for the elderly, Medicare, is run in a more disciplined way than the Canadian health insurance system. Consistent with the division of responsibilities set out in the constitution, Canadian law recognizes and encourages provincial initiatives in the organization of care and the delivery of services. It does not limit the right of the provinces to modify their own approach to health care funding. However, it does require that a separation be maintained between contribution and use—that is, between what we pay for health care (either through taxes or premiums of various kinds) and the actual costs of the services we receive.

The package of publicly funded services varies from one province to another, aside from a core of predictable health care essentials. This is the reason that Quebec has its own universal system of drug insurance, which is provided in partnership with the private sector. We could cite numerous other examples. In fact, the experts like to say that the Canadian health care system is a simple juxtaposition of ten provincial systems, three territorial ones and three different federal plans for First Nations people, the armed forces and prisoners. It is as far from comprehensive as could possibly be imagined.

This asymmetry is at the same time beneficial and necessary. It is beneficial because it allows for innovation and initiative. The elements of the Canadian system were developed by individual provinces before being adopted nationally, including those two pillars of the system, hospital insurance and medicare, which originated in Saskatchewan.[11] And the provinces showed that they were able to learn from each other; innovations as important as the regionalization of health services spread across the country without the federal government or any other central or national organization playing a major role in this reform movement. Most of the time, it is true, the dissemination of these new systems required Ottawa's active support, primarily because of the central government's financial capacity but also because of the interaction of the different interest and opinion groups. In the 1950s and 1960s, it would have been hard to overcome the initial resistance of medical associations to the idea of a public system if the politics had been limited to the power structures within Quebec or Ontario.

It is also possible to show that asymmetry is necessary. The conditions that determine a population's state of health are local ones, which means crafting solutions tailored as closely as possible to the specific needs and resources of the community. In a country the size of Canada, it is easy to see that the conditions and the ways of life vary enough from one region to another to require different priorities. Human resources (the doctors or nurses) are not equally distributed either from one province to another or within a given region. Furthermore, in a modern health system we expect that citizens will have something to say about the organization and management of their health care services. We also expect that patients will provide feedback on the care they receive. In effect, the delivery of these services depends on a solid understanding of the local political culture—or even just the culture in general—because it is at this level that the expectations and rules that govern civic participation are decided.

The asymmetry of the Canadian system has generally served Quebecers well, and I do not believe I have ever heard anyone seriously suggest that we put the brakes on this approach. Elsewhere in the country, however, asymmetry is not entirely accepted.[12] When we are persuaded that we know the truth about something—an attitude that is unfortunately widespread among experts—we tend to view all other ideas as demonstrations of ignorance or as a resistance to change. As a result, Ottawa is often called upon to impose rules, standards and procedures with rigid sanctions attached. This process is typically constructive and positive. However, a certain measure of vigilance is required to both maintain the capacity to innovate and to prevent the risk of isolation to which asymmetry may give rise.

The arguments in favour of centralization always come up in a more difficult, more polarized context. This is partly the federal government's fault, because it is not always very adroit or very consistent in choosing its priorities. Health care matters have a great capacity to sway public opinion, and Ottawa often gives the impression that it is running from one problem to another, without any analysis other than occasional surveys and without any strategy other than a cheque book and a few generally accepted ideas.[13] The provinces often become a bit irritated in the face of all this dithering, each new proclamation of national objectives bringing with it new provincial obligations, at least moral ones. The recent offensive around wait times is a good illustration of the federal government's approach and the problems it generates. The campaign commitments of federal politicians on this issue do not make any sense unless they are taken up by the provinces, which inevitably give the impression of negotiating poorly and at the expense of average citizens on issues and standards they had not even considered to begin with.

A certain amount of centralization is necessary, however, for a few reasons. First, there are several classical arguments supporting this view. For example, some health care issues transcend provincial boundaries and cannot be dealt with by improvised solutions. The creation of the Public Health Agency of Canada after the SARS epidemic in 2003 is a perfect example of this thinking. Some matters also require substantial budgets and a critical mass of specialists and technicians. Drug testing and approval comes under this heading. In Europe, for example, countries have decided to respond to the financial and technological demands required for pharmaceutical innovation by setting up an increasingly large number of multinational organizations and agreements. Other health care issues are the result of structural or even natural inequalities, which arise from differences in demography or geography. In this case, a central government's powers of taxation and redistribution are indispensable tools for re-establishing a measure of fairness and correcting the most glaring discrepancies. Finally, certain aspects of health care dictate practical approaches. It is clear that Ottawa does a few things very well, from gathering and processing statistics to scientific and technical policy-making. In the past ten years, federal initiatives have radically revolutionized health research, by setting up world-class centres of excellence. Quebec has had to do nothing more than simply reap the benefits of these efforts.

And yet it is certainly possible to exaggerate the influence Ottawa can have. Even in the smallest provinces, the administration of health care does not depend on the federal government, which has neither the human and financial resources nor the juridical and administrative authority to control anything at all. In Quebec's case, it should be fairly clear that Ottawa usually plays a secondary role in the elaboration of public policy, which is developed on the basis of consensus among interest groups and experts in the province. When they do exist, Canadian national standards are the result of compromise among "partners" that do not always share the same values and that seldom have the same objectives. Do not be deceived on this point, however: if the partners agree to agree, even with much grumbling and accusations of meddling, it is because they have everything to gain. For the provinces, it is money, information and powers; for Ottawa, the vital recognition of its national role and its leadership.

The strength of federalism does not lie *only* in its capacity to accommodate differences. In the long term, as our knowledge

and our social and economic realities inevitably keep changing, it is useful to be able to compare the solutions of different
governments. Experience shows that lessons learned in one location spread effectively across a national framework. I would go
as far as to say that contemporary federalism is characterized by
the distribution and sharing of knowledge, and the comparative
evaluation of policies and public decisions. The Constitution Act,
1867 anticipated that there would be conflicts around the balance and divisions of power, and it established mechanisms such
as that absurd power of disallowance, which gave the federal
government the ability to strike down provincial laws. Today, the
reality is quite different: the norms and standards are born of endless negotiations in which knowledge is the principal tool. When
interest groups, even doctors or insurance companies, imagine
they can impose their wishes regarding health policy on the
nation, they have to present and debate their views in the public
arena. When governments want to change the rules, as Alberta
has several times proposed to do under Ralph Klein, they do not
rush off to Ottawa, they convene a large symposium.[14] Certainly,
as is the case with most federations, the Canadian federal government is often more conservative than the provinces, which is
frustrating to the innovators. But it is also more progressive than
the conservative provinces, so overall the system benefits citizens by protecting them from experiments that are risky or, at
least, not well thought out. In a political world in which a government's position changes frequently according to the time period
and the stakes, this balanced federalism has a global benefit.

Conversations about Reform

This dynamic that I have just been suggesting assumes that discussions about health system reform will be concerned with
issues other than just the distribution of powers. This is true not

only for Quebec. Throughout the country, there are people help-ing to redefine health care policies and programs with a primary focus on results, and with little or no concern for the old worries about jurisdictions and structures. And so there is a sort of wider community discussing cancer, and another, recently established one, talking about children's health.[15] Other communities are beginning to form—or are trying to do so—by bringing together groups and organizations in a given field, around a theme or a proposal. I am hesitant to think of them as coalitions, although they sometimes look and act like that. Fundamentally, they are "conversations" of a special kind, which allow participants to share their views on problems and solutions.

These conversations are important for two reasons. First, I think they will form the basis of a new program of reforms for the Canadian health care system. As I have already pointed out, so few were the advances made by the program of the 1990s, which was mostly focussed on structural change (management, agencies, boards), that it is not far from being considered a total failure. But reform is always pressing and not only for financial reasons. It continues to be essential to better integrate care sys-tems, to review the distribution of professional roles, to limit waste and errors in the delivery of services, to mediate the bal-ance between prevention and treatment, to reduce inequalities in health care. We have never wanted to face the difficult issue of rationing health care: is there a reasonable limit of care, beyond which everyone is on their own? Basically, to paraphrase Dr. Duncan Sinclair, the former chair of the Ontario Health Services Restructuring Commission, is it possible to conceive of a health care system that really operates as a... system? The participants in these national conversations on health care are obsessed with this question.

Second, it is indeed because these national conversations take place in a completely free atmosphere that they are fruitful.

Traditionally, the least departure from the (unwritten) rule that forbids turning to the private sector for health care has been met with all the open-mindedness that the Inquisition showed to the Cathars. However, as a part of these conversations some leaders in the struggle against cancer have been able to suggest—as much for reasons of social justice as compassion—the concrete and immediate possibility that *some* patients might pay for hospital services, without those leaders being immediately exiled or condemned as members of the extreme right. Other more technical and less emotionally charged debates are also taking place, characterized by this same freedom. Of course, this attitude is fed by the frustrations that the delays of the past decade have engendered, but also by the very nature of these professional communities. Instead of the traditional ceremony of the federal-provincial roundtables, in which protocol keeps most citizens except for a few hand-picked guests from participating, these dialogues are, on the whole, open to all interested groups and networks, in a sort of necessary pluralism.

This networking did not come about by chance. Those working in the fields of cancer, children's health and drug policy actively seek the support of every ally they can recruit: experts, charitable organizations, the private sector. And they stay in close contact with public institutions directly interested in their field, at the local and regional levels as well as at the provincial and federal ones. The last step is obtaining the participation of the public and achieving the democratization of health policy that will surely follow. Since health care priorities inevitably compete with other public priorities, it is essential that there be open debate on these matters and that the expectations and preferences of all citizens be fully understood. It is this next step that will undoubtedly determine the fate of this experiment. I should note here that, in this big picture that we have of health care today, policies on children's health or drug testing and approval reach far beyond the health care system, often extending into the fields of education or industrial policy. As a result, this is a debate that cannot limit itself purely to questions of provincial responsibility; it must involve a whole range of factors at every level of responsibility.

So where is Quebec in all this? Neither totally absent nor truly present, depending on the issues and the stakes. Jean Charest's government has stuck to the party line, which prevents any involvement in "national" health initiatives, in the name of respecting the boundaries of exclusive jurisdiction. In fact, there has been, all the same, a whole series of small events that indicate a kind of thaw, in matters ranging from public health to the processing of medical information, as well as drug policy and strategies for preventing and treating cancer. Discussions with the other provinces have increased too, and it is often suggested that the blatant similarities between measures adopted both by Quebec and by other provincial governments are perhaps not just a matter of chance. But, as in any kind of glasnost, what counts most is not what the officials agree to say or even to do but rather what the civil society decides to undertake. In this particular case, it is clear that the message is spreading and that individuals and groups are now taking part in more substantial and more readily apparent ways across the entire country. It remains to be seen whether we will know what to do with the benefits from these initiatives: new ideas, new alliances, new projects.

The Rules of Engagement

Conversations are still just conversations, and I am not so naïve as to think that is enough to effect real change on the health care scene. But this is an interesting dynamic to watch. It is helping to lend support to local experiences while using to best advantages the enormous possibilities in a system as powerfully asymmetrical as the Canadian one. In several of the instances I have referred to, shifts of this kind are leading to changes in the overall health care system more surely and sometimes more radically than some of those national projects that arose from compromises between the provinces and Ottawa over the past decade. The reaction of Philippe Couillard, Quebec's minister of health and social services, to the *Chaoulli* judgement, in which the Supreme Court overturned Quebec's ban on private medical service, could be a useful example here: instead of a radical overhaul of the rules of the game, he claimed, the answer lies in a more limited and well-defined arrangement, which clearly looks at a sector and identifies the particular problems within it. Other provinces are making similar decisions about access to medication, public health or the organization of front-line services. I think it can be shown that these policies are always the product of a long gestation period, during which an entire community has weighed and debated the different options—including, of course, options proposed in other provinces and even in other countries.

.Besides, the other useful aspect of these national debates is that they circulate information. In a federalism where authority is primarily based upon knowledge, not even established standards can withstand challenges based on fact. And this means that purely ideological or self-interested propositions have no chance of being imposed on anyone, *especially if they are limited to a single province*. Alberta, which was on such a path, soon backed down from private for-profit health care when it became impossible to find conclusive evidence that supported the measures announced by Premier Klein. As I have been insisting, perhaps a little too forcefully, the benefit of centralization lies in the political and juridical recognition of the expectations and rights of citizens, for there do exist some foolproof protections against ill-conceived initiatives. And not just in a single direction. These expectations and rights must also be subjected to the test of reality, including the presumption that every kind of care must be available unconditionally—whether or not its benefits are demonstrable and regardless of its consequences for the system in its entirety.

The policy of the empty chair had its own internal coherence. By limiting the exchange of information and the sharing of knowledge, by exercising a kind of control over ideas, we gave— and we gave ourselves—the impression that it was possible to have a completely autonomous health care system, separate from the standards and norms that prevailed elsewhere in Canada. This era has finally passed, but the new approach will have its own repercussions. I suggest we accept these with an open mind, without immediately crying foul about conquest or imperial federalism. On the one hand, the burden of proof will always fall to those who would like to limit our freedom to innovate and experiment. And on the other, it seems to me that we are now ready to defend our policy choices on the basis of fact and the best available knowledge. Those should be the only rules of engagement within the federation.

PIERRE-GERLIER FOREST *is President of the Trudeau Foundation, an independent and non-partisan foundation supporting advanced research in human and social sciences. He was Research Director for the Commission on the Future of the Health Care System in Canada (the Romanow Commission) and Chief Scientist at Health Canada.*

Notes

1. The report that formally established this conceptual and practical idea was published in 1974 as *A New Perspective on the Health of Canadians*. This report is known worldwide as the Lalonde Report and was named for the health minister at the time, Marc Lalonde.
2. The Canada Health Act establishes the conditions that the provinces and territories must respect in order to receive transfer payments from the federal government towards the cost of providing public health insurance.

The principles enshrined in this document are also embedded in the Quebec legislation, and Quebecers defend them with as much passion as citizens in other parts of the country. In Quebec, however, this federal legislation does not hold the same iconic status, and it is recognized primarily because it prohibits two long-standing practices: extra billing and user fees.

3. A well-documented example, about patient wait times, appears in one of the field's most respected scientific journals. See Sharon Willcox, Mary Seddon, Stephen Dunn, Rhiannon Tudor Edwards, Jim Pearse and Jack V. Tu, "Measuring and Reducing Waiting Times: A Cross-National Comparison of Strategies," *Health Affairs* 26 (July–August 2007), pp. 1078–1087.

4. Canada always scores well in surveys on the health of its population, with the scandalous exception of First Nations peoples. But this is only because we live in a more just, more egalitarian and more peaceful society than many of the countries with which we are being compared, the United States being one of them, of course. Let me repeat that health is in large part a product of social policy.

5. Douglas Brown, "Who's afraid of asymmetrical federalism?", speech given at "Asymmetrical Federalism: Is Reviving an Old Idea Good for Canada?", a symposium sponsored by the Royal Society of Canada, held at the Institute of Intergovernmental Relations, Queen's University, May 12, 2005.

6. Guy Laforest, "La génération post-souverainiste: pour Mario Dumont et l'ADQ, le résultat d'hier soir relève à proprement parler de l'exploit," *La Presse*, March 27, 2007. (translation)

7. The forthcoming biographies (by John English and Max and Monique Nemni) will perhaps identify the exact point at which Mr. Trudeau's thinking changed, but, for me, there is a difference in the Mr. Trudeau we knew *before* the Victoria Conference (1971) and the one we came to know *after*. The former wrote remarkable essays about the rights and responsibilities of the provinces; his indictment of fiscal imbalance still figures among the most brilliant analyses on the subject. The latter spoke of the equality of the provinces and the ability of the central government to fulfill all the obligations necessary for a democratic country. Moreover, after 1982, the question of the future of the Charter of Rights and Freedoms was addressed with a rare urgency. I sense in his words at the time of the Meech Lake and Charlottetown Accords a real anxiety that these agreements were tantamount to a full-scale assault on the fairness and widespread use of the Charter.

8. Pierre Trudeau suggested this idea in the 1960s: "But I add here that they might one day, as computerized planning becomes possible, constitute the primary bastion against the new despotism of a central government, either against its law and order or against its parliamentary bureaucracy." Pierre Elliott Trudeau, *Federalism and the French Canadians*, Toronto: Macmillan of Canada, 1968, p. 140.

9. To be fair, I would add that Professor Harvey Lazar, who developed this classic typology of intergovernmental relations (collaboration, co-operation, competition), has long disagreed with this propensity to hide the differences and the conflicts (personal interview).

10. André Pratte, "La longue marche de l'Europe," *La Presse*, July 16, 2007.

11. It is not completely accidental that the Commission on the Future of the Health Care System in Canada of 2000–2001 was chaired by Roy Romanow, a former premier of Saskatchewan. In Quebec, Mr. Romanow was best known for his role in the repatriation of the constitution, but elsewhere in Canada, no one could ignore the fact that he was the direct political heir of Tommy Douglas, the founder of the original public health insurance plan. The air of legitimacy that surrounded him served the commission well, as he was able to affirm his independence from Ottawa. This was, in fact, the first commission to be based away from the federal capital.

12. For more on this subject, see the article by an influential group of specialists from the University of Calgary published in the prestigious *British Medical Journal* in 2001 (Steven Lewis et al., "The Future of Health Care in Canada," BMJ, vol. 323, no. 7318 (October 20, 2001) pp. 926–929), in which they make the case for standardizing the Canadian system under Ottawa's direction. We cannot take for granted that asymmetry is an unchangeable and uncontested feature of our system.

13. During my four or so years in Ottawa after the Royal Commission, I saw the government become excited about, one after the other, drug policy, public health and wait times. Each time, the government claimed with conviction that it had found its role in the system.

14. The conference took place in May 2005 in Calgary at the instigation of Alberta's premier. The conference board published a summary of the presentations and the debates under the title *Unleashing Innovation in Health Systems: Alberta's Symposium on Health*, Ottawa, September 2005.

15. In 2006, Michael J. Prince published a brilliant article about the Canadian strategy on cancer and federalism. See Michael J. Prince, "A Cancer Control Strategy and Deliberative Federalism: Modernizing Health Care and Democratizing Intergovernmental Relations," *Canadian Public Administration*, vol. 49, no. 4 (December 2006), pp. 468–485. The issue of children's health was the subject of a pan-Canadian get-together in April 2007 organized by the Canadian Medical Association (see the proceedings at www.ourchildren. ca/summit.htm).

10

HERVÉ RIVET AND FABRICE RIVAULT

THE QUEBEC NATION

*From Informal Recognition to
Enshrinement in the Constitution*

From Denial to Recognition

The most recent saga of Quebec's place in the Canadian federation began on October 21, 2006, when the federal Liberals in Quebec passed by a vast majority a resolution recognizing the Quebec Nation[1] within Canada. This event, which many found outstanding, triggered an extensive debate across the country, which led the House of Commons to pass, a month later, a resolution by Prime Minister Stephen Harper recognizing the "Québécois nation" within a united Canada.

Of course, the federal Liberals were not the first to express themselves on the recognition of Quebec as a nation. The main provincial parties, the Bloc Québécois and the New Democratic Party (NDP), had already broached the question. All the same, the fact that the party of Pierre Trudeau and Jean Chrétien would propose such recognition was enough to set off a pan-Canadian debate that polarized public opinion for several weeks.

We had received the mandate to allow the Quebec wing of the party to renew its governing structure, its image and its vision. And indeed, following its crushing defeat in the general election of January 23, 2006, there was no doubt in our minds that the Liberal Party of Canada (LPC) absolutely had to renew certain aspects of its "Liberal catechism," which had become obsolete and somewhat disconnected from the Quebec population and indeed from the modern world.

As fate would have it, our consultations on renewing the Liberal vision continued until June 19, 2006, just a few days before Prime Minister Harper stumbled on the issue of the Quebec Nation. On the very eve of St. Jean-Baptiste Day (Quebec's National Day), Bloc Québécois leader Gilles Duceppe had the pleasure of backing Mr. Harper into a corner by asking if he was ready to formally recognize the Quebec Nation. Mr. Harper preferred to refer the question to the Quebec National Assembly and declared that the national identity issue was not the "real question" regarding Quebec politics.[2]

Taking advantage of the prime minister's obvious embarrassment, the candidates in the federal Liberal leadership race began to increase their public appearances and speak out in favour of recognizing Quebec's nation status. Michael Ignatieff was the first, immediately followed by Stéphane Dion and Bob Rae, right on St. Jean-Baptiste Day. One way or another, all the other candidates expressed their receptiveness to the recognition in principle.

Furthermore, during the candidates' debate held in Quebec City in September 2006, they all seemed to agree that Quebec and all its people do, indeed, constitute a nation within Canada. This apparent consensus encouraged the militant federal Liberals who wanted to pass a motion to this effect.

After much discussion and internal debate, the text they had drafted was passed by more than 80 per cent of the delegates to the Quebec Liberals' Special General Council. In the province, the resolution was very warmly received by the great majority of editorialists and columnists. But, in the rest of Canada, most of them disapproved of the party members' decision, believing that it went against the spirit of the Canadian federation. Using the same arguments heard during the debates over the Meech Lake and Charlottetown Accords, some federalist-centralists— from all political parties—once again wheeled out the whole conventional arsenal of tactics in an attempt to discredit such recognition.

It was in this turbulent atmosphere that Gilles Duceppe decided to take a miscalculated risk and propose to the House of Commons a motion demanding the recognition of the Quebec Nation[3]—a bluff that will certainly be remembered as one of the worst blunders of his political career. He especially underestimated the political flair of Prime Minister Harper and the potential for openness among the other federal parties. After being assured of the support of the interim Liberal Party leader Bill Graham and the NDP leader Jack Layton, Mr. Harper had the ingenuity and the pluck to cut the ground out from under the Bloquistes' feet and propose a motion with the same intent as the one the Quebec Liberals had passed, specifying that "the Québécois constitute a Nation within a united Canada." A few days later, Prime Minister Harper's motion passed in a historic vote, 266 to 16.

It is possible to suggest that this recognition of the Quebec Nation contributed to the feeble performance of the Parti Québécois during the general election in Quebec on March 26, 2007. The use that both the provincial Liberals and the Adéquistes (members of the Action démocratique du Québec) made of this recognition seems to at least suggest this. In fact, the latest polls show that Quebecers no longer believe that independence is a pressing issue, which suggests that they may be ready to give a renewed federalism another chance.[4]

For the first time in nearly twenty-five years, the federalists have again taken a leadership role on the question of Quebec's place in Canada and the thorny issue of Canadian unity. For the first time in a long time, it is not just a matter of reacting to attacks from the sovereignist movement but rather of acting in a proactive and constructive way. Finally, it has become possible to hope that this historic recognition, initiated by a few militants in the Quebec branch of the Liberal Party of Canada and adopted by Prime Minister Harper, will mark the start of a long dialogue between federalists and nationalists with the object of reaching a definitive reconciliation between Quebec and the rest of Canada. At last, we will be in a good position to tackle, together, the great challenges we will face in the course of the century to come.

What Is a Nation?

Throughout the debate over the Quebec Nation, the fiercest opponents of the idea positioned themselves as the defenders of an orthodoxy according to which Canada should never grant any recognition whatsoever to the special character of Quebec—a doctrine that grew out of the anti-nationalist philosophy that Pierre Trudeau was preaching in the 1960s and 1970s.

In our view, it is entirely legitimate to consider some aspects of "Trudeauism" with admiration and maybe even a touch of nostalgia. Mr. Trudeau was a visionary who did great things for Quebec and for Canada, there is no denying it. However, the former prime minister was not immune to making faux pas. Moreover, he alone did not embody the Liberal ideology. For instance, we have to remember that the former Liberal prime minister Lester B. Pearson stated, "While Quebec is a province in this national confederation, it is more than a province, because it is the heartland of a people: in a very real sense it is a nation within a nation."[5]

Faced with this dilemma of a dual nationality—Quebec and Canada—Liberal Party of Canada leader Stéphane Dion has always seemed a little ill at ease, a discomfort that does not seem to us to be justified. Mr. Dion is certainly right to emphasize that today's Quebec is a society that is open to the entire world, which implies a Quebec that is made up not only of French descendants.[6] The English-language version of Mr. Harper's motion on the Quebec Nation uses the word "Québécois" rather than "Quebecers." This term carries an ethnocultural connotation which, in the right time and place, will have to be corrected.

This said, we also feel that it could prove dangerous to try to promote debate around a definition of the Quebec Nation that is too specific. After all—and this is a good example—did the House of Commons ever need to explicitly spell out the idea of "a clear question" and "a clear majority" when it passed the Clarity Act?

Moreover, the word "nation" is quickly becoming a nightmare for anyone wanting to risk a universally workable definition. Canadian federalists may be on their way to discovering this. But Europe—the very cradle of nationalism—has given up, citing "the difficulty, indeed the impossibility, of giving a universally accepted definition of the concept of a nation."[7]

The United Nations recognizes some two hundred sovereign states, each of which has its own idea of the word "nation," consistent with its own language and sociocultural traditions. In some countries, the concept of "nation" has to do with citizenship, that is, the juridical connection between the state and a person, independent of that person's ethnocultural origins. In other countries, the word designates a specific community occupying a more or less well-defined territory, speaking a particular language, characterized by a series of cultural and historical traditions as well as by a shared concept of the past and shared aspirations. And finally, there are some countries where the two concepts are both used.

In other words, the term "nation" is deeply rooted in the culture of different peoples and built into the fundamental elements of their identity. It is closely tied to the political ideologies that have used it—and, unfortunately, have sometimes corrupted its original meaning. Furthermore, a concept like "nation" is often untranslatable in many countries where there exists only an approximation of the word. Conversely, the words used in one national language do not always find any adequate translation into the words of another national language—as seems to be the case in Canada.

Even though the term "nation" is commonly used by anglophones as a synonym for "sovereign state," it is a usage that serves the demagogic purposes of some people who are trying to scare Canadians by extinguishing any hope of national reconciliation with Quebec. It is the language of a past era, of a Canada and a Quebec that ceased to exist a quarter of a century ago. The reality of contemporary Canada is that Quebec shows all the traits of a non-state nation, like thousands of others that do not necessarily aspire to become nation-states. Spain and the United Kingdom are two examples of modern sovereign states within which different non-state nations cohabit; these are commonly called "nations"—or "constituent countries" in the United Kingdom or "autonomous communities" in Spain.

In Spain, Catalonia has just been granted nation status in the preamble of the Spanish constitution. It is an act that is more than just symbolic and is of enormous importance to a great many Catalans. In the United Kingdom, England, Wales, Scotland and Northern Ireland have been recognized as nations for decades now. Like Quebec, these nations have a rich collective history marked by a variety of challenges. Scotland and Catalonia were even sovereign states at different points in their history. And yet, today, the political autonomy that these two nations enjoy is a great deal more limited than that of Quebec within Canada.

In any case, these examples clearly show that it is entirely possible to think of a sovereign state as being composed of one or more non-state nations. However, before we adapt this model of "nations within a nation," Quebec and Canada will have to learn from these foreign experiences. These show us that, far from being an outdated notion, the quest for national recognition by peoples around the world is very much contemporary.

However, many still feel that the recognition of special status for Quebec, implied or stated, is a direct affront to the multicultural view of Canada that Pierre Trudeau proposed. It is easy for a Liberal to succumb to the charm of his vision of federalism. Indeed, this advocate of the just society, of a bilingual and multicultural Canada with a strong central government, was one of the main actors in the Quiet Revolution, a persuasive French Canadian, intelligent and charismatic. However, he also expressed a profoundly anti-nationalist sentiment, derived from those ethnocultural and separatist conflicts that raged in many places around the world during the second half of the twentieth century.

Federalists today owe it to themselves to look at Canada and the world around them with an open mind in order to draw conclusions about the present reality: Quebec is a different place than it was more than a quarter of a century ago. Quebec nationalism has changed too. Since the Quiet Revolution, it has evolved for the better, becoming, bit by bit, a moderate nationalism that is inclusive and open to the world. Evidence of this slow metamorphosis can be seen in the term "nationalist-federalist," which is being used more and more in reference not only to a growing number of francophone Quebec federalists but also to anglophones and allophones.

Let us not have any illusions! These "nationalist-federalists" are certainly proud Canadians. But they are also proud Quebecers who are not the least bit timid about claiming their dual allegiance, to both Quebec and Canada. Some Quebec anglophones are even wondering, and rightly so, why Mr. Harper's resolution does not yet also allow them to call themselves "Proud Quebecers." As for new immigrants, they see no contradiction between belonging to Quebec and to Canada, both of which they are proud to call home. And finally, more and more Quebec francophones doubt the relevance of the sovereignist approach and are ready to give the Canadian project another chance. It will be up to the next generation of federal leaders not to disappoint them.

In the meantime, those critics who suggest the Quebec Nation is a concept of the past could not be more mistaken. As the Quebec Minister of Intergovernmental Affairs, Benoît Pelletier, recently noted, "It is not the idea of Nation that is retrograde, it is the idea suggesting that it necessarily has to be sovereign."[8]

In this sense, it is entirely unjustified and even irresponsible to claim that the concept of "nation" is synonymous with "sovereign state," or even "sovereign-state-in-the-making." Those who use this logic to raise the spectre of Quebec sovereignty demonstrate little awareness of what modern Quebec is all about.

Contrary to the impression some might give, the "Canadian" recognition of the Quebec Nation is in no way a device for legitimizing the kind of radical nationalism that promises the utopia of an independent Quebec that is obsessed with itself. As stated by Canada's first prime minister, Sir John A. Macdonald, in 1856, "If we treat them [the people of Lower Canada] as a nation, they will behave as free people usually do, generously. Treat them as a faction and they will become factious."[9]

The burden of proof is thus going to be heavy for all those who see the recognition of the Quebec Nation as a Trojan horse that threatens the stability of Canadian unity. But those who favour a reconciliation between Canada and Quebec must also be united. They must demonstrate persuasiveness and perspicacity if they want to change the prejudices that some still hold, in the rest of Canada as well as in Quebec.

As long as we agree that when we use the word "nation" to describe Quebec, it is for its historic, sociological and civic importance rather than for any legal connotation equating Quebec with a sovereign state in the making, then we will never find ourselves facing the disasters feared by those who advance the anti-nation thesis. In other words, we must not allow ourselves to be paralyzed by our fears and our past mistakes. It is time to take the bull by the horns and continue building Canada with a fresh outlook and a positive attitude.

Towards the Enshrinement of the Quebec Nation

The recognition of Quebec as a nation was a first and essential step towards the reconciliation between Quebec and the rest of Canada. To this end, we can even hope that, one day, it will lead to the renewal of the constitutional agreement of 1982. That will depend in large part on the willingness of the key political players to drive the process towards the next step.

For more than half a century, Canadians have been bombarded with multiple visions of the special status of Quebec. As the years have passed, so too have the concepts used by each premier, from the *"maîtres chez nous"* (masters of our own home) of Liberal Jean Lesage, through the "equality or independence" of Union Nationalist Daniel Johnson and the "sovereignty-association" of René Lévesque and the Parti Québécois to the "distinct society" of Liberal Robert Bourassa. However, one thing is certain: the wish to recognize Quebec's unique character within Canada is deeply rooted in the psyche of Quebec society.

Which leads us to wonder whether the formal recognition of Quebec's special status in the Canadian constitution is actually necessary and whether it might not contradict the spirit of the Canadian federation as conceived by the founding fathers. Our federation is based on a pact among the different peoples who live on Canadian soil: the First Nations, the Acadians, the French Canadians, the English Canadians, and so on. This pact is the expression of a shared desire to unite, to live together and to prosper, while maintaining those features that are unique to each of the constituent sociopolitical entities.

As former United States president James Madison put it brilliantly in his eighteenth-century essay *Federalist Papers No. 51*, a federation is above all a sociopolitical structure that serves the sovereignty of its citizens.[10] In the case of a country like Canada, we can say that a system of "shared sovereignty" is implied, which allows some effective forces at both the provincial and federal level to maximize both the quality of life of the individuals who live there, as well as that of the whole collectivity.

In that same essay, James Madison also proposed the idea that this two-level system of government is characterized by a series of "checks and balances" that allow the different constituent parts to manage themselves in a way that avoids potential abuse by an overly centralized central power, or the tyranny of the majority over minorities. In sum, federalism should lead to the best protection for, as well as the flourishing of, minorities within a well-balanced structure.

In this perspective, we can say that the "special status" is not hostile to the federal spirit, quite the opposite. And even more so in the case of the Canadian federation, where the constituent nations, provinces and territories have different languages, religions, histories and legal systems.

Having said this, is it really necessary to explicitly recognize Quebec's special status in the Canadian constitution? If that is the case, how can we reconcile the recognition of the Quebec Nation with today's dominant vision of a Canada that is just, bilingual, multicultural and pluralist, as proposed by Pierre Trudeau in the Canadian Charter of Rights and Freedoms? And if such explicit recognition is not necessary, how can we deal with the wish of the signatories of the Constitution Act, 1867 to unite several peoples within the same federation so that they could work together for the common good and still maintain their individual characteristics?

Those who no longer fear the concept of the Quebec Nation but are still against enshrining this recognition in the Canadian constitution generally maintain that reopening the constitutional debate would be much too dangerous. In their eyes, the recognition of the Quebec Nation is undoubtedly desirable but certainly not necessary. Canada is a stable political system that works very well as it is;[11] why provoke false debates, they wonder.

We will not discuss here the feelings of bitterness and exclusion that many Quebecers still feel following the repatriation of the constitution in 1982 without the agreement of Quebec's National Assembly. All the same, if the epic of the Liberal resolution on the recognition of the Quebec Nation teaches us anything about Canada, it is that it is a somewhat unstable political system. Indeed, to the great displeasure of those who hold that "all is for the best in this best of worlds," it took only one short month for that Liberal recognition of Quebec—a simple sheet of paper!— to set off an unforeseen and irreversible political process that changed, in all probability, the history of Quebec and of Canada.

Let us admit it, it may not yet be the auspicious moment to rewrite our founding documents. But let us not fool ourselves. Eventually, our national reconciliation and the unity of the country must necessarily entail the enshrinement of the recognition of the Quebec Nation within the Canadian constitution. As the Quebec philosopher Michel Seymour put it, not so long ago, "The Canadian problem, we must remember, is not the Quebecers' refusal to recognize their Canadian civic identity, but Canada's refusal to recognize the Quebec nation. And this refusal constitutes a powerful argument in favour of Quebec's independence."[12]

One thing is certain, the need to see Quebec's special status recognized by Canada is deeply rooted among the great majority of Quebecers, of every political persuasion. No gesture or action by the federalist leaders over the last twenty-five years has managed to reduce or appease this need. Quite the opposite, the repatriation of the constitution, the failure of the Meech Lake and Charlottetown Accords, the narrow victory of the No side in the 1995 referendum on sovereignty and most recently the sponsorship scandal have instead undermined Canadian federalism in Quebec.

Of course, for some, there is always the House of Commons motion recognizing Quebec as a distinct society within Canada, which was adopted immediately after the 1995 referendum.[13] For others, there is also the Clarity Act that established the conditions under which the Government of Canada would enter into negotiations that might lead to *secession*. All the same, these actions are more reactions to the sovereignist threat rather than proactive and constructive proposals contributing to Canadian unity. Thanks to the unqualified recognition of Quebec as a nation, symbolic though it may be, the federal parties have finally returned with a new message of reconciliation, a new model, a new social project.

As we saw earlier, Canada is not the only state to be made up of several nations. With the Commons motion on the Quebec Nation, however, Canada proposes a new model to the world: a sovereign federal state that is bilingual, multicultural and "multi-national." Nothing in that model prevents the recognition of Quebec's special status from coexisting with the principle of a strong and egalitarian federation that favours the rights of the individual. Quite the opposite, we can say that such coexistence can only strengthen Canada, which could even become an example for other countries in the world whose nationalist tensions are more conflictual than our own.

Today, it has become an illusion to think that Quebecers will ever let go of this legitimate desire they have to see the special nature of their national identity recognized. With this in mind, every federalist of good faith who believes in a proud and strong Canada that includes a Quebec that is just as proud and strong should be working towards the permanent resolution of this dilemma, which for too long has threatened the stability of the country.

However, how do we move towards this end without repeating the failures of the past? More particularly, how do we convince Canadians that such an exercise constitutes not a threat to Canada but rather an act of reconciliation that will make it stronger?

First of all, it would be useful to recall that such a constitutional change does not require the unanimity of the provincial partners. The agreement of seven provinces representing 50 per cent of the population of Canada is enough to enshrine the recognition of the Quebec Nation into the constitution.[14] It goes without saying that the support of Quebec's National Assembly for this new agreement would be necessary in order to give it the required moral authority to bring about a definitive reconciliation. But as we will argue below, it would also be helpful to avoid putting this recognition of special status into a broader agreement that includes other matters—and which then would strongly risk requiring unanimity.

Once having accepted the fact that Quebec's special status should be constitutionalized, we will still have to work out the form this recognition should take. This is where the recent motion of the House of Commons becomes especially meaningful. Indeed, it raised the debate to another level, for the concept of the Quebec Nation is now part of the language of federal political discourse. Contrary to what some have said, it has become unthinkable to revert to being satisfied with "distinct society."

The term "Quebec Nation" should be retained because it expresses a historic, sociological and civic reality. And besides, the notion of "nation" is more inviting and inclusive and less threatening than "distinct society," which, from the beginning, had a divisive effect across the country.

Unlike "distinct society," the notion of "nation" is familiar and widely used. It can even be charted in a purely historic, sociological and civic sense. It offers no surprises, and very much reflects Quebec's reality within the Canadian federation.

As we have already noted, the modern Quebec Nation is inclusive and has nothing to do with the ethnic and retrograde nationalism that Pierre Trudeau opposed with so much passion. This concept has even led some of Mr. Trudeau's former colleagues, such as Marc Lalonde and Alf Apps, to say that the former prime minister would not have objected to the recognition of the Quebec Nation in either the historic, sociological or even civic sense of the word.[15]

Another substantial argument that Pierre Trudeau advanced against the idea of a "distinct society" had to do with the exclusivity it implied.[16] Could there be other "distinct societies" in Canada? With a term as vague as this, it is easy to anticipate a measure of discontent arising among the First Nations, the Acadians, the Newfoundlanders, and so on. If Quebec is a "distinct society," then what are they? Recognizing Quebecers' sense of belonging to the country as a whole must not, however, prevent similar recognition of the other nations that make up Canada.

As much as Quebecers do, members of the First Nations, the Acadians and even Newfoundlanders all have good reasons to affirm a particular national identity. Within this new model of "nations within a nation," the peaceful coexistence of all the partners in a united Canada inevitably has to start by accepting that our differences are not weaknesses but indeed are strengths. This acceptance particularly implies that all Canadians should recognize their differences while appreciating their similarities and their shared sense of belonging. All this fits perfectly with the ideal of a united, bilingual and multicultural society.

One of the biggest sources of disagreement in the debate over the "distinct society" clause had to do with the increased special powers and responsibilities that it bestowed upon the government of Quebec. More specifically, due to the principle of linguistic duality built in as a fundamental characteristic of both Quebec's and Canada's social structure, the National Assembly and the Quebec government saw themselves as having the responsibility for guarding and promoting the distinct character of Quebec. This looked like a backward step to a lot of Canadians, who saw it as the confirmation of two Canadas: a French Quebec versus the English rest of Canada (ROC).[17] This division, which is based on ethnolinguistic considerations, is markedly different from what the recent recognition of the Quebec Nation implies.

It is erroneous, if not dishonest, to claim that the backdrop of the debate over the Quebec Nation is a collision between the concepts of linguistic duality and bilingualism, two concepts that seem to some people to be diametrically opposed. The recognition of the Quebec Nation is in no way a declaration—even less so the promotion—of linguistic duality at the expense of bilingualism. Bilingualism is a source of pride in Canada, and it is here to stay. Recognizing the Quebec Nation has more to do with a historic, sociological and civic reality that is agreed upon by all Quebecers. In no way does it call for or promote differentiation based upon language or ethnicity.

The Canada of tomorrow will never again be what it was in the past, namely a country built upon two nations with two languages and two cultures. Pierre Trudeau was right to believe in a pluralist and cosmopolitan Canada. However, contrary to what some still think, the flourishing of Quebec's principal language is altogether compatible with bilingualism and multiculturalism. The coexistence of these two principles—reinforcing and developing the French language in Quebec while maintaining Canadian bilingualism—only makes Quebec as well as all of Canada both stronger and richer in human and cultural capital. After all, today's Quebec is made up of people who have come from all over the world to be part of the shared values and traditions of Quebec and of Canada.

Does the formal recognition of the Quebec Nation grant supplementary powers or additional responsibilities to the National Assembly and the Quebec government? In our view, it would be dangerous to repeat the mistakes of the past by linking Quebec's special status to a series of further demands. The recognition of the Quebec Nation is above all a symbolic act of national reconciliation. In this respect, and contrary to what the sovereignists want, it must not be accompanied by other demands, for the simple reason that it is not negotiable. Either it is offered in good faith or it will be acquired with determination, but in no way can it be bargained for.

Understood in this sense, the recognition of the Quebec Nation is just a stepping stone towards eventually reopening the constitutional debate. If there is going to be such a reopening, it is only once this premise—Quebec's recognition as a nation—is clearly agreed upon that all the other issues can be addressed within the framework of respectful negotiations among equal partners.

A Strong Central Government

Once the special status of Quebec is recognized, if there is going to be a debate on the reorganization of the distribution of jurisdictions, then it is imperative to maintain a fair balance between the powers of the central government and those of the provinces. Too much centralization would suffocate local initiatives, and too much decentralization would substantially risk weakening the Canadian federation. In other words, there has to be an equilibrium between the two levels in such a way as to allow the central government to guarantee common standards and citizenship rights for everyone across the country, as well as shared values.

A strong Canada needs a strong central government because of its vast territory and the great diversity of its population. The federal government has the particular responsibility to look out for the interests of the Canadian collectivity as a whole, more than simply to defend an amalgam of ten provinces or varying regional interests. Of course, the federal government must have the necessary tools with which to defend the integrity of its territory, to support and promote national commerce, to build lasting and high-quality pan-Canadian infrastructures, to encourage common standards of citizenship and to guarantee, at the federal level, respect for the Canadian Charter of Rights and Freedoms.

Ironically, Canada is already recognized globally as one of the most decentralized of all federations. Accordingly, it seems difficult to make the case that even greater decentralization is needed in order to better serve the interests of Canadians throughout the country. In fact, one could argue that greater decentralization would bring about more regionalization and, consequently, a marked dilution of our shared Canadian values as well as a growing disparity of wealth and of the public services available to all Canadians. In such a Canada, the less well-off provinces—such as Quebec—might well see their human capital quietly slipping off towards the richer provinces. In short, an exodus of brains, youth, capital, and so on.

Our opinion is that it is a duty of the Canadian government to ensure the continued existence of basic services all over the country, both in terms of accessibility and quality. To achieve this essential goal, the federal government needs some "special powers," such as the powers of reserve and of spending that are given it by the preamble to section 91 of the Constitution Act, 1867.

Clearly, it is also perfectly legitimate to examine the possibility of limiting the central government's spending power in the provinces' exclusive areas of jurisdiction, of developing a flexible recovery formula with full financial compensation subject— or not—to precise standards or conditions, such as respect for national priorities. This kind of change is all the more appropriate in our era, given that the provinces are subject to strong financial pressures resulting from their particular constitutional responsibilities.

We must also bear in mind that these pressures may be temporary. As such we should not arbitrarily restrain the federal government's spending power to the point of emasculating, briefly or over the long term, its capacity to meet its responsibilities, especially to guarantee common standards and values for every region in Canada.

In a flexible and open federal system, this kind of debate is demonstrably very healthy and should be welcomed. Whatever its conclusions, we have to recognize that Quebec has already seen its autonomy reinforced much more than an overall constitutional agreement ("a package deal") would ever have accomplished—without the need for any constitutional amendments—thanks to the numerous adjustments negotiated between the Quebec and Canadian governments over the last half century.

Over and above the delegation of wider powers, which led, for example, to the creation of Quebec's own department of revenue or to Quebec's enlarged role in the admission of immigrants as a result of the Canada-Quebec Accord of 1991—under which Quebec alone is responsible for "the number of immigrants destined to Quebec and the selection, reception and integration of those immigrants." Also, in the last few years, Quebec has made some important advances in its relationship with the federal government. We can think particularly of the following: the Labour Market Development Agreement (1997); the Health Agreements of 2000 and 2004; the Agreement on Early Learning and Child Care (2005); the agreement regarding Quebec's seat at the United Nations Educational, Scientific and Cultural Organization (UNESCO) (2006); and then the Agreement on Fiscal Imbalance (2007).

The 2004 Health Agreement between the governments of Paul Martin and Jean Charest is particularly important because it also ratified the concept of "asymmetrical federalism," former premier Robert Bourassa's old dream of a federal system that would be flexible, adjustable and respectful of each member's different priorities, thus allowing a federal policy to be put into effect differently from one province to another.

These examples demonstrate that Canadian-style flexible federalism, whether it is called "asymmetrical" or "open," works very well when it comes to serving the interests of Quebecers and other Canadians. The various gains that Quebec has made over the past fifty years show how a constitutional agreement that is global, static and frozen in time would probably not serve Quebec's long-term interests as well as a renewed and flexible federal system.

Dialogue: The Way of the Future

During the next discussions on Quebec's place in Canada, it goes without saying that it will be absolutely vital to avoid stale confrontations. Debates can generate disagreements that are not necessarily destructive as such, because they can also allow us to better understand ourselves and to move forward. Above all, we have to maintain a positive and a constructive attitude.

Without question, the official recognition of Quebec's specificity can come about only in an atmosphere of confidence, good faith and dialogue. If our recent experience with the Liberal Party of Canada reveals anything, it is that the whole question of Quebec's special status is charged with emotion and can quickly go off the rails.

Fortunately, now that the House of Commons has adopted a motion recognizing the Québécois Nation, the groundwork has been laid for a return to the larger discussion on Quebec's specificity and its place in Canada. The symbolic aspect of this recognition, so decried by the sovereignists, should not be trivialized. Indeed, in terms of history, this motion represents a major move forward for all Canadians and Quebecers. On the political front, it also offers a measure of reassurance to the federalist leaders, who are in the driver's seat for the first time in a long time.

It is up to us now to show inventiveness and to avoid the mistakes of the past—the futile and emotional internal wrangling—and to act with integrity so as not to divide public opinion over personal pride or for purely electoral purposes. It is an exercise that is easier to describe than to execute, of course, but does Canada deserve any less?

In the short term, perhaps the House of Commons motion will give some strategic advantage to the federalist forces over the sovereignist movement. However, it also places the burden of moving on to the next step squarely on the shoulders of these same federalists.

In order to pave the way for future success on both sides in the next round of constitutional discussions, it is vital that we reflect upon what this recognition brings in the short term. We must explore the long-term benefits. We must also take advantage of this new climate of peace and openness towards Quebec nationalism, and pursue, together, this constantly evolving dialogue on the modernization of Canada.

In this perspective, it becomes imperative that our political leaders, federal and provincial, across Canada, exorcise the demons of the past and shore up their support for our common cause: the consolidation of our country. They must not hesitate to question their own beliefs in order to find, together, a well-thought-out alternative to the status quo, not only for the coming years but for the coming generations.

This debate could be highly charged. In our view, however, it is healthy and essential. The country's unity will come out of it stronger, and we will be in better shape to meet the great challenges of the twenty-first century, such as the aging of the population, global warming, the effects of globalization and the peaceful settlement of armed conflict around the world.

This dialogue among Canadians should start without delay. Like tiny sparks, they will feed the debate and thus promote an even greater understanding of the concept of a Quebec Nation.

We advocate a consensual and constructive approach whose aim is not an upheaval but rather "a very quiet revolution," a prudent and pedagogical initiative with solid, long-term results. It is a recipe that some may consider simplistic. But let it not fool you: it requires rigour, discipline and above all patience.

A number of signs suggest that this move towards more dialogue has already begun: the House of Commons has passed a motion recognizing the "Québécois nation"; editorialists and columnists across Canada continue to write about the idea and its short-, medium- and long-term consequences; universities are already holding conferences to discuss its impact on Quebec, Canada and the world. The debate has started and the dialogue is well under way.

Like an old married couple that is recultivating its relationship after years of living together, happily but also with some conjugal quarrelling, Quebec and the rest of Canada have to start "flirting" with each other again, in order to rekindle the flame of unity. But like a young couple that is still getting to know each other, they cannot rush things. As was the case with the "fight against the deficit," Canadians will come around to the idea when they begin to feel at ease with the concept of the Quebec Nation.

It is still too soon for us to undertake large-scale initiatives such as the Royal Commission on Bilingualism and Biculturalism (the Laurendeau-Dunton Commission), the Task Force on Canadian Unity (the Pépin-Robarts Commission) and, most recently, the 1991 joint committee on constitutional amendment (the Beaudoin-Edwards Committee), which was struck after the Meech Lake setback. It is an even less appropriate time to hold constitutional conferences like the ones in Victoria in 1971, at Meech Lake in 1987 or in Charlottetown in 1992.

The political will is not there yet. Moreover, Canadians do not have much more appetite for the kind of politico-juridical melodramas that have nearly cost them their country a few times already. Nevertheless, this should not stand in the way of beginning a dialogue, a discussion, a constructive statement of hopes and concerns that goes beyond the traditional question of "What does Quebec want?"

If we are patient, this exchange of views is a more moderate approach—and realistically the only valid option—that allows us to believe we will reach a solution that is mutually beneficial to Quebec and the other provinces and territories in Canada.

In this way, we can hope that, a decade from now, a new generation of Canadians and Quebecers will tackle the question of

Quebec's place in Canada with an open mind and a new outlook. It is also possible to hope that time will have healed old wounds, so that a new generation of political leaders, unmarked by past experiences and present beliefs, will emerge. Only then will we be ready to launch a new initiative with the aim of enshrining in the constitution the official recognition of the Quebec Nation within a more united and stronger Canada.

A consultant in public affairs, HERVÉ RIVET *was executive director of the Liberal Party of Canada in Quebec from 2004 to 2007. He has worked in federal politics for more than ten years, notably as chief of staff for the Honourable Yvon Charbonneau and legislative assistant to the Honourable Lucienne Robillard.*

FABRICE RIVAULT *is a consultant and project manager in communications strategy. He has worked in the national office of the Liberal Party of Canada and was that party's Quebec Director of Communications and Policy until March 2007.*

Notes

1. In this chapter, we use the term "Quebec Nation" to refer to both the Québécois's and Quebecers' nation, that is to say to Quebec and all its population.

2. Antoine Robitaille, "Harper dit non à la nation québécoise," *Le Devoir,* June 24, 2006.

3. Joël-Denis Bellavance, "Le Bloc sauté dans la mêlée," *La Presse,* November 1, 2006.

4. Hugo de Grandpré, "L'option souverainiste serait en regression," *La Presse,* June 23, 2007.

5. Lester B. Pearson, "Allocution au congrès de l'Association des hebdomadaires de langue française du Canada," Bibliothèque du Parlement, August 17, 1963.

6. Radio-Canada, "Nation québécoise: Stéphane Dion revient à la charge," June 24, 2007.

7. Council of Europe, Parliamentary Assembly, Recommendation 1735: The concept of "nation" (2006). See also www.assembly.coe.int/Main.asp?link=/ Documents/AdoptedText/ta06/EREC1735.htm (accessed May 27, 2008).

8. Radio-Canada, "Nation québécoise: Un débat d'actualité, pour l'avenir," November 3, 2006. (translation)

9. John E. Trent, *Trying to Understand Distinct Society,* Ottawa: University of Ottawa Press, 1997, p. 14. Donald Creighton, *John A. Macdonald: The Young Politician,* Toronto: The MacMillan Company of Canada Ltd., 1952.

10. James Madison, "The Structure of the Government Must Furnish the Proper Checks and Balances Between the Different Departments," *New York Packet,* February 8, 1788.

11. Chantal Hébert, "Ignatieff contre Rae et Dion," *Le Devoir,* September 18, 2007.

12. Michel Seymour, *La Nation en question,* Montreal: Editions L'Hexagone, 1999. (translation)

13. The wording of the agreement presented by Prime Minister Jean Chrétien was the following: That Whereas the people of Quebec have expressed the desire for recognition of Quebec's distinct society; 1) the House recognize that Quebec is a distinct society within Canada; 2) the House recognize that Quebec's distinct society includes its French-speaking majority, unique culture and civil law tradition; 3) the House undertake to be guided by this reality; 4) the House encourage all components of the legislative and executive branches of government to take note of this recognition and be guided in their conduct accordingly. Parliament of Canada, *Journals,* no. 267, Government Orders, Government Business no. 26, Wednesday, November 29, 1995.

14. Article 38(1) of the Constitution Act, 1982. It is also necessary to take into account the regional vetoes accorded in *Constitutional Amendments,* L.C. 1996, c. 1, par. 1(1), which outlines that "no Minister of the Crown shall propose a motion for a resolution to authorize an amendment to the Constitution of Canada" unless it "has first been consented to" by the provinces representing five regions (Atlantic Canada, Quebec, Ontario, the Prairies and British Columbia).

15. Joan Bryden, "Aide says Pierre Trudeau would have supported Ignatieff's position on Quebec," *Canadian Press,* November 22, 2006.

16. Donald Johnston and Pierre Trudeau, *Pierre Trudeau Speaks Out on Meech Lake,* Toronto: General Paperbacks, 1990, p. 73 and following.

17. *Ibid.*

11

MARC GARNEAU

FIRST, LET US UNDERSTAND EACH OTHER

I AM VERY PROUD to be Canadian. And that is not surprising. On my father's side I have deep roots in Quebec, and on my mother's side my ancestors come from New Brunswick and Nova Scotia. My paternal grandfather fought for Canada during the Great War, and my father did the same during the Second World War. I have had the honour of serving in the Canadian Navy to defend my country and flying into space to represent Canada at the planetary level.

No one should be surprised to learn, then, that I believe in Canada and that I think of it as an exceptional country. Our forerunners tamed an often inhospitable land, adapted to an extremely harsh climate and overcame huge distances in order to build the impressive country we live in today. Since then, we have declared the primacy of the rights of the individual in our Charter. We have dispatched our soldiers to foreign lands to defend the freedoms that we cherish. We have made our diplomatic voice heard in international conflicts. Indeed, we can be proud of our accomplishments in building a great country and playing a significant role on the international stage, contributions that have sometimes cost us dearly. Our political structure has allowed us to achieve these gains.

All my life, I have believed that the provinces and territories can work best within a federation that evolves over time and within which the benefits are mutual. Thus, the federal government deals with certain matters, such as national defence or fisheries and oceans, that are important for all the provinces and territories but best handled at the national level. At the same time, Ottawa undertakes to maintain a kind of "economic equality" from one end of the country to the other by redistributing some of the nation's wealth to the less prosperous regions. The provincial and territorial governments manage certain other sectors as they see fit, to accommodate the particular needs of their own citizens. Finally, the responsibility for a third category of concerns, such as the environment and natural resources, is shared between the two levels of government. This symbiosis can be very beneficial for everyone, but it requires a spirit of co-operation and compromise in which each partner is prepared to contribute to the common good. Finding that balance is not always easy.

The sovereignists dream of an independent Quebec. My own dream is of a united Canada that works well. Our country came into being four hundred years ago, and despite the many difficulties encountered throughout its history, it has become an exemplary democracy. Personally, I believe in Canada and I do not want to see anyone spoil this great success story. And on a purely practical level, there are simply more advantages in being big than in being small, especially when it comes to our economic prosperity and our social security net.

In the past decade, I have spent a lot of time thinking about my identity and reflecting on my role in this federation. It has taken me some time to become fully aware of this fact, but today I am proud to identify as much with Quebec as I do with Canada. For many years I never felt the need to declare this feeling of dual identity. My pride in being Canadian probably won out a bit over my pride in being a Quebecer. I certainly loved Quebec and I appreciated being able to live and work in that province. But what counted most was my Canadian heritage. Moreover, I have to admit that the increasing violence of the Front de Libération du Québec during the sixties led me to reject any kind of Quebec nationalism, even its most moderate forms.

I have never felt oppressed in this country. Even during the years of polemical debates about Quebec sovereignty that took place while I was at university, I have never shared the hatred some of my fellow students felt. One of them went so far as to call me a "sellout" because I hung around with anglophones as well as with my francophone friends. The fact is that I have lived seventeen years of my life abroad and several years in Canadian provinces other than Quebec. So it is no surprise that my perspective is at the level of the whole country and that my attitude is more open than the insular view of those who live in isolation.

When I ran as a candidate for the Liberal Party of Canada in Vaudreuil-Soulanges in 2005, a reporter asked me if I would still be able to live in Quebec if the referendum on sovereignty returned a Yes vote. I responded in the negative, without hesitation. Although I would not answer in the same way today, this reaction is a good example of my thinking at that time of my life. These days, I am committed to staying in Quebec, and I will always do whatever I can to make sure Quebec continues to play its essential role in Canada.

To be a political candidate in an election in Quebec is a visceral experience. One exposes oneself, but there is great potential to grow if one takes the trouble to listen, to read and to question assumptions. The most important thing I learned in my "kitchen-table" discussions, my door-to-door conversations and my face-to-face sessions (sometimes during very highly charged exchanges) was that many Quebecers, without being sovereignists, have bit by bit turned their backs on Canada because they are hurt by the lack of recognition the rest of Canada has for Quebec, with the sad result that they identify less and less with federalism.

It was only during this election that I began to fully understand this deep sense of Quebec nationalism—a nationalism that is strongly anchored in Quebec's history, that is fiercely proud without being reactionary and that does not necessarily mean separation. I have to add that my frequent meetings with sovereignists were very important in this context, since they allowed me to better understand the whole spectrum of opinion that exists in Quebec. One positions oneself better when one knows where the extremes are.

I now know that many fervent federalists are also genuine nationalists, and I am proud to count myself among them. But I also realize that many nationalists need to be convinced of the merits of federalism. Unfortunately, the debate on Quebec's place in Canada has taken on a more acrimonious tone since the very mitigated success of the repatriation of the constitution in 1982. Not surprisingly, the sovereignists exploited this historic event to attract disillusioned nationalists who no longer saw such great value in a united Canada and who were unimpressed by its defenders, who were entirely unable to reconcile the concepts of nationalism and federalism.

Today, federalism and Quebec nationalism do not seem to me to be contradictory. Impassioned by the claims of both camps, I am proud to be both a Quebecer and a Canadian. Moreover, if there is, in the rest of Canada, one common misunderstanding about Quebec nationalism, it is the idea that a nationalist is a sovereignist, or, at best, an individual who exploits the fear of sovereignty in order to obtain better deals for Quebec. In my experience, this is definitely not the case with most nationalists. For many Quebecers, the nationalist sentiment is just an expression of their pride in their identity, the affirmation of a social and historical reality, the desire that it be recognized as such and respected. It is important for those who mistrust Quebec nationalism to clearly understand this fact.

A Difficult and Unacceptable State of Affairs

However, it is clear that Canada, this great country so admired by others, is not running as smoothly as it should be. Canada still has not succeeded in escaping the threat of separation, indeed of being dismantled. So it is imperative that we ask what it is that continues to strain the relations between Quebec and the rest of the country.

On the one hand, during the past twenty years and despite cyclical fluctuations, surveys indicate that about 40 per cent of Quebecers feel little or no pride in Canada. Having forgotten the historical contribution and the pioneer spirit of their French Canadian ancestors, they remain huddled behind their provincial borders, their backs turned to the rest of Canada—including other francophone Canadians.

On the other hand, most Canadians simply will not accept that Quebecers should be treated differently from any other citizens of the country. They believe that to do so violates the idea of fairness that says we should all be treated as equals and that no group deserves special treatment, a typically Canadian approach that I recognize very well because, until quite recently, I thought that way myself. However, this is a point of view that escapes a lot of Quebecers.

Without laying blame on anyone, we have to agree that this current situation is difficult and unacceptable. The tensions that exist between Quebec and the rest of Canada will persist unless we agree to a major effort to better accommodate our differences. The other option is a complete breakup. Our growth as a country will always be hampered by our inability to work constructively together.

So what has to be done to reset our course towards a more promising future?

The provincial election of March 26, 2007, ended with both good and bad news. The good news was that about two thirds of Quebecers had voted for parties that claim to oppose separation (the Liberals and the Action démocratique). The bad news was that about two thirds of Quebecers had voted for parties that believe Canada owes them something without requiring anything in return (the Parti Québécois and the Action démocratique).

This result is not all that surprising when we bear in mind that, since the start of the Quiet Revolution, the Quebec government has never stopped making demands and it has generally obtained what it was seeking. In my view, our current situation should be seen as positive and, in the long term, good for Canada. That is, significant demands have been met, and after more than forty years of hard work, failures and successes, Quebec has shed its inferiority complex. Nowadays, the province is confident and largely manages its own affairs. So where is the problem?

Unfortunately, being in the habit of always making demands leads the giving reflexes to atrophy. As a result, many Quebecers no longer see federalism as a two-way street. The emergence of the Action démocratique du Québec is revealing in this respect. We are in the presence of a party that threatens the Parti Québécois without showing any sign of a strong attachment to Canadian federalism.

The idea that the province benefits from federalism and that as a result it has some obligations to the rest of Canada is almost never raised in Quebec. And yet, would it not be a breath of fresh air to hear a Quebec government say out loud that the province derives some important advantages from its participation in the Canadian federation!

For too long in Quebec, "federalism" has seemed to be a word to avoid—or at least to utter only in a hushed voice. This silence has to stop! Today there is a pressing need to clearly demonstrate the value and the strengths of federalism and to present them simply and objectively so that Quebecers understand without a doubt that Canada is the best future choice for Quebec.

Independence and the Unidentified Flying Objects

Sovereignists do not rely primarily on ideas and policies to sell independence, though both the Parti Québécois and the Bloc Québécois have shown some ability in this field. Their appeal is fundamentally emotional, an approach that repeatedly calls up the yoke of oppression and the threat of the extinction of the Quebec culture. The sovereignists carefully cultivate the mentality of the French Canadian martyr and glorify those historic moments when they were humiliated at the hands of their English "masters."

This appeal to the emotions of the electorate has been very effective up to now. But Quebecers are beginning to realize that there is nothing constructive about such an approach. It deliberately cultivates a sense of inferiority that has nothing to do with the reality of today's Quebec. It is time, then, to counter this argument, to show the rest of the country that many Quebec nationalists are ready to move on to other matters and work towards Canada's growth and development. They must simply be convinced that this is the best road to take.

Of course, Quebecers who want separation at any cost are not going to be dissuaded from this goal by reason. Some would be ready to accept the heavy sacrifices that attaining independence would demand. As for the vast majority, however, I think they simply do not realize the real economic consequences of separation.

This refusal to accept any rational explanation and to take an objective look at the arguments against Quebec's sovereignty may perhaps lead some of my detractors to accuse me of intimidation or of digression. During the last election, some of them even had fun suggesting that I go back out into space... But joking aside, this willing blindness does make me think of all those people who believe in unidentified flying objects (UFOs). It is exciting to imagine there might be extraterrestrials whose society is sufficiently advanced that they could come to visit us from time to time. But until there is proof to the contrary, this idea belongs quite simply to the realm of science fiction. And yet, no argument will ever dissuade those who believe UFOs are real. Some are so convinced they even go so far as to accuse the scientists who contradict them of being part of a conspiracy!

Like it or not, I am well and truly a Quebecer! A Quebecer who lives in Quebec and is profoundly convinced that Quebec's future is to be found within Canada and not outside of it.

A Messy Divorce

It is not hard to show that Quebec gains a lot from belonging to the federation. All the same, even though the specialists agree on the evidence, the Parti Québécois has only to claim that Quebecers would be better off if they kept all their money in Quebec, and this assertion is swallowed hook, line and sinker by the sovereignists. The reason is simple: that is exactly what they want to hear. When we believe in a dream, we have a tendency not to stumble over the facts. Quite the opposite, we are often outraged by anyone who dares present these facts as evidence of another view.

Two other reasons may explain why many sovereignists are taken with this illusion that life would be rosy in a sovereign Quebec. Both are connected to a lack of understanding about the real impact of separation. First, many sovereignists point out only the advantages of independence without looking objectively at the many disadvantages. Of course, it is only human to act in this way when passionately committed to a cause. But it is dangerous too, for in refusing to weigh the disadvantages we leave out an important part of reality—with the certainty that it will catch up to us sooner or later.

For example, many sovereignists still believe that if Quebec becomes independent, the rest of Canada will somehow still be there—connected to Quebec by an invisible umbilical cord—rather than being an autonomous and sovereign country as the United States is in relation to Canada today. Indeed, it is difficult to imagine a situation that has never been clearly defined by the *indépendantistes*. Since Quebecers have been exposed to several concepts, such as pure independence, sovereignty-association and national affirmation, it is not surprising to see them a bit confused. They are having a hard time assessing the real consequences of sovereignty, not only for their day-to-day lives but also for Quebec and for the rest of Canada.

Personally, I believe that if independence became a reality it would resemble a messy divorce. The idea of a friendly separation is terribly naïve. The reason is very simple: each side has so much to lose that a civilized approach is not realistic. After a divorce, both partners find themselves worse off. That is the sad reality. Divorce negotiations can start out in a spirit of civility, but that phase does not last. How could it be any different when Canada is torn apart and Quebec realizes what it has just lost?

The second reason has to do with the famous five years of turbulence that Parti Québécois leader Pauline Marois has said we should anticipate after Quebec's separation. Remember the virulent reaction of the sovereignist camp when she had the audacity to say that? In my view, Madame Marois's forecast is optimistic! I believe the turbulence would last between ten and twenty years.

Certainly, forty years ago, Quebec's demands were legitimate. But today we can no longer claim that Quebec is unfairly treated by the rest of the country. It could even be said that Quebec's language and culture would not be better protected in a sovereign Quebec. Take Bill 101, an instrument that was conceived for the protection of the French language and the Quebec culture. Most agree that this law has value and recognize its legitimacy. In my experience as the former president of the Canadian Space Agency, a federal agency located in Quebec, I also believe that the Canadian government's policy on official languages represents a big step in the right direction. In a united Canada, these two laws powerfully contribute to the cause of the French language in North America, even though in some *exceptional and isolated* cases, they can cause some difficulties.

But following a divorce, would the French fact be better served? No. And why not? Because this objective has already been met! We could not go any farther without impinging on the rights of the individual, isolating all Quebecers, provoking more emigration, depriving ourselves of the potential offered by people who do not speak French and damaging our business and other relationships with the rest of the world.

The comedian Yvon Deschamps recently declared himself once more to be an *indépendantiste*, explaining that he fears the disappearance of Quebec's culture. We could legitimately ask whether Mr. Deschamps has noticed the profound changes that have taken place in Quebec since 1960. Quebec culture would not be better protected in a sovereign Quebec than it is already within the Canadian federation. How can the sovereignists still believe this antiquated argument when Quebec's culture is clearly so vibrant?

Of course, not everything is perfect. But today, Quebec no longer has a huge long list of demands. Even if the sovereignists are out hunting for new arguments to bolster their cause, most of these are weak or even laughable. The leaders of the independence movement have been forced to bring out their ultimate weapon: the emotional appeal of sovereignty to create a country in which they are the only "masters in our own house." Do they not see that this approach cultivates a deep sense of inferiority among Quebecers? The truth is that Quebecers are already largely the masters in their own house. We are self-confident and we are not looking for excuses.

Questions Without Answers

Picture for a moment this new independent country: a Quebec with a population of almost eight million inhabitants, of whom slightly more than half would have voted for sovereignty. A Quebec that is proud of its identity but also aware that there are a great many challenges still to be met, not unlike those facing a Canada newly without Quebec. Has the sovereignist camp explained to us in detail and with any measure of credibility just how a sovereign Quebec would be more prosperous outside of Canada? Have they described specifically how they would govern this country? Apart from a few general statements whose lack of rigour lays them open to criticism, the answer to each of my questions is no. We know why: credible responses would spread doubt about the value of separation.

Why do Quebecers not insist on such explanations?

How could an independent Quebec count on internal harmony, knowing that almost half of Quebecers had voted against sovereignty?

How would we compensate for the loss of revenue coming from the rest of Canada, given that Quebec, under the present arrangement, is a province that receives more than it gives?

How would a sovereign Quebec meet the growing economic challenge of an aging population, a challenge that exists everywhere in Canada and will not magically disappear whether Quebec is independent or not? A recent Quebec study entitled *Oser choisir maintenant*[1] (Dare to Choose Now) describes a future that will be difficult unless the province begins right now either to cut programs or to increase taxes. The most optimistic scenario forecasts a deficit of more than fifty billion dollars in 2050 if no changes are made in the short term.

How would an independent Quebec go about countering the effects of globalization, including the absorption of Quebec and Canadian companies by international conglomerates and the loss of jobs to developing countries—one more challenge that Canada is already facing as a whole?

Would a sovereign Quebec, already Canada's most indebted province, continue to champion unreasonably low costs for electricity, for post-secondary education and for child care? Policies like these work against responsible financial management and would be even more unrealistic without a continual flow of federal funds.

What would be the foreign policy of a sovereign Quebec vis-à-vis the United States? Although our neighbour to the south has no say in the matter of our sovereignty, we can be sure that the United States would prefer to deal with one rather than two countries on its northern border. The government of Quebec would have to negotiate agreements on North American security (a priority issue for our neighbour), on international trade, on aviation and maritime policy, and plenty of others. Would that mean the creation of a Quebec armed forces? All indications suggest the *indépendantistes* would like to create such forces (at a considerable cost) in order to affirm Quebec sovereignty. What kind of influence would an independent Quebec realistically have within the North Atlantic Treaty Organization (NATO) and the North American Aerospace Defense Command (NORAD)?

There is room for the idea that the electorate is beginning to understand the dimensions of these challenges, which might explain the results of the March 26, 2007 election, in which a great many Quebecers decided that the Action démocratique approach, which proposes a larger measure of autonomy without separation (that is, the illusion of being able to have your cake and eat it too), was more attractive than separation itself.

A Lack of Understanding

It is one thing to hammer away at the negative effects of separation (effects which, let us be clear, would be just as detrimental for the rest of Canada), but it is a completely different matter to advance positive arguments that would make federalism more attractive to the skeptics. I am not just referring here to Quebecers, but also to certain other Canadians who are frankly exasperated with the secessionists' threats and who are increasingly raising doubts about the value-added that Quebec's presence within Confederation allegedly brings.

I travel the country a lot and I listen to what Canadians in the other provinces have to say about Quebec. Among those who do not hesitate to express themselves, the well of sympathy for Quebec is just about dry. The dominant view is this: Quebecers never stop demanding more while taking advantage of the attention they receive from federal politicians, especially at election time. After all, here is a province with its own federal party dedicated to sovereignty. Here is a province that receives substantial sums of money from the federal government, and indirectly from the other provinces, and still keeps asking for more. Here is a continually dissatisfied province.

Those who complain this fervently are in the minority, but it is a more and more exasperated minority. For obvious reasons, this frustration is more openly expressed in the richer provinces, which feel they are subsidizing a province of ingrates.

The outraged remark made by a Saskatchewan government minister after the 2007 federal budget could be the most eloquent example of this frustration. In the minister's view, Ottawa was merely the transit point for the transfer of his own province's wealth to Quebec to pay for the tax reduction that Premier Charest was in such a hurry to announce. It was of little consolation to the minister that other provincial governments have done the same in the past.

Thus, some provincial politicians are less and less hesitant to express their anger against Quebec. In some cases, this outcry is just a way to advance their province's own interests. Sometimes, however, they sincerely feel that Quebec is receiving preferential treatment from the federal government.

Between English Canada and francophone Quebec there exists a real lack of understanding. The reason is simple: as Canadians, we just do not know each other very well and we seem in no hurry to change this. Although this gulf results mostly from a closed attitude, a lack of interest and an absence of good will, in some cases it springs from pure apathy. If this lack of understanding continues, we will keep on advancing new federalist formulas—whether openness, asymmetry or centralization—without ever moving forward. The success of Canadian federalism depends above all upon good will on the part of all the players, who, a priori, must see themselves as members of the same team. That is, unfortunately, not always the case at the moment.

In sum, we are facing a serious problem with only two possible outcomes:

1) to learn to know each other better, which demands a lot of work on both sides; or 2) to allow the gap to become even wider.

Governments can undoubtedly help us begin to know each other better. In the end, though, it is each one of us that must make the effort.

In my view, the following steps are necessary:

1) Quebecers who have already turned their backs on Canada must take the time to objectively re-evaluate what federalism has to offer, and therefore what they risk losing if they renounce it. More than anything, this means that every single person must make the effort to become informed, impartially, so as to be able to distinguish between what is true and what is false. Each person must insist that their elected representatives, on both sides of the debate, provide enough information to enable a well-reasoned decision. After that, each person must ponder the facts and make their own choice. Politicians must rise to the challenge of communicating clearly and honestly with the public.

Quebecers have to insist that the politicians of the sovereignist parties provide in-depth explanations as to the modus operandi of an independent Quebec. At the same time, they must push the proponents of federalism to provide proof, as well as clear and specific explanations, of the advantages of that option.

2) In September 2006, I wrote a piece for the *Globe and Mail*[2] in which I argued that it is not possible to fully understand Quebec if all the sources (newspapers, television, radio, Internet) are in English. It is essential that English Canadians seek out French-language reports in order to understand what Quebecers are thinking. This argument is as valid in the other direction: Quebecers should be reading and listening to English Canadian media if they really want to understand the rest of their country.

Canadians who believe that Quebec does not deserve special treatment within Canada should study the history of Canada, to better familiarize themselves with Quebec and its culture. They should remember that alongside the First Nations and the Acadians and the first Newfoundlanders, Quebec *was* Canada for the first century and a half of its history. In the context of globalization, they should understand francophone Quebecers' preoccupation with their language, their culture and their identity. But beyond all that, they should accept that Quebecers' desire to be recognized as *different* does not mean a desire to be treated *better* than the rest of Canadians.

3) English Canada should quickly and unreservedly condemn the malicious remarks made by certain anglophone commentators towards Quebecers and French Canadians. At the same time, in order to help discredit those who show such prejudice, Quebecers have to resist the temptation to play the martyr when such inane comments are expressed. Reason must always prevail over emotion.

4) Although it is, of course, necessary to better explain the economic arguments that favour federalism, Quebecers must also be given other arguments that support remaining in Canada.

During the last federal election campaign, I said that if Bloc Québécois leader Gilles Duceppe and then–Parti Québécois leader André Boisclair could join me on the space shuttle and see Canada in all its glory, they would certainly never want to destroy our country. I soon realized that expressing this idea in the middle of an electoral campaign was naïve (even if it has always been well received by the general public when I invite our leaders, in a different context, to make this same trip in order to promote a greater harmony around the world).

This incident taught me two things: 1) that it is important to speak carefully in the political arena because comments can easily be taken out of context and 2) that hard-and-fast separatists feel no attachment to Canada whatsoever. The appeal for unity will always resonate with Quebecers who also think of themselves as

Canadians but find no support among the sovereignists. Steadfast sovereignists do not have nightmares about losing the Rocky Mountains or the Great Lakes. They have no difficulty sleeping at night knowing that Quebec's independence would tear the rest of the country in two. They do not even try to seriously imagine what the potential effects of dismantling Canada might mean for Quebec over the longer term.

What I have concluded from all this is that the only arguments that have any chance of being listened to are practical ones. The economic advantages alone should be sufficient, but there are many other strong arguments as well.

Science and Technology: A Critical Issue

I can certainly demonstrate the merits of federalism in my own field of expertise, namely science and technology (s&t). It is a field in which I have worked throughout my career and which I understand well. Even if s&t is only one issue among other equally important ones, it is crucial for the economic and social future of Canada, and thus, by that fact alone, for the future of Quebec.

Right now, Quebec is benefiting from a very large number of federal programs that support scientific research and the development of new technologies. At the same time, Quebecers contribute to the financing of these programs through their federal taxes. What would change if Quebec became an independent country?

For the sake of comparison, let us look at the United States. Our relationship with our neighbour is generally very good. We also have to acknowledge, however, that in s&t we are adversaries or—more politely—competitors. We are in competition with each other because, wherever there is the potential for commercial applications, it is the "everyone for themselves" theme that wins out. The relationship between a sovereign Quebec and the rest of Canada would take the same form as the one we have now with our neighbours to the south: we would become rivals, caught up in competition.

Every year, federal S&T programs grant billions of dollars to universities, hospitals and research institutions across Canada.[3] Suppose that at the time of a hypothetical Yes vote on sovereignty, Quebec was receiving its fair share of this financing; and suppose, too, that Quebec continued to support such programs—or maybe other targeted programs requiring similar investment— then the financial impact on S&T programs of independence would be minimal, though there would be extra management costs because of some job duplication.

However, and this is more serious, there would be far less exchange of information between Quebec researchers and those in the rest of Canada. Make no mistake; those exchanges are of great scientific value. Worse, we would inevitably see some Quebec researchers going off to Canada or to other countries. The size of that exodus is impossible to gauge, but its impact could be considerable.

The Canadian government also finances the development of new technologies; for instance, in the aerospace industry in Quebec. Given that half of the Canadian aerospace sector is housed on Quebec land, the impact of the disappearance of such programs from a sovereign Quebec could be considerable. In fact, in this field Quebec receives more than an equal share of federal funds, for strategic reasons. We should also note that the aerospace industry in Quebec has clearly benefited from certain political decisions over the years. To name just one example: the contract awarded in 1986 to Canadair, a Montreal-based company, for the maintenance of the CF-18s, even though the tender from Bristol Aerospace in Winnipeg was judged by a panel of government experts to be more advantageous. This decision still rankles Manitobans today.

We also have to look at the principal federal organizations in Quebec that co-ordinate certain essential scientific research programs. Fifteen such organizations exist across the province, including the Canadian Meteorological Centre in Dorval, the Canadian Space Agency in St. Hubert and Defence Research and Development Canada in Valcartier. These establishments and many others would certainly be closing their doors if Quebec became independent. Why would the Canadian government continue to finance research centres in another country?

So the Quebec government would find itself with some unused and immovable infrastructure, but what about the scientists, technicians and support staff who used to work in these buildings? And what about the Quebec manufacturing and service industries that benefited from the presence of these federal organizations? Some scientists would leave Quebec when their laboratories closed, if, lacking the financial resources, the government of an independent Quebec gave up supporting these research centres. This possibility would be even more likely if, as it would seem logical to do, the Canadian government decided to relocate these same laboratories to other provinces. Other scientists would leave simply by choice. It is certain that, even in the research centres that the Quebec government decided to keep going, there would be an upheaval among the scientific staff. We could call this a temporary situation, but the transition period, here too, could stretch to ten or twenty years.

The financial impact could also be substantial as a result of certain decisions made by Quebec. Take defence research, for example. Would the government of a sovereign Quebec want to equip itself with armed forces, and would this decision include a parallel decision to maintain a defence research centre? Other examples: within a new financial structure, would the Quebec government want to create its own National Research Council? Its own Space Agency?

Some businesses in Quebec now, Canadian or multinational, benefit enormously from—when they are not totally dependent upon—the presence of these federal institutions. The Canadian Space Agency, for example. If the government of a sovereign Quebec decided not to finance such an agency, a large part of the space industry would certainly move to Canada. In contrast, if the Quebec government did decide to maintain a space agency, it would probably be of a modest size and of a lesser scope than the one that currently exists in Quebec. A space program requires a considerable budget, and countries the size of Quebec can manage only modest programs in this field... if they can manage one at all.

Quebecers in Space

Countries that have set up a space program consider it an important example of their technological maturity. In addition to such leaders in space research as the United States, Russia and Europe, countries like China, India and Brazil are undertaking some very ambitious space-related projects. So a space program, beyond its strategic, economic and social dimensions, has great symbolic importance.

I am raising this point because I know that the Canadian space program is a matter of pride for *all* Canadians. After more than twenty years promoting this program, I can attest to the fact that Quebecers share this pride, all the more so since the Canadian Space Agency is so well established in Quebec.

Our successes in the field of space research are remarkable. Canada was the third country to launch a satellite into space, with the flight of Alouette 1 in 1962, the first to use its own national domestic communications satellite (Anik AI, in 1972), the first to build an operational radar satellite for observing Earth (Radarsat-1, in 1995), the first to build a robot arm (the Canadarm, first used in space in 1981) as well as being a space pioneer in several other scientific and technological areas. So Quebecers have good reason to take pride in the long list of advanced technologies developed by the space sector in Quebec and admired around the world. And I would even dare to say that some are proud that Quebecers have gone into space.

Getting Rid of Prejudices

The solutions proposed here deal more with eliminating the mutual misunderstandings among Canadians than with the issue of which federal model is most likely to effectively serve Quebec and the rest of Canada. Eventually we are going to have to agree on a flexible and modern approach that acknowledges the special nature of a Quebec that is fully engaged within a dynamic federalism. But to get there, we must first understand and mutually respect each other.

Canadian federalism is certainly not perfect. It can and should be better. Whether it be "open," "asymmetrical" or "centralized," we must not shy away from debating the issues that will allow us to arrive at a realistic consensus over the course of the twenty-first century. Whatever formula we come up with, we will, in any case, have to shed our old prejudices and our jaded attitudes. For various reasons, some provinces want more autonomy whereas other less prosperous ones worry about being left behind. The form of confederation we choose will have to take into account all of these differing needs.

After forty years of productive change in Quebec, we have to realize that the debate on sovereignty has become stale, carried on by aging dreamers who have invested a good part of their lives trying to persuade their fellow citizens that independence is necessary at any price, in order to preserve the French language, culture and way of life. Moreover, this handful of devotees has already shown itself to be very good at the job, distorting Quebec's politics and history in order to carry forward this dream of a better world, especially among our youth.

The truth is that the language, culture and way of life of francophone Quebecers will never be as secure as they are now inside of Canada. As well, today's Quebecers possess all the confidence they need to rebuff the seductive isolationist rhetoric of the sovereignists. Therefore the time is right to re-evaluate Canadian federalism, to prove its worth for Quebec.

MARC GARNEAU *was the first Canadian to go into space (1984, 1996, 2000). He was president of the Canadian Space Agency from 2001 to 2005. In the 2006 federal election, he ran as a candidate for the Liberal Party of Canada.*

Notes

1. Luc Godbout, Pierre Fortin, Matthieu Arseneau and Suzie St. Cerny, *Oser choisir maintenant: Des pistes de solution pour protéger les services publics et assurer l'équité entre les generations,* Quebec: Les Presses de l'Université Laval, 2007.

2. Marc Garneau, "My views have changed: Recognize Quebec as a Nation," *The Globe and Mail,* September 16, 2006, p. A15.

3. The organizations responsible for granting and managing these funds include the Natural Sciences and Engineering Research Council of Canada (NSERC), the Canadian Institutes of Health Research (CIHR), the Social Sciences and Humanities Research Council of Canada (SSHRC), Genome Canada, the Canada Foundation for Innovation (CFI), Canada Research Chairs (CRC), the Indirect Cost Program (ICP) and the Networks of Centres of Excellence (NCE).

12

MATHIEU LABERGE[1]

A COUNTRY FOR MY GENERATION

Towards a Canada 3.0

PATRIE *(Homeland): noun [Latin patria] Political community of individuals living on the same land and connected by a feeling of belonging to the same collectivity (especially cultural and linguistic); a country inhabited by such a community.*

PATRIOT: *adjective and noun [Greek patrios] One who loves his country, who tries hard to serve it.*[2]

MUCH HAS been written about "the children of Bill 101," those young people born since 1977 who have never known Quebec without the extra language protection brought to them by that law, the work of Quebec premier René Lévesque's first government. We often look on the Charter of the French Language as one of the most significant pieces of legislation in contemporary Quebec history. However, the changes it brought about do not seem to be reflected very much in our political debates.

Now as before, the various Quebec political parties never stop demanding ever-greater powers, especially in the name of protecting Quebec culture. And still today, the debate is polarized between federalists who want more autonomy and sovereignists who are waiting for the "Big Night" when Quebec will finally achieve sovereignty from Canada. To the point where sometimes I ask myself, "Where are those Quebec federalists who believe in Canada, not just to demand new powers but also to contribute to building this country?"

If there is one generation that can be the incarnation of change, because its political life evolved within a radically different Canada, it is certainly the one of the children of Bill 101. Now that the Charter of the French Language has celebrated its thirtieth year, and the generation born with it is entering its thirties and beginning to see what its political role will be, maybe it is time to spell out how this generation is so different. This political generation—made up of the children of Bill 101—is my generation.

A GENERATION THAT IS PROUD OF ITS DUAL IDENTITY

We understand generational differences in voting preferences quite well, but pollsters only rarely broaden their surveys beyond current political questions. So the analysis of generational difference remains largely based on impressions rather than on facts. However, in June 2007 the firm Skidmore, Owings and Merrill (SOM)[3] polled Quebecers about their attachment to Canada, to Quebec and to their respective symbols. And it appears that young people aged 18 to 35, roughly the children of Bill 101, have an outlook that is fundamentally different from their parents' when it comes to their feelings towards Canada.

More than half of young Quebecers between the ages of 25 and 34 recognize themselves when playwright and film director

Robert Lepage says he feels "Québécois in Quebec and Canadian abroad."[4] Among the 18 to 24 year olds this percentage drops slightly, to 45.7 per cent. But they still call themselves Canadians in significantly larger numbers than their elders do. Responding to the same question, less than one third of the 45 to 64 year olds said that they would identify themselves as Canadians first when travelling abroad.

Young Quebecers are not only more likely to call themselves Canadians but are similarly more attached to Canadian symbols than their elders are. More than four out of five of those between the ages of 25 and 34 said they were either "very proud" or "fairly proud" of their Canadian passports when they were travelling outside the country. Among the 18 to 24 year olds, that feeling of pride climbed to 91.1 per cent of respondents. For comparison's sake, only a little more than three quarters of the baby boomers gave similar answers.

So, contrary to the popular assumption that has greater numbers of young people identifying with the sovereignist idea, the poll suggests they feel at least as much pride as, if not more than, their elders in being both Canadians and Quebecers. I also have the feeling—and the survey seems to support this—that my generation is less reluctant to talk about its attachment to Canada and its symbols than was my parents' generation. It is as if, from now on, we are allowing ourselves to affirm our dual identity loudly and clearly: we are Quebecers within Canada. As if this unspoken identity, formerly seen as a sign of ambivalence, has now become a source of pride.

And because our political existence makes us more ready to conciliate and to assume our identity as both Quebecers and Canadians, our generation is the one that has the power to change the Canadian political dynamic, on a long-term basis and beyond what has been done in the past. It is the leaders of our generation who will have the best tools to offer a sound response to proposals and criticisms coming from the rest of Canada, avoiding de facto the kowtowing that took place until the mid-1960s but also steering clear of the stage management that has replaced it. Comfortable growing up in a global environment, these new leaders will be able to break from the navel-gazing that has been so common in Quebec for many years and look outwards and help Quebec make the most of its assets. In short, my generation has the ability to lead Quebec from its role as the official opposition of Canada towards an active role in defining and building it in the future.

THREE FOUNDING MOMENTS

If we pause to review the outstanding political events since the birth of those young people who turned thirty in 2007, we can identify three founding moments that had a real impact on their understanding of the political dynamic of Quebec within Canada: the adoption of the Charter of the French Language, the shift of power from Ontario and Quebec towards Western Canada and the emergence of flexible federalism. When we look closely, we can see that these three events have had a lasting effect.

For both the most committed sovereignists as well as those who want to maintain the existing political order, it will be easy, after reading the following paragraphs, to assert that young people lack the necessary historical awareness to understand actual political games. We can always cite situations that have been overlooked or exaggerate the importance of marginal events. But that would be going down the wrong path. The reality is that even knowing exactly the same history, two observers of contemporary political realities will draw radically different conclusions, given their interpretation of historical events and their respective life experiences. I could never read today's historical events through my father's or grandfather's lenses, because my life experience has been too different.

The Charter of the French Language

In 1977, before I was born, the Charter of the French Language was passed by the new Parti Québécois government. René Lévesque had come to power less than a year before, and the political atmosphere was highly charged: for the first time ever, a secessionist party was in office in the National Assembly. Among the first pieces of legislation introduced by the new government, Bill 101 was intended to entrench the rights of the francophone majority and become the centrepiece of a political and social program that has left a permanent mark on Quebec's political world. The first referendum on sovereignty was at hand. Having just been born, those first children of Bill 101 could not have known that this was their first founding moment.

Today's thirty year olds—and those of us who followed—never knew the time when downtown Montreal was plastered with English signs. Similarly, we have never been served in English at Eaton's, and some of us do not even know that this store once existed! Any more than we knew first-hand the ferocious struggles for the emancipation and recognition of the rights of francophones. Instead, we have lived in a Quebec where French is recognized as the language of public exchange and where the rights of francophones are guaranteed. The Quebec we know is free of confrontation between the anglophone and francophone communities, apart from a few passing squabbles over language that, to our eyes, look more like anachronisms than real conflicts between the two groups. The harmonious coexistence of Quebec's francophones and anglophones in this new generation is such that the Canadian rock group Arcade Fire, which has been successful around the world, was founded in Montreal and made up of musicians who originally came from Greater Montreal, of course, plus Toronto, Guelph and Texas!

And so why does this absence of conflict and of the awareness of tough historical times constitute a founding political moment for my generation? Clearly, this shift makes all the difference between the baby boomers and my generation in terms of our perception of the political stakes. My parents always saw the French language as the principal embodiment of Quebec specificity, probably because of that sense of urgency they felt to protect and defend their language. After all, Quebec is the main francophone community in North America, a French enclave in an Anglo-Saxon world. In the absence of any effective legislative protection even on Quebec territory, the battle in defence of the French language became a major political issue. And that justified a whole collection of measures in favour of francophones in Canada, such as the historic alternation between francophones and anglophones in certain strategically important jobs. When these kinds of measures do not exist, it is still a kind of reflex for people of my parents' generation to demand them.

In short, the French language became, over the years, a distinct trait that seemed to justify demands for more favourable treatment for Quebecers. The absence of protection for French plus the generally defensive attitude of Quebecers had the effect of polarizing Canada. For those who knew Quebec before the Charter of the French Language, there always was, and there still is, "them"—the Canadians of the rest of Canada—and "us"—Quebecers. Quebec's whole political strategy is still aimed at preserving that delicate balance between "them" and "us" and, if possible, gaining still a little bit more for the Quebec side.

Having never known the urgent need to protect the French language the way my elders did, my generation cannot have the same outlook. That sense of urgency is no longer as omnipresent. Even if most thirty year olds love the French language and want it to be protected so that it will endure, we do not believe it to be in such imminent danger. Some of us now feel those measures intended to ensure positions for Quebecers in federal institutions actually hamper the full development and recognition of Quebec rather than contributing to the province's political and social self-affirmation. What is the point of favouring a francophone at the expense of hiring a more able candidate? To say nothing of how measures that give preference to Quebecers over English Canadians are going to set off some resentment among our neighbours... and with good reason!

The same thinking applies to Quebec culture. Over the last few decades, Quebec has had much cultural success internationally. Le Cirque du Soleil puts up its big top all over the planet and even has an entry in some dictionaries. Denys Arcand's films have seduced the Cannes Festival. Robert Lepage's stage plays have become a synonym for international success. Luc Plamondon is the author of some of the best-known song lyrics and Céline Dion is still a resounding international success story. Far from endangering the development of Quebec culture, globalization has in fact contributed to a new feeling of confidence among people of my generation. English is no longer seen as a symbol of colonial oppression but rather as an indispensable tool in our daily working lives. Our culture has become Quebec's business card on the world stage.

Our parents fought for the survival of Quebec's culture; it is now our duty to secure its progress. And although Quebec's cultural ambassadors do not need anyone to hold them by the hand, Quebec still needs to develop new talents who will continue to carry our reputation beyond our own borders. I am in no way minimizing the importance of the struggle of those who have come before us, but we have to admit that by concentrating all our energies on our past achievements, we risk losing the opportunity to build new ones. Now we have to affirm, and not just defend, the international role of Quebec's culture and the French language.

French—and even more importantly our culture—are still the most defining characteristics of Quebecers, there is no doubt about that. This is not to say that these are superior traits or that Quebecers can justifiably claim preferential treatment at the expense of other Canadians. My generation has less difficulty accepting that Quebec be considered on an equal footing with the other provinces rather than being put on a kind of pedestal.

In fact, the perception of the debate around the recognition of Quebec as a distinct society is taking an entirely different shape. Whereas the debate used to focus on Quebec's exclusive character, this exclusivity is no longer a prerequisite for the younger generations. If Quebec does constitute a distinct entity within Canada, other groups have distinctive characteristics that are equally valid. And although giving special status to another province or another group used to be seen as questioning Quebec's special status, it is now simply a recognition of contemporary Canadian reality.

There is a second difference in the point of view between Quebecers aged 45 to 64 and those 18 to 34, regarding the adoption of the Charter of the French Language. The former, having lived through the bitter political and juridical fights that surrounded the Supreme Court's ruling on Bill 101, consider its survival as a triumph wrested with great difficulty from federal institutions. Some sovereignists still claim that the Charter was mangled by the courts. But unlike our parents and our grandparents, my generation has never lived without Bill 101. As a result, even though we know about its adoption and the battles that followed, we did not witness these ourselves. We know only what has been told to us, more or less skillfully, by those who had a stake in the debates. Several people—and I am one of them—now see the Charter of the French Language as demonstrating our ability to defend Quebec culture and the French language within the Canadian constitutional context. The fact is that it achieved the purposes for which it was put forward.

It has already been said: French is now recognized as the official public language of Quebec, and the francophone face of Quebec has been well preserved. Whatever trivial exceptions we might find, the reality is that any tourist landing in Montreal—for that is the ground on which the core "linguistic battle" is being fought—will have no doubt that the language in everyday use in Quebec is French. And we have to admit that the most recent declines in the use of French by newcomers is the result of provincial policies adopted in Quebec City. It was, for example, the government of Quebec that closed the doors of the Centres for the Orientation and Education of Immigrants.[5] We cannot blame Ottawa for some odious policy that our own politicians came up with! As far as I am concerned, the adoption of Bill 101 and the realization of its fundamental objectives amount to a Canadian federal achievement in terms of recognizing and accommodating provincial particularities. As I see it, it demonstrates the flexibility of the Canadian system, even before the days of asymmetry and openness!

The Shifting Centres of Influence

It is an undeniable fact that, since the end of the 1990s, Western Canada has become an increasingly dynamic economic centre in Canada. This region attracts more labour than any other, regularly sees its share of investment increase and, consequently, watches its overall wealth grow.

The evolution of provincial shares in investment is a good illustration of the way our economic activity has been sliding towards Alberta and British Columbia at the expense of Quebec and Ontario. Whereas Quebec and Ontario were attracting 53.4 per cent of the country's private investment in 2001, by 2006 they were receiving only 47.3 per cent, a drop of more than six points in five years. Meanwhile Alberta and British Columbia saw their share of private investment climb from 33.7 per cent in 2001 to 40.9 per cent in 2006, a rise of more than seven points over the same period. What is especially interesting is that the other provinces' shares barely changed. And the picture is essentially the same when you look at the distribution of public investments.

The balance of migration has changed along with this: labour has begun to leave central Canada for the West. From 2002 to 2006, British Columbia received a total of 19,024 immigrants from other parts of Canada; Alberta, 161,929. In the same period, Quebec lost 25,800 inhabitants to other provinces; Ontario, 58,939. In fact, British Columbia and Alberta are the only provinces to have had an inflow of immigrants from the other provinces between 2002 and 2006. And, although less striking than the above figures, the growth of gross domestic product and business starts since the beginning of the century supports this picture of a shift of Canadian economic activity from the centre to the west.[6]

This displacement of the centres of power towards the west is primarily an economic phenomenon. Nonetheless, it will have a serious impact on the political outlook of the children of Bill 101. Whereas those who have been running Quebec politics up to now have always lived with the competition between Montreal and Toronto for the title of the largest and most important Canadian city, my generation has witnessed stock market transactions leaving the Montreal Exchange for the Toronto Stock Exchange, and trading in natural resources moving to... the Winnipeg Commodities Exchange! Quebecers have had no choice but to specialize, and become experts in, derivatives. This chapter in the financial history of Quebec is a particularly strong indicator of Montreal's decline in terms of Canadian economic primacy.

The ferocious battles between Montreal and Toronto during the mid-1990s more or less embodied the struggle between the two solitudes for economic, political and social control in Canada. It was a daily and very tangible reminder for Quebecers of the battle they were waging to preserve their position in Canada's future. For my parents' generation, this struggle was real evidence of the idea of the two founding peoples who had to live together, for better or for worse. It was a warning to Quebec's political leaders of the importance of containing the other solitude if they were going to uphold their own position.

I was too young to witness this clash between Montreal and Toronto for the title of the country's pre-eminent city. When I started to become aware of all the ongoing political debates, the drama had already played out. Now, the thesis of the two founding peoples sounds to me more like a relic of the past than a current reality. After all, did the census of 1996 not show that 46.5 per cent of Canadians are of an ethnic origin other than French or British?[7] How can we continue to claim that the two founding peoples are the only political forces in the Canadian debate?

I am more inclined to see all the different ethnic groups in Canada on an equal footing and to acknowledge that there are now more than two distinct societies in Canada. This includes, especially, the First Nations, who have been excluded from Canada's public debates for too long, and though they are starting to be better acknowledged, we must do more from now on.

Furthermore, I firmly believe that what Quebecers refer to as the "rest of Canada" is not a uniform entity. I suspect that there is not a "rest of Canada" as such, but rather a whole collection of groups who, while they hold to the great Canadian principles, all have their own characteristics: a collection of... distinct societies!

Some years ago while I was studying in England, I had the opportunity to talk with a colleague from Vancouver about the Canadian political climate. Apart from the unusual nature of the scene itself—two Canadians, one francophone and one anglophone debating national politics over a pint of beer in a British pub—I was able to learn something from these discussions. And some of them completely changed my original image of Canada.

In our minds, there was no doubt that we shared a common past and that we both were committed to the same humanist values, which could be called the "Canadian values." We were equally in agreement about the main points of difference, namely language and cultural history, but also our ways of approaching pan-Canadian political issues. The single most important difference between the two of us was our respective views of the actual makeup of Canada. Newly arrived from Montreal, with a minimal knowledge of the Canada west of Ottawa, I had an unshakable belief in the idea of the two founding peoples. And so I believed that there had indeed been two solitudes: "we"— Quebecers, and "they"—the rest of Canada. And though he freely admitted that Quebecers are different from English Canadians, my colleague insisted that it is not possible to lump the latter into one basket and claim that they amount to the "rest of Canada." After many very heated discussions, I was forced to accept the facts: he was right.

Do the Acadians not have their own national day? In a recent speech, did Premier Danny Williams not talk about the

"Newfoundland Nation"? Other groups of Canadians have their own shared cultural traits. Albertans have the Calgary Stampede, whose purpose is to preserve and promote the values and the heritage of the Canadian West. And British Columbians are leaders in sustainable development in Canada, a characteristic that is particular to the West Coast, both of Canada and of North America. Those are only a few examples of the defining features, of the "distinctions," within Canada. Language aside (it is certainly a distinctive trait but I do not see it as necessarily more important than others), what links a Canadian from Vancouver to a Canadian from Charlottetown that does not also tie them to a Quebecer or to any other Canadian? There are at least as many differences between a Manitoban and a Nova Scotian as there are between a Vancouverite and a Montrealer!

Although this fact is difficult to admit at first, so deeply anchored in our political mores is the myth of the two founding peoples, if we take the time to reflect on this question with an open mind, we can only arrive at the same conclusion: the rest of Canada is at least as diverse as the different regions of Quebec. To grasp the full implications of this statement, we have to switch starting points: if a British Columbian is different from all the other Canadians, then a Quebecer is part of his or her "rest of Canada." As Quebecers, we would find being blended into this "rest of Canada" a bit questionable. On second thought, I even think that the expression the "rest of Canada" has something fundamentally reductionist about it, if indeed it does not convey a condescension towards all those who make up "the rest."

In sum, since my generation has never actually lived with the polarization between the two solitudes, I think we are better disposed to look on Canada as a whole that contains a collection of different groups that share a history and some common values, while at the same time accepting that there are some fundamental differences among them. And I like to think that not only do these differences not stop Canadians of every background from living together harmoniously, but that this coexistence is in itself one of Canada's greatest strengths. An asset that too few of my fellow citizens, Canadians and Quebecers, are fully aware of. An asset that we, as tomorrow's leaders, accord much more value to.

The Emergence of a Flexible Federalism

Whether we use the Liberal line about asymmetrical federalism or the Conservative line about open federalism, the emergence since the beginning of the century of a new way of managing the Canadian federation, one that is more flexible and more open to regional disparity, constitutes the third founding political moment for the children of Bill 101. Unlike our baby-boomer parents, we never knew the most dysfunctional moments of the Canadian federation, characterized as they were by those epic confrontations between the sovereignist and the federalist camps. The last chapter in this struggle was written in 1995, at the end of the recession of the early 1990s that saw huge cuts in the federal transfers to the provinces and a marked reduction in access to employment insurance. We can bet that the oldest among us, at that time celebrating their eighteenth birthdays, were busier cruising the bars to toast their arrival in the adult world than they were with informing themselves about the country's failures.

So what attitude should we take towards this new federal government's openness to provincial demands, given that we have only a vague notion about the stumbling blocks that lined the path of those past debates between Quebec and Ottawa? I believe we can only applaud that flexibility and question this urgent need to make Quebec independent. In my view, the burden of proof rests with the *indépendantistes*. They will have to show me again that sovereignty would bring Quebecers more benefit than staying allied with the other provinces. If this is not the case, why even consider the painful transition from the status of province to that of country, when, as long as I have been alive, Canada has been sensitive to Quebec's demands?

If my thinking is sound, we are probably more disposed to respond to a new *beau risque*[8] (beautiful risk) than our parents are. Faced with the uncertain future of an independent Quebec, maybe it would be better to try and work out a reformed Canadian federalism. Considering what we have lived through politically, this attempt to salvage the confederation could not be considered the "nth try"—as it might have been for the preceding generations. In fact, this attempt to renew the Canadian federation ought to be our first conscious generational political act.

THE CHILDREN OF BILL 101: THE PATRIOT GENERATION?

Because we did not live in pre-Charter Quebec, nor in the darkest periods of the Canadian federation, and because the confrontation between the two solitudes never assumed a concrete form for us, we make up a political generation that is different from all those that preceded us. I dare to think that this makes us less anxious to demand a disproportionate share for Quebec in national political decisions, and that we are similarly better positioned to acknowledge that Canada is made up of a collection of distinct groups. Above all, I am convinced that it is up to us to clear the slate of the darkest chapters of our past in order to build anew on the foundations set in place by the preceding generations. We should begin by defining a new plan based on contemporary Canadian realities and meeting the expectations of our fellow citizens. Defining and executing this new Canadian plan will take time and commitment. There is no guarantee that it will succeed, given the number of pitfalls and the opposition that will befall its builders. All the same, our generation does have the necessary tools to carry out the task.

During discussions with several of my friends about the politics and the future of Canadian federalism, one name kept coming up: Charles Blattberg, the professor of political philosophy at the Université de Montréal. His book *Shall We Dance? A Patriotic Politics for Canada*[9] seemed to have deeply affected several of the people with whom I spend a lot of time. So much so that the starting point of my thinking about this essay began with reading his book, which proposes a fundamental change in the political relationships between provinces, between the provincial governments and the federal government, and even among Canadians themselves, in order to set in motion a real dialogue instead of the usual confrontation that always seems to come with federal-provincial negotiations. He calls for a patriotic approach to Canada, in which we can all affirm that we belong to Canada, without interfering with our connection to other groups.

If there is a generation capable of responding to Charles Blattberg's call, I am persuaded that it is ours. All of our political experience has predisposed us to respond to this appeal for a Canada in which all citizens can develop feelings of belonging to the country they have helped to build, while in no way rejecting their membership in distinct ethnic or national groups. What follows is clearly not a claim to have found all the themes that should be included in this new plan but rather to suggest several directions in which to search for them.

It goes without saying that to launch the thinking on a new plan for Canada means proposing a starting point that is true to its reality. This implies a recognition of the connection, however tenuous, that binds Canadian citizens to their country. A form of acknowledgement of the "Canadian values." As a corollary, we need to understand that being part of Canada is based on more than just this shared unity, and that as a result there is no single shared perception of the whole nature of Canada that is the same from sea to sea. Far from weakening the country, admitting this fact demonstrates the real strength of Canada: our ability to welcome and facilitate the coexistence of several distinct groups, while always maintaining a sense of membership in the whole.

In my view, the key idea for this new Canadian plan, then, must be to radically change the dominant political culture of the last several decades. Namely, to move from interactions based on confrontation among the different groups that are developing within Canada towards dialogue, where careful listening replaces the power struggle.[10] Although most of Quebec's interaction with the rest of Canada since 1867 has been under the banner of negotiation, which implies confronting an adversary, we should now be trying to create a climate of dialogue among the different Canadian "distinctions." Far from expecting to win ground from the other provinces, it is up to us to seek to develop a mutual understanding of what brings us together and a mutual tolerance of what divides us. In short, it is our task, above all, to act in such a way that the Canadian solitudes stop developing in parallel and start living together.

It seems to me that there are at least two steps that we should take to promote an environment of exchange among citizens and among our leaders. The first is more institutional in its nature: that is, to fully empower the Council of the Federation so that the provincial leaders can discuss issues on an ongoing basis outside the formal structure of federal-provincial meetings, which tend too much towards bargaining and confrontation.

To begin with, the members of the council should aim to make it the instrument of mediation regarding interprovincial disputes. Traditionally the role of arbiter—not mediator, I have to add—in those episodic conflicts among the provinces and territories has fallen to the federal government. This has meant mobilizing Ottawa's resources to put out fires that were started by regional misunderstandings and to deal with threats from one side or another whenever the federal government's decisions cause an upset. As long as they are settling these interprovincial conflicts, federal politicians cannot be working effectively towards the social, political and economic development of the country as a whole. And Canadians, like the country itself, come out the losers after these cockfights, which serve only to exacerbate tensions among the provincial leaders and work against building real dialogue among the provinces, focussing instead on the short-term concerns of competing provincial interests. If they made a commitment to resolving their disagreements, the provinces and territories would have no choice but to establish a real dialogue and demonstrate the benefits of a new approach to pan-Canadian relations. Although the council might, at first, only apply this mechanism for mediation and constructive dialogue to a limited list of disagreements, it could eventually be expanded to many different issues.

And that is why the second step we have to take regarding the Council of the Federation is to provide it with a clear mandate that allows it to make recommendations to the federal government. Canadians of all backgrounds benefit whenever the provincial and territorial leaders engage in informal dialogue, as we saw with the recent signing of the Trade, Investment and Labour Mobility Agreement (TILMA) between Alberta and British Columbia. So the Council of the Federation would be not only a place to solve interprovincial issues but also a centre to study the future of Canada and the new Canadian plan. The responsibility for building interprovincial connections would no longer rest only with the federal government but equally with the provincial and territorial governments, who would be obliged to produce results. And so the provincial and territorial leaders would have no choice but to step out of this stage manager role they are too often content to play and engage with the issues in order to develop a new understanding of Canada and its future. The curtain has fallen on that time when the federal government proposed and the provinces disposed of money and ideas without having to answer for their decisions!

Eventually, we should even demand the establishment of a genuine interprovincial diplomatic network, in which dialogue would occur between official meetings of the Council of the Federation. How can we explain that Quebec has twenty-two offices, posts or delegations abroad, including two in Germany, two in China, two in Italy and five in the United States,[11] while there are only four in the whole of Canada, two of them in Ontario, only one for all of the Atlantic provinces and another one for all of the West? Even worse, now that Alberta is the economic development centre of Canada, how do we explain that the only Quebec office west of Toronto is in Vancouver, not Calgary![12] It seems paradoxical that Quebec devotes so many resources to developing its international connections when there is such potential for interprovincial exchange within our own country. The best way to strengthen exchanges among the provinces and territories is precisely by increasing the diplomatic ties among them.

Dialogue among the provincial leaders is crucial to defining the new plan for Canada, but it is not enough. Canadian citizens must see themselves as part of the solution. How can we expect voters to elect politicians who are interested in debating the future of Canada if they, themselves, have no interest in opening up to other Canadians?

Several programs could help us reach this objective, but none will be sufficient all on its own. Having said that, there is one solution that seems especially promising to me. I would like to see the federal and provincial governments put in place an interprovincial student exchange program, a Canadian version of Europe's European Community Action Scheme for the Mobility of University Students (ERASMUS). This program pays for students and professors of the European Union (EU) to teach or study in a European university outside their own country. In 2006, 1 per cent of the European student population, or more than 150,000 students, took advantage of this program. There are also similar programs at other educational levels, all of which come under the umbrella of the EU's Socrates program (now known as Lifelong Learning Programme).[13]

Having met several European students who have benefited from the ERASMUS program, I am persuaded that this EU initiative in student exchange has contributed significantly to the development of a feeling of belonging to Europe and to the potential for constructive dialogue among the various European nations. After all, Europeans have more obstacles to overcome in this regard than we Canadians have. The Second World War has left scars that are still visible in the relations among citizens of different nationalities.

There are some language exchange programs sponsored by the Council of Ministers of Education Canada, such as Explore, which offers bursaries to college-level students so they can learn a second language in another province. Or Odyssey, which provides university students with jobs as official language monitors. The Explore program granted 7028 bursaries in 2005–2006, responding to just over half the applications.[14] As for the Official Languages Monitoring Program, it hired 871 monitors in 2004–2005, less than half of the 1890 applicants.[15] If a Canadian ERASMUS program had financed a student exchange program for 1 per cent of Canadian students, 10,144 more young Canadians would have had the chance to discover another province and build connections to begin a dialogue with their compatriots.[16] If the Socrates program has been able to bring together students from European nations that were delivered from a terrible war barely decades ago, we can be sure that better co-ordination of the existing student exchange programs and the development of new interprovincial exchange programs would greatly benefit dialogue among Canadians.

During a speech to the European Group of Public Administration in 2005, the former deputy prime minister of The Netherlands (and minister for governmental reform) Thomas C. de Graaf expressed the view that Western governments are under fire because of their inability to respond to their people's expectations. He explained these failures as resulting from government claims they can manage everything, and citizens counting too much on these unrealistic claims. In his opinion, the solution lies in a greater transfer of decision-making power from the central government to citizens themselves, in short, a new division of responsibilities between governments and citizens, a better equilibrium between rights and duties, and between demands and legislation... between reality and expectations.[17]

We can certainly draw a parallel between the situation described by the Dutch minister and our Canadian constitutional context. For decades now, Canada's stability has rested almost entirely on the shoulders of the federal members of Parliament. As if a country could construct itself based on directives issued in Ottawa! This approach to Canadian development has been characterized by resounding failures and very rare successes, with the result that, today, even provincial politicians are withdrawing from the constitutional game. I believe it is time to move on to a new concept of Canada in which citizens lead the dialogue and their country. The time is right: only now, with the members of my generation coming into our thirties, are we ready to revive the Canadian project.

If, as I have argued throughout this essay, our life experiences inevitably colour our interpretation of political events, it also seems that they have a marked influence on the political environment within any given generation. Whereas the baby-boomer generation brought with it demands, struggles and referenda, my generation, I believe, can make lasting changes in the way we look at Canada. Eschewing the era of confrontation, economic and political stagnation and constitutional pessimism that followed the golden age of the sovereignist movement, my generation can bring about the co-operation, dynamism and optimism that belongs to people to for whom the world is full of hope. It is up to us now to take advantage of our lived political experience in order to build the Canada we would like to live in. Maybe we can bring the country what it needs the most: a genuinely patriotic generation ready to work towards its growth. All we have to do is pick up the torch and do what is necessary to pave the way towards a patriotic Canadian future.

MATHIEU LABERGE *is an economist at the Montreal Economic Institute and holds a master's degree in economics from the University of Nottingham.*

Notes

1. He wishes to thank Ariane, Martin and Paul-Émile for their support and wise advice and to emphasize that all the opinions in the piece remain his sole responsibility.
2. Definitions from *Le Petit Larousse* and freely translated.
3. Alain Dubuc, "Entre deux fêtes," *La Presse*, June 30, 2007, p. 4.
4. Nathalie Petrowski, "Robert Lepage: la face cachée d'Andersen et de la souveraineté," *La Presse*, April 11, 2006, online at www.cyberpresse.ca/ article/20060411/CPARTS04/604110783 (accessed May 27, 2008).
5. Centres d'orientation et de formation des immigrants: COFI
6. Institut de la statistique du Québec, http://www.stat.gouv.qc.ca/donstat/ econm_finnc/conjn_econm/TSC/index.htm (accessed May 27, 2008).

7. *Ibid.*

8. This term was used by René Lévesque after Brian Mulroney became prime minister in 1984.

9. Charles Blattberg, *Shall We Dance? A Patriotic Politics for Canada*, Montreal and Kingston: McGill-Queen's University Press, 2003.

10. *Ibid.*

11. Relations internationales Québec (Ministry of International Relations), www.mri.gouv.qc.ca/en/index.asp (accessed May 27, 2008).

12. Secrétariat aux affaires intergouvernementales canadiennes (Secretariat of Canadian Intergovernmental Affairs), www.saic.gouv.qc.ca/bureauduquebec/index_en.htm (accessed May 27, 2008).

13. European Union, http://ec.europa.eu/education/index_en.html (accessed May 27, 2008).

14. Council of Ministers of Education, *2005–06 Annual Report* (Spring and Summer 2005), www.cmec.ca/publications/Explore_Annual_Report_2005-06.en.pdf (accessed May 27, 2008).

15. Council of Ministers of Education, *2004–05 OLMP Annual Report*, www.cmec.ca/publications/OLMP_Annual_Report_2004-05.en.pdf (accessed May 27, 2008).

16. Statistics Canada: www40.statcan.ca/l01/cst01/educ54a.htm (accessed May 27, 2008).

17. Thomas C. de Graaf, "Necessity and Difficulty of Government Reform," keynote speech delivered to the European Group for Public Administration, Bern, Switzerland, September 2, 2005.

ANDRÉ PRATTE

AFTERWORD

A Federalist and a Nationalist Plan

THE AUTHORS of this collection are proposing to reinvent the relationship between Quebec and Canada. Every chapter offers concrete suggestions to this end. But what is most important is the overall change in the approach that we are recommending.

We, Quebecers, have succeeded in too many fields, have overcome too many obstacles, to remain trapped in a victimist and isolationist political culture. Our affirmation of this nation has to move to another level. First, by tackling head-on the issues that face Quebec right now. Then, by looking well beyond our own provincial borders and investing our culture, our resources and our energy in building the Canada of the twenty-first century. This approach is resolutely federalist because we are persuaded that the federal idea—contrary to what too many have said too often in Quebec—is the exact opposite of the status quo. With its generous spirit and its capacity to adapt, federalism is unquestionably the form of government best suited to the diversity and the internal complexity of a modern state. Our approach is also nationalist, in that it calls upon the particular genius of the Quebec Nation, inviting it to surpass itself—and to reconquer Canada.

Above all, we want to see Quebec move forward. We want this nation, *our* nation, to achieve its full potential. We are convinced that if Quebecers roll up their sleeves everything becomes possible, without their having to wait for the Canadian constitution to incorporate every single aspect of their vision of the country or for their state to achieve complete independence—which, in any case, is nothing but a fantasy in this age of globalization.

JOHN RALSTON SAUL is an award-winning essayist and novel-ist best known for his commentaries on politics and economics. Winner of the Governor General's Award for *The Unconscious Civi-lization* (based on his CBC Massey Lectures), he is a Companion of the Order of Canada and lives in Toronto, Ontario. His most recent book is *A Fair Country: Telling Truths about Canada.*

ANDRÉ PRATTE has been a journalist for thirty years and is currently Editorial Pages Editor at *La Presse.* He has written five books on politics and the media. In 2006, he was a signatory to a manifesto presenting a "clear-eyed vision" for Quebec. Last year, he received the National Newspaper Award in the Editorials cat-egory. He lives in Boucherville, Quebec.

Nationally known for *This Hour Has Seven Days* and *The Watson Report,* translator PATRICK WATSON has been producing, direct-ing, writing, hosting and interviewing for television, in Canada and the U.S., for more than fifty years. His recent book *The Canadians,* based upon the his HTV series, is a collection of biog-raphies. He is a Companion of the Order of Canada and lives in Toronto, Ontario.